Writing the Past in Twenty-first-century American Fiction

Writing the Past in Twenty-first-century American Fiction

Alexandra Lawrie

EDINBURGH
University Press

Edinburgh University Press is one of the leading university presses in the UK. We publish academic books and journals in our selected subject areas across the humanities and social sciences, combining cutting-edge scholarship with high editorial and production values to produce academic works of lasting importance. For more information visit our website: edinburghuniversitypress.com

Edinburgh University Press Ltd
The Tun – Holyrood Road
12(2f) Jackson's Entry
Edinburgh EH8 8PJ

Typeset in 11/13pt Adobe Sabon by
Cheshire Typesetting Ltd, Cuddington, Cheshire, and
printed and bound in Great Britain

A CIP record for this book is available from the British Library

ISBN 978 1 4744 6344 7 (hardback)
ISBN 978 1 4744 6346 1 (webready PDF)
ISBN 978 1 4744 6347 8 (epub)

Contents

Acknowledgements

I am very grateful to friends and colleagues who have offered advice and encouragement at various stages of this project; particular thanks are owed to Sarah Carpenter, Simon Cooke, Andrew Taylor and Jonathan Wild. I am also indebted to Randall Stevenson, not just for his support of the project, but also for reading and commenting on one of the chapters at a key stage of its development. And I am very grateful to Lee Spinks, who was kind enough to read several chapters in their draft form and offer insightful suggestions each time. I've also learnt a great deal from our conversations about American history and culture. Edinburgh University Press's two anonymous reviewers provided careful and constructive feedback which helped shape my thinking throughout the project, and my editor Michelle Houston was enthusiastic and supportive right from the start. My thanks also go to staff at the Edinburgh University Library and the National Library of Scotland, to students on my Twenty-first-century Fiction course, and to my mother Lavinia and my sister Hope. This book is dedicated to Marlowe.

Introduction

In an essay for the *New York Times* in June 2021, the novelist Jonathan Lee declared that a reawakened commitment to historicity was now shaping the contemporary novel. He described how 'For the past two decades, the novels celebrated for defining our time have almost always been books set *within* our time', with historical fiction perceived as 'fusty' and 'easy to caricature'. Yet more recently 'the tone of such conversations has begun to change', with the historical novel undergoing a revival, increasingly 'embraced and reinvented': witness, for instance, Colson Whitehead's 2017 Pulitzer for *The Underground Railroad*, and his second for *The Nickel Boys* three years later. Even authors usually drawn to contemporary contexts, such as George Saunders and Lauren Groff, have 'swerved into the past' for their most recent works, driven backwards by a feverish cultural mood that feels altogether too transient to narrate. The current study examines a group of twenty-first-century novels profoundly shaped by the historical consciousness Lee describes, yet they also remain anchored, at least in part, to a present-day setting. In that sense they accomplish two feats at once: firstly, they reflect on the tumultuous events that have punctuated the new century, with references (both oblique and overt) to the wars in Afghanistan and Iraq, President Obama's election victory, the 2008 financial crash, the Black Lives Matter movement, and the climate emergency. And secondly, alongside this sustained attention to the politics and culture of the new century, these novels are conceptually linked through their shared engagement in historical archaeology: each of them examines how aspects of America's past exert various types of pressure on the contemporary moment. This forms the central concern of this study: it takes a group of novels largely set in a recognisable, present-day

America (C. E. Morgan's *The Sport of Kings*, Hari Kunzru's *White Tears*, Ben Lerner's *10:04*, Dana Spiotta's *Eat the Document* and *Innocents and Others*, *What Belongs to You* by Garth Greenwell, *Christodora* by Tim Murphy, *Zone One* by Colson Whitehead and Omar El Akkad's *American War*), and explores how scenes and memories from an earlier period or periods repeatedly interrupt the contemporary narrative in ways which underline the past's continued relevance to the characters' lives.

These historical parallels and evocations, which are either recalled by the characters, described in narrative flashbacks, or emerge through recurrent images and motifs, compel the protagonists to regard their own contemporary experiences (and in many cases, their own struggles) as part of a broader pattern. In some cases, this is the re-emergence, in another place and time, of dormant feelings of shame or of centuries-old structures of discrimination; in another, less disturbing example, a narrator's encounters on the streets of New York are reinterpreted through the redemptive influence of an earlier writer. Across five chapters the impact and focus of this historical awareness varies widely – from the ways in which political decisions relating to Vietnam half a century ago continue to be felt today, to the legacy of the HIV/AIDS crisis in narratives of queer identity, to the spectre of historical racism in contemporary structures of race-based oppression. In several of the novels the characters themselves are required to carry out the excavation work, as they unearth historical parallels, long-since buried, which help them make sense of their current circumstances: acknowledging past crises is for many of the protagonists a necessary step towards understanding the position they currently find themselves in, even if this does not lead directly to positive change. The novels use extended flashbacks and non-sequential narrative arrangements which appear to dissolve the distance between decades and even centuries, momentarily closing the gap between events and circumstances which are temporally far apart. These instances of temporal slippage allow the novels to foreground the recurrence of structural inequality, violence and discrimination, and (in response to those issues) political resistance through protests and demonstrations.

This interest in how structures and ideas from earlier decades rematerialise in the present day is not of course unique to writing of the new century: to varying ends, American authors including (but by no means limited to) James Baldwin, Michael Chabon, Don DeLillo, E. L. Doctorow, John Dos Passos, William Faulkner, Norman Mailer, Toni Morrison, Bharati Mukherjee, Tim O'Brien,

Richard Powers, Thomas Pynchon, Philip Roth, Susan Fromberg Schaeffer, Kurt Vonnegut, Alice Walker and Richard Wright have traced how individual lives are reshaped and even blighted by the reappearance of historical pressures. To take one example from that list: Schaeffer's 1989 novel *Buffalo Afternoon* describes the horrors of the Vietnam War and its lasting effect on veterans such as Pete Bravado, an Italian American from Brooklyn who enlisted at the age of seventeen and spent a year on combat duty. While Pete's disturbing experiences in Vietnam take up much of the novel, a long final section depicts his life after returning to America, where for the next two decades he is haunted by what he has seen and done – trauma which manifests itself in nightmares, hallucinations and acts of extreme and unprovoked violence. One of the novel's final scenes takes place at a reunion dance for former soldiers; in a dreamlike sequence, Pete stumbles into a room where veterans can go back and redo a particular ambush or patrol over and over again. Pete's friend Mickey, who has tried it three times already, marvels at how real it feels: 'The foliage's so thick in there you can hardly see your hand in front of you. Nothing's changed, man' (635). While Mickey wants to relive those experiences, Pete fears their reappearance, later telling Sal, an old army friend, that 'The past's a minefield, man. You learn more about life, you walk on new ground, you set something off. It turns out you didn't forget after all' (644).

Schaeffer's novel is an earlier example of historical pressures (in this case, war trauma) stubbornly re-emerging in different contexts – a useful reminder that the collapse of temporal boundaries is not, by any means, a new contrivance in fiction. Nevertheless, this study identifies a heightened awareness within contemporary novels of the permeable boundary linking past and present, and – in some cases – of the possibility for a productive relationship between the two. The increased focus on historical sedimentation in novels published this century, this book suggests, is partly down to the level of disruption in American cultural and political life over the past two decades. But the somewhat paradoxical effect of this turmoil is not to impress on each character the sense that their own period is unique in terms of the changes taking place; rather, it encourages them to place these events in correspondence with historical precursors and consider their ongoing impact. The year 2020 seems particularly momentous, encompassing as it did a global pandemic, mass protests calling for racial justice following the murder of George Floyd, and the defeat of President Donald Trump after four divisive years. But the crises started mounting up almost as soon as the twenty-first century had begun: the contested election of 2000, which led to President George W. Bush's victory by the narrowest of margins; thereafter the terrorist attacks of 11 September 2001 and the subsequent War on Terror, with wars in Afghanistan and Iraq; Hurricanes Katrina and Harvey; the financial crash of 2008; mass shootings, including at Sandy Hook Elementary School; and Trump's presidency, which was mired in scandal and disarray – the Russia investigation, two impeachments, the white supremacist rally at Charlottesville and the rise of the alt-right, nuclear tensions with North Korea, the detention of migrant children on the US–Mexico border and, finally, Trump's false accusations of voter fraud and his claim that the 2020 election was 'stolen'. As later portions of this introduction will explain, moments of contemporary crisis depicted in the novels under discussion push the narratives backwards: when characters attempt to make sense of their disordered lives, this means taking a broader historical view, laying bare how past events persist in shaping the here and now.

Because the novels examined in this book are set predominantly in the twenty-first century, they tend to be categorised as literary fiction, contemporary realism or (in the case of Ben Lerner) autofiction. Their present-day setting also sets them apart from the more 'conventional' historical novels published in this century, which tend to remain within a specific historical period or periods, rather than base part of their narrative in the present moment. Jonathan Lee's examples include Jennifer Egan's *Manhattan Beach* (2017), which takes place in 1930s and '40s New York, and George Saunders's *Lincoln in the Bardo* (also 2017), set during the Civil War. To these we might add Rachel Kushner's first two novels, which are notable for their vivid depiction of specific historical settings: *Telex from Cuba* (2008) follows a group of American expatriates in 1950s Cuba prior to Castro's revolution, and *The Flamethrowers*, published in 2013, is set largely in the 1970s New York art world, with stretches in Italy and Nevada, and shifts back in time to fill in the story of T. P. Valera, who grew up in Alexandria and Milan at the turn of the century, and went on to found a motorbike company, Moto Valera. Parallels between the 1970s and the years before 2013 (when the novel was being written) may be inferred – both were times of significant financial crisis, with New York as a case study in wealth inequality – but the novel stops short of any explicit comparisons. Marilynne Robinson's second novel, *Gilead* (2004), shifts between earlier historical periods in ways that are more fragmentary and elusive: it is set in 1956, when John Ames, a Congregationalist minister in the small rural town of Gilead, Iowa, sits down to write an account of his life for his young son to read after his death. But the letter also includes details of Ames's family history, in particular his grandfather's friendship with John Brown, and his violent participation, on the abolitionist side, in Bleeding Kansas during the 1850s. His grandfather's actions, and the consequent dispute between him and Ames's father over the ethics of responding to the violence of slavery with further violence, forms a type of double narrative, with Ames's advice to his son interrupted by often charged moments of recall. Like Kushner's *The Flamethrowers*, the events described in *Gilead* might usefully be placed in dialogue with present-day issues – for example the Republican Ames's repudiation of racial inequality during a key moment in the civil rights movement could reasonably be shown to anticipate the re-emergence, during the Trump era, of the rhetoric of white resentment. But this possible contemporary parallel is extrinsic to Robinson's narrative, which never strays later than the 1950s.

This study draws a distinction between the category of historical novel where the narrative takes place in an earlier period or periods (even if contemporary resonances might plausibly be perceived), and texts which move freely and overtly back and forth between the twenty-first century and past decades or even centuries. This interweaving of past and present is just one of the features that sets them apart from the historical novel as conceived by Georg Lukács in his 1937 work *The Historical Novel*. For Lukács, the historical novel was an essentially realist form, epic in scope, and occupied by issues of nascent nationhood. He presented Walter Scott as his archetypal historical novelist, who portrayed historical struggles through ordinary individuals: these characters were 'mediocre', tending towards the 'decent and average' (36), but also representative, 'in their psychology and destiny', of 'social trends and historical forces' (34). By narrating history through the lens of ordinary people, Scott's readers could see themselves represented on the page: he showed how the everyday lives of people like them were altered by the major crises and conflicts of their age, and they were also portrayed as active participants in those historical struggles; this lends the novels an immediacy and ongoing resonance. Lukács wrote that Scott 'makes history live', as his writing 'brings the past close to us' (53); the novels are 'both humanly authentic' and 're-liveable by the reader of a later age' (40). Lukács also emphasised Scott's sense of 'historical necessity' (58), a progressive understanding of historical development which views the outcomes of past conflicts as having a positive transformative effect on the nation, while at the same time perceiving history as ongoing and developmental; Lukács's point was that history is an 'uninterrupted process of changes' and 'has a direct effect upon the life of every individual' (23). Lukács's book remains a classic account of the historical novel which still occupies a prominent position in more recent discussions of the form, such as Perry Anderson's 2011 article 'From Progress to Catastrophe', which begins with Lukács and Fredric Jameson, and argues for the historical novel as having been born out of the 'romantic nationalism' (24) generated across Europe in response to the Napoleonic Wars. Anderson describes how, from the highpoint of *War and Peace* and the 46-volume *Episodios Nacionales* by Galdós, as well as later examples by Robert Louis Stevenson and Edward Bulwer-Lytton, the genre went through a long period of decline, so that by midway through the twentieth century it was a purely lowbrow form: popular, formulaic and mass-produced. But Anderson's account of how historical fiction has fared in recent decades is perhaps more relevant and certainly more arresting, as he describes how 'abruptly, the scene changed', and 'in one of the most astonishing transformations in literary history . . . the historical novel has become, at the upper ranges of fiction, more widespread than it was even at the height of its classical period in the early 19th century' (27). Anderson attributes this remarkable 'resurrection' to the 'arrival of the postmodern', noting that 'the most striking single change it [postmodernism] has wrought in fiction is the pervasive recasting of it around the past' (27). And while he acknowledges that not all historical fiction of the past three decades contains postmodern features, he draws his most recent examples from among their ranks, including Thomas Pynchon, Don DeLillo, William Styron and Toni Morrison.

While Anderson's article is reluctant to look beyond the 'postmodern revival' (28), Alexander Manshel has identified, in a 2017 article, a more recent development in historical fiction, as he sets out to answer the question posed by Jameson in his 2013 *The Antinomies of Realism*: 'What kind of History can the contemporary historical novel . . . be expected to "make appear"?' (263). Manshel's response to this is: very recent history. He describes the emergence of a 'new literary sub-genre' which he terms 'the recent historical novel'; these are novels which narrate twenty-first-century events such as 9/11, the Iraq war, the 2008 financial crisis and Obama's election victory (n.p.). Manshel's three examples are *10:04* and *Leaving the Atocha Station* by Ben Lerner, and Ruth Ozeki's *A Tale for the Time Being* – novels which contain specific details and events which situate them in a recognisable time and place. Instead of depicting an 'amorphous present', these novels are 'precisely datable' (n.p.). For Manshel, this allows them to seem both relevant and authentic ('the work is elevated by its contact with capital-H history'), but also means they contribute to the process by which recent events are historicised. Readers are invited to compare their own memories of a disaster with its novelised version, although in this re-telling they know how the event ends; this has a dual function, in that they perceive themselves as witnesses to history – their memories are now 'the stuff of history and, what's more, literary history' – while reassuring them that those events are now firmly in the past, 'marked through writing as a bounded and closed period of history' (n.p.). Manshel's article can be placed alongside Theodore Martin's *Contemporary Drift* (2017) as recent explorations into how we might periodise 'the contemporary' through fiction and film. The current study carefully examines the present-day context for each of the novels under discussion, but is generally less concerned with conceptualising the period than with establishing some of the parallels and resonances between earlier decades and the present time. The exception to this mostly 'backward turn' is the final chapter of this book, where portions of the 'past' under consideration are 'now' – the early years of the twenty-first century. Omar El Akkad's *American War* and Colson Whitehead's *Zone One* are both set in a near-future America blighted by decisions made in the present time; they explore how foreign policy manoeuvres and several decades' worth of indifference about climate change could play out in the years to come. Mitchum Huehls would regard these as examples of the 'historical novel of futurity', a post-2000 approach which 'renders the present as the prehistory of the future' (146). But whereas Huehls regards this novelistic approach as a pragmatic response to 'history's inaccessibility' in an era still marked by traces of postmodernism (148), my final chapter suggests that in a near-future America, 'history' – or more simply 'the past' – continues to hold sway as a compelling and ultimately *fathomable* presence. And just as the rest of this study explores how images, structures, and responses from multiple temporal periods might reappear within a single novel set in the present day, the novels by El Akkad and Whitehead do not confine their historical consciousness to the twenty-first century, but also contain allusions to earlier events such as the Civil War and Reconstruction.

   The approach to literary historicity taken by the authors in this study might usefully be termed historical recursion or archaeology, and is emblematic of a larger novelistic drift already noted by a number of critics. Robert Eaglestone has suggested that 'the past's grip on the present has become even stronger' in recent fiction; he terms this 'the resurgent past', by which he means 'an intense concern for the impact of the past on the present' (311), and the 'ever more diverse and contradictory array of modes by which the past is represented, forms which far exceed the historical novel as usually conceived' (312). Adam Kelly writes that 'twenty-first-century novelists who attempt to connect past and present' are generally 'disinclined to see the present as a radical break from the past' (50). And lastly Peter Boxall has argued that novels of the new century are attempting to 'gain a new understanding of the way that historical material asserts itself in the contemporary imagination'; this 'emergent mode of historiography', he suggests,

> is characterised by a fresh commitment to what we might call the reality of history ... grounded in a keen awareness of history as event, history as a material force which is not simply produced by narrative, but also shapes and determines it (41).

Boxall makes the important point that twenty-first-century novels tend to treat history as a fixed and coherent reality, and this is true of the novels this study explores: aspects of the past might have been repressed, hidden or left unexplored in these fictions, but this does not mean that that history cannot finally be accessed, or that it remains irresolvable. This conception of historicity distinguishes these novels from much postmodern fiction, where received history is often regarded with profound distrust. Jameson famously declared, in *Postmodernism, or, the Cultural Logic of Late Capitalism* (1991) that the 'postmodern' is characterised by a 'weakening of historicity' as it grapples with the 'disappearance of the historical referent' (6, 25). E. L. Doctorow is Jameson's exemplar of this position: *Ragtime*, he suggests, 'float[s] in some new world of past historical time whose relationship to us is problematical indeed', underlining 'the evident existential fact of life' that there is no longer 'any organic relationship between the American history we learn from schoolbooks and the lived experience of the current multinational, high-rise, stagflated city of the newspapers and of our own everyday life' (22). Jameson's account of postmodernism's 'crisis in historicity' (22) is taken up by Mitchum Huehls, who describes how novels by Doctorow, DeLillo, Morrison and Pynchon betray a 'pervasive skepticism toward all foundational truth claims', portraying history as fragmentary, indeterminate and beyond comprehension (141). In books such as *Ragtime*, *Libra*, *Beloved* and *Gravity's Rainbow*, these authors present counterhistories – re-writings of historical events that not only problematise the received narrative, but also the process by which those 'truths' were constructed in the first place.

History, in these and other postmodern writers, is presented as 'flamboyant cartoon', 'magical myth', 'paranoia', 'metafiction' or 'unknowable trauma' (Huehls 141). In *Libra* (1988) the historical facts are available in voluminous piles; the mistake is in imagining they might generate a single and unambiguous interpretation. DeLillo presents the assassination of John F. Kennedy as a CIA plot orchestrated by a group of former agents still smarting from the failed Bay of Pigs invasion, who determine that the US government could be forced into a second invasion if they can choreograph an event 'that will make it appear they [Cuba] have struck at the heart of our government' (27). In Lee Harvey Oswald they find their ideal assassin: a former marine and communist sympathiser who defected to the Soviet Union. Now back in America, he produces a trail of evidence the CIA men would have otherwise had to create in order to make him seem a feasible assassin, and he therefore seems a 'quirk of history ... a coincidence', who 'matches the cardboard cutout they've been shaping all along' (330). Oswald too feels 'swept up, swept along' by history, as a series of coincidences, premonitions and patterns convince him that his 'destiny' (277) is linked to Kennedy's death. But the 'third line' which 'bridges the space' (339) between the CIA plot and Oswald's own plan is impossible to make out: in a substrand of the novel, Nicholas Branch, a retired CIA analyst who spends years attempting to write a secret history of the assassination, finds that while the facts of the case are available to him, their connection to each other seems to defy logic and deny meaning.

   DeLillo, alongside his contemporaries Toni Morrison and Thomas Pynchon, continued to produce major work in the 1990s and beyond: their respective novels *Underworld, Paradise* and *Mason & Dixon* were all published the same year, 1997. These novels' construction of alternative histories, and their inclusion of conspiracy theories and magical elements, contribute to the sense that historical fiction of that decade still tended to regard history as inconclusive and subject to revision; Huehls suggests that historical novels of the 1990s 'struggle to escape residual postmodern forms', and this 'threatens to foil these novels' various attempts to capture history and produce historicity' (140, 142). As Huehls acknowledges, this broadly accords with arguments put forward by Samuel Cohen in his 2009 study *After the End of History: American Fiction in the 1990s,* which considers how 1990s authors set out to reassess ideology-driven 'truths' about America's national character and its victorious past. Cohen suggests that between the end of the Cold War and 11 September 2001, American culture 'took on a markedly retrospective quality' (10). Finally released from the decades-long threat of nuclear war, writers took the opportunity to reconsider America's 'continuing reliance on particular narratives', particularly the 'triumphalist school of American history' (7) which re-surfaced after the Cold War. Cohen takes a group of mainly postmodern writers (Pynchon, DeLillo and Morrison, but also Roth, Didion and O'Brien) who, in contradistinction to Francis Fukuyama's famous 1989 declaration, refuse the reassuring sense of closure that comes with that 'end of history' narrative. These authors construct 'counternarratives' (28) which suggest history 'might have turned out differently, or might still' (52), and explore 'the effects of myth' (the stories America tells about itself) 'on the way history is understood' (83). For Cohen the 1990s was an 'interwar decade', coming as it did between 'the fall of the Wall and the fall of the Towers' (4). Stephen J. Burn, in *Jonathan Franzen and the End of Postmodernism* (2008), considers the decade to be 'transitional' (9) in the development of the American novel: while the surviving first-generation postmodernists raged against the dying of the light, a new generation of writers (whom Burn terms the 'post-postmodernists') tended towards realism over metafiction, and plot over formal experimentation, though they shared with their predecessors the 'ambition to produce an encyclopedic masterwork' (20), and included 'knowing winks to the reader' about those older writers in their own novels (19). Most importantly in this context, Burn identifies that we get a 'fuller sense of a character's personal history' in the work of post-postmodernists like Jonathan Franzen, Richard Powers and David Foster Wallace, because they 'more freely interrupt time's passage through strategically deployed analepses' (24) – the flashbacks represent 'a younger generation's more fundamental belief in the shaping influence of temporal process – that the things that happen to you in the past make a difference to who you are in the present' (25).

In Franzen's *The Corrections* (2001), each of the novel's long sections focuses on a different member of the Lambert family, usually beginning in the present day of the narrative before rewinding to significant moments in the previous days, weeks or years which help illuminate their current circumstances. The novels examined in the current study also make substantial use of analepsis, but these flashbacks are not only a means of revisiting an episode that felt significant for an individual character; often they return to periods and events which had far-reaching implications for the nation as a whole. Some of these flashbacks are therefore embedded, at least partly, in specific events and organisations – in Spiotta's *Eat the Document*, the protagonist is a former member of 1970s militant group the Weatherman Underground Organization; in Murphy's *Christodora* one of the central characters was a leading figure in ACT UP (AIDS Coalition to Unleash Power). Each novel also stages its non-linearity differently. In *Christodora* the narrative is presented largely non-chronologically, with the date given at the start of each chapter. This non-sequential arrangement produces a range of effects: at the most obvious level it encourages the reader to modify their view of a character or situation once the back story has been filled in, but a more significant consequence is the redirection of emphasis away from a character's trajectory (because that has already been established), and onto the reasons behind the often startling alteration in their circumstances. (Even when a pair of chapters are presented in order, they might be set several years or even decades apart, and this too emphasises the changes that have been wrought.) But the most important effect of this non-linear structure, and one which is common to all of the novels in this study, is to call attention to the porous relationship between past and present: in the case of *Christodora* and of *What Belongs to You* the distance between historical periods seems to melt away altogether as the shame and grief of an earlier era continues to shape the responses of the central characters. This is perceptible in Morgan's *The Sport of Kings*, too, where the temporal shifts are less clearly marked: the novel consists of long sections which move across the period 1783 until 2006, the roving narrative eye taking in slavery, Reconstruction, Jim Crow, the civil rights era in the South and the War on Drugs movement. In each section the reader has to piece together references to the wider historical context in order to establish the exact setting, and in a sense that is exactly the point: the novel captures how racist structures and violence endlessly repeat, regardless of year or context, over more than 200 years, including in the contemporary period. In Lerner's *10:04* the various temporal shifts are even more subtle and indistinct: Ben, the narrator, is on a writing retreat in Marfa when his identity starts to merge with that of Walt Whitman during the Civil War era; meanwhile lines from modernist poetry and prose also occur to him seemingly at random, suggesting he is subconsciously eliding his own experiences in twenty-first-century New York with those of prior interpreters of urban life. Ben slides uneasily between the 1860s, the 1920s and the 2010s; at one point he describes himself as 'falling out of time', a phrase which usefully captures the thematic concern of this study as a whole, as well as the structural devices employed in each of the novels. The point to be made is that in each of the novels those earlier scenes or motifs do not exist only in the past, but are continually reconfigured in new contexts, interjecting themselves into the contemporary in ways which range from the revelatory and affirmative to the frightening or simply demoralising: in *Eat the Document* (which ends in 2000), a new generation of teenagers seems unwilling to protest against globalisation and corporate greed, and the novel juxtaposes this with the energy and commitment (but also violence) of their parents' anti-capitalist stance some twenty-five years earlier. The connection between past and present has a more destructive effect on Allmon Shaughnessy, the young Black man at the centre of Morgan's novel: when he discovers how long-established those racist structures of control really are, he judges them insurmountable, and starts to lose hope.

Morgan's novel would be considered realist, although the narrative is capacious enough to incorporate numerous different styles of writing, with long diversions into equine genetics, a seven-page sermon from Allmon's grandfather, and even brief passages of metafiction. And *10:04*, the subject of Chapter 2, is an example of autofiction: the narrator is also called Ben and shares some of Lerner's biography; at the start of the novel Ben is celebrating a large advance for his second novel, which appears to be the novel we are reading. *10:04* is probably the most formally innovative among the books discussed here, most of which largely eschew experimentation at the level of form, opting for broadly realist approaches to narrative and characterisation. This is another means by which these texts offer a contrast to the 'highly mediated and self-conscious nature' of much postmodern narrative (Huehls 140): while each of the novels are formally *interesting*, they remain committed to the idea that reality (and indeed history) can be represented in a relatively straightforward manner. In Adam Kelly's essay on 'Formally Conventional Fiction', he presents 'historical novels of the 2000s' as a pertinent example of the 'spirit of skepticism' (50, 47) regarding formal experimentation more generally: these novels 'tend to be accessible on a narrative level, disinvested in an overly experimental approach to language', and feature protagonists who 'attempt to attain and share historical understanding' (50). This explicitly involves the reader, who is 'appealed to first and foremost as a partner in the construction of shared meaning' (51). That last point seems particularly pertinent to the end of *10:04*, when Ben reaches for lines from Whitman's poem 'Crossing Brooklyn Ferry' in order to speak directly to the reader in a moment of shared sympathy and reassurance: 'I know it's hard to understand / I am with you, and I know how it is' (240). In the poem, Whitman's appeal to his future readers is rooted in their common experience of city life; Ben not only finds personal solace in this cross-temporal connection, but also borrows the poet's words to construct with his own readers an empathetic vision of urban experience.

While each of the novels discussed in the following pages have a shared investment in moments of historical recursion, their focus varies widely, and across five chapters this book explores a range of thematic concerns through the lens of historical consciousness. Chapter 1 takes Morgan's novel *The Sport of Kings* (2016) and Hari Kunzru's *White Tears* (2017) in order to explore the persistence of racist structures across different periods in America's history, and its contemporary manifestation in discriminatory policing, arrest, and sentencing. *The Sport of Kings* has a wide historical sweep which is presented in a non-linear fashion, ending in 2006 with the story of Allmon Shaughnessy, a young Black man who takes a job as a horse groom on a Kentucky Thoroughbred farm. The limits on Allmon's freedom and choices replicate several aspects of post-enslavement experience, with his life following a trajectory analogous to that of his ancestor Scipio, who had been enslaved on the same farm in the 1820s; nearly 200 years later, in 2006, Allmon predicts that little will change for him under Obama's presidency. *White Tears* similarly parodies the notion of a 'post-racial' America: two white college friends, Carter and Seth, remix an old blues song and market it as their own, before discovering that the song had belonged to Charlie Shaw, a Black singer in the 1920s who was arrested for vagrancy and forced to work on a levee under the system of convict leasing. Charlie's reappearance in ghostly form forces Seth to consider the structural connection between Charlie's fate in the Jim Crow period and that of contemporary Black men, targeted by the police, and handed excessive prison sentences. Taking its lead from Michelle Alexander's *The New Jim Crow*, Saidiya V. Hartman's *Scenes of Subjection* and Christina Sharpe's *In the Wake*, this chapter will consider how the continual collapse of temporal boundaries in these two novels demonstrates how structural and often violent resistance to civil liberties tends to be reconfigured, rather than dissolved, across different periods.

Chapter 2 examines Ben Lerner's 2014 novel *10:04*, which is set in New York around the time of the Occupy Wall Street demonstrations in 2011. The narrator, a writer called Ben, has benefited directly from the financial system currently in place (his second novel having become an expensive commodity for which he lands a six-figure advance), yet he remains ambivalent towards the structures of neoliberalism which are physically rendered on the Manhattan skyline, and is intrigued by the contemporary mood of protest stemming from the 2008 financial crash. As this chapter describes, Ben's sense of unease leads him to draw parallels between the Occupy demonstrations and the dissatisfaction voiced by modernist writers, around a hundred years earlier, regarding the impact of new industrial processes. But while Ben's experience of urban life appears to replicate the chaos and alienation represented at the level of form and theme by Virginia Woolf, T. S. Eliot and John Dos Passos, these literary antecedents eventually prove inadequate, and he turns instead to Walt Whitman, particularly his 1856 poem 'Crossing Brooklyn Ferry', which provides a redemptive vision of New York and a mode of resistance to neoliberal totality, authorising Ben to recast his place in the contemporary city. The history Lerner excavates in this novel is literary history: Ben identifies in Whitman's writing (and in Whitman himself) a precursor for his own withdrawal from ordinary temporal routines during his long periods of writing, and a model for a more sympathetic mode of social behaviour when he re-emerges from this retreat.

Chapter 3 explores the long-term impact of militant protests carried out by New Left activists in the 1970s. The protagonist of Dana Spiotta's 2006 novel *Eat the Document*, Mary Whittaker, is a member of the notorious Weatherman Underground Organization, an anti-capitalist and anti-imperialist militant group formed in 1969. Mary's terrorist activities as part of the Weatherman force her to withdraw from society altogether, changing her identity and living as a fugitive. The lethal protest tactics of her youth are assessed against the much less effective, but also less violent protests planned by teenagers in her hometown of Seattle nearly thirty years later, where she has settled under a different name. By continually eliding the differences between these two periods of activism (the 1970s and the late 1990s), Spiotta frustrates the reader's urge to take sides, and to see either response as more legitimate. Similar tensions are at work in her 2016 novel *Innocents and Others*, which considers the role of commitment in the context of filmmaking. Meadow Mori is a documentary maker with an uncompromising approach to her subjects, but the films also cause other people immense pain, as she coerces participants into reliving painful moments from their pasts. This forces us to consider whether these inflammatory documentaries, which come from a position of commitment, are necessarily more commendable than the mainstream comedies made by her friend Carrie Wexler. This chapter will consider how we judge a committed but ultimately destructive approach, whether in politics or in art.

The Kentucky horse farm where Allmon takes a job in *The Sport of Kings* is owned by Henry Forge, who can trace his own family line back to the first settlers to make it through the Cumberland Gap. But this proud family lineage erases the family's enslaver past, its support for the Ku Klux Klan, and its murder of a Black employee in the 1950s: these stories have been 'whitewashed' out of history. Chapter 4 tackles another instance of historical amnesia, looking at Tim Murphy's novel *Christodora* and Garth Greenwell's *What Belongs to You* (both 2016) to consider the long-term impact of the HIV/AIDS crisis on those who experienced it first-hand. Like the novels examined throughout this study, *Christodora* is presented out of sequence during a narrative which stretches over forty years, from 1981 until 2021. The after-effects of those years of trauma are traceable in most of the characters, but particularly Hector, a leading figure in ACT UP during the 1980s and early '90s, who campaigned for funding into research while friends and lovers fell ill and died. The deaths of so many of Hector's friends exist as textual absences in the novel, replicating the official silence about the crisis, and its partial erasure in subsequent decades. In Greenwell's novel, feelings of shame and disgust the narrator had internalised as a gay teenager in 1980s and '90s Kentucky continue to shape his responses as an American abroad. During a long flashback midway through the novel, he recognises that the homophobic environment of his youth, and the conflation of same-sex desire with disease, has been replicated in contemporary Bulgaria, which at first had seemed an escape from such prejudice.

In Chapter 5 the 'past' is, in part, the early years of the twenty-first century. If, as the previous chapters have suggested, the past continues to have a profound effect on individuals in the contemporary period, then it seems reasonable to expect that the consequences of major events over the last two decades will still be felt in the years to come. This final chapter looks at two novels that opt for an anxious near-future setting in order to examine how decisions relating to climate change, foreign policy and neoliberalism are likely to play out in later decades. Colson Whitehead's *Zone One* (2011) takes place after a zombie apocalypse, with 'skels' still roaming across America as the country tries to rebuild from the ground up.

Whitehead's protagonist Mark Spitz has so far survived the plague, and has found work helping to clear New York of zombies, so that other survivors can begin moving back to the city. Yet as with the other novels examined in this book, *Zone One* also reaches further back: Mark Spitz is confronted with memories and artefacts of his past life, and these allow him to resist the government's propagandist narrative that post-plague America is simply a continuation of life before, as they paper over the full extent of the crisis. The burning of zombie bodies in post-plague New York has generated toxic rain, filled with human particles, which Mark Spitz's fellow sweepers claim not to notice; the second novel this chapter explores, Omar El Akkad's *American War* (2017), is focused more explicitly on climate change: the novel begins in 2074, when rising sea levels have worn away the Southern coastline, while the landlocked states are scorched by drought. Meanwhile the country is locked in a second civil war, with the Northern government deploying drone strikes and ground assaults against the Southern states, and foreign agents infiltrating the region to build their own strategic alliances. As well as reflecting on the damage wrought by US foreign policy decisions in the present time, El Akkad's novel is also backward facing: his fictional conflict is pitched as an anachronism, closely resembling the 'first' Civil War in terms of the rhetoric used by each side. In substantive terms this is also a country in retreat, decades of in-fighting and a stubborn attachment to fossil fuels having occasioned its decline from superpower to impoverished nation.

This book does not aim for extensive coverage, and nor does it claim that the novels under discussion are unique in their preoccupation with historical sedimentation and recursion; Eaglestone's suggestion that this is a 'distinctive and dominant theme' (311) in contemporary fiction is borne out by American novels such as Teju Cole's *Open City*, Michael Cunningham's *Specimen Days*, Junot Díaz's *The Brief Wondrous Life of Oscar Wao*, Jennifer Egan's *A Visit from the Goon Squad*, Jeffrey Eugenides's *Middlesex*, Yaa Gyasi's *Homegoing*, Aleksandar Hemon's *Nowhere Man* and *The Lazarus Project*, Denis Johnson's *Tree of Smoke*, Edward P. Jones's *The Known World*, Nicole Krauss's *The History of Love*, Jonathan Lethem's *The Fortress of Solitude*, Viet Thanh Nguyen's *The Sympathizer*, Ruth Ozeki's *A Tale for the Time Being*, Jonathan Safran Foer's *Everything is Illuminated* and Ocean Vuong's *On Earth We're Briefly Gorgeous,* as well as those older writers who have continued to produce work this century such as Marilynne Robinson, Philip Roth and Sarah Schulman. One notable point of commonality linking the novels discussed in this book is the theme of protest, and this becomes a minor thread running through the chapters. A September 2018 article in *Vulture* which attempted to put together a 'canon of the 21st century' (not just of fiction, but also books of essays, poetry collections, and memoirs), described how the chosen novels in particular capture the 'waves of hope and despair' that have gripped America since 9/11; the editors concluded that 'instability' is the 'hallmark of the era', with the first eighteen years of the new century having witnessed 'wars, economic collapse, permanent-seeming victories for the once excluded, and the vicious backlash under which we currently shudder'. And Americans have taken to the streets in unprecedented numbers to protest these divisive government policies, as L. A. Kauffman explained in an article for the *Guardian*, also from 2018: she pointed out that 'We are in an extraordinary era of protest' as a result of Trump's presidency, during which 'more people have joined demonstrations than at any other time in American history' ('We are living'). This began the day after Trump's inauguration, when '4.2 million or more people took to the streets in more than 650 coordinated Women's Marches all around the United States', making this 'almost certainly the largest coordinated protest ever in US history' (Kauffman, *How to Read*, 59). Just three years later, in 2020, the Black Lives Matter movement was reignited following the murder of George Floyd by a white policeman in Minneapolis, an event which sparked several weeks of protests across the US and around the world. An estimated 15 million to 26 million people in the US attended a BLM demonstration, according to a *New York Times* article, many of them new to protesting.[1]

While the Black Lives Matter movement gained huge global support in 2020 (and brought about some immediate, though all too limited changes in police policy), the movement actually began in 2013 after George Zimmerman's acquittal for the death of Trayvon Martin, and rose to prominence the following year after the deaths of Eric Garner and Michael Brown. The novels by C. E. Morgan and Hari Kunzru (both published before 2020) draw direct parallels between the treatment of Black men in contemporary America and the murder of Black men in the Jim Crow South around the time of the civil rights movement – the era which witnessed the first and most iconic mass protest in US history: the 1963 March on Washington for Jobs and Freedom.[2] Two years later, in 1965, protesters converged on Washington once again – this time for the March Against the Vietnam War, organised by the Students for a Democratic Society

(SDS). Chapter 3 considers Spiotta's portrayal of the late 1960s and '70s militant group the Weather Underground, an anti-imperialist splinter group of the SDS which engaged in violent antiwar protest activity including the 'Days of Rage' in Chicago in 1969; this chapter also compares the Weather Underground's tactics with the WTO protests in Seattle in 1999, which saw 50,000 anti-globalisation protesters gather in the city. Meanwhile in Chapter 2 Ben allows an Occupy Wall Street protester to use his shower and washing machine before he cooks him dinner – a gesture which forces him to interrogate his default to the 'bourgeois household' and to consider, perhaps for the first time, 'a world in which moments can be something other than the elements of profit' (47). Chapter 4 considers another, more effective example of protest activity: the tactics and achievements of ACT UP, which was established in New York in 1987 and led the fight against AIDS, using high-profile stunts and demonstrations to demand federal funding for research and access to experimental drugs. While the novels in Chapter 5 do not explicitly reference any protests, the issues they address – foreign policy, global capitalism, climate change – have each triggered mass demonstrations of varying effectiveness: on 15 February 2003 millions of people across the world protested against the United States-led invasion of Iraq; and growing anger about the climate crisis, particularly among young people, has sparked waves of protest activities which have brought the climate emergency to public attention, and vastly increased pressure on politicians to make meaningful pledges to reduce emissions. The Global Week for Future strikes in September 2019 took place in the days leading up to the UN Climate Action Summit, a deliberate piece of planning designed to focus global leaders' minds.

Protests become necessary when individuals and groups are excluded from the decision-making process, their concerns ignored by those in power. Often these protests have no discernible effect on government policy: they register the sense of anger, but fail to bring about change. Not all of the protagonists discussed in this book are protesters, but each of them is characterised by a degree of restlessness and unease, as they struggle to locate themselves comfortably within their contemporary moment. In the chapters that follow, their anxieties, and the context for those concerns, are placed in dialogue with some of the most lasting and tumultuous episodes in America's past.

Notes

1. The same article suggests that the largest demographic of participants in the BLM protests were those who were young and wealthy, with much more support from white Americans than previous BLM protests: 'nearly 95 per cent of counties that had a protest recently are majority white, and nearly three-quarters of the counties are more than 75 per cent white' ('Black Lives Matter May Be the Largest Movement in U.S. History', *New York Times*, 3 July 2020).
2. Kauffman's book *How to Read a Protest* looks in depth at the planning of this march, and the impact of the signs that were carried by protesters.

Chapter 1

Historical Racism and Contemporary Incarceration in C. E. Morgan and Hari Kunzru

The opening pages of C. E. Morgan's second novel, *The Sport of Kings* (2016), describe a young boy, Henry Forge, attempting to run away from his father and the punishment he can expect for having killed one of the neighbour's bulls. When he is eventually caught by Filip Dunbar, a Black farmhand on the Forge estate, Henry's father, John Henry, beats him with his belt having first tied him to an old whipping post for enslaved people – an early indication both that the Forge family had been enslavers, and that this racist history has a tangible ongoing presence on the estate. This opening scene takes place in Kentucky in 1954, but the novel as a whole, which is a complex, multigenerational exploration of slavery's aftermaths, is set in both Kentucky and Ohio, and spans the period 1783 to 2006. As the novel develops, the focus remains for a time on Henry's growing interest in breeding Thoroughbreds, as he transforms his father's estate from corn production to a horse farm. By the 1980s, Henry is inculcating his daughter Henrietta with his own obsession with genetics and evolution; together they set about trying to breed the perfect racehorse. But the novel contains a parallel to this narrative of ambition and privilege: around a third of the way through the reader is introduced to Allmon Shaughnessy, the son of an absent white father and low-income Black mother, whose childhood and adolescence, roughly contemporaneous with Henrietta's, is spent in the poorest parts of Cincinnati. When his mother's sickness forces him out on to the streets to sell drugs for money, he is made to countenance the stark truth about his lack of choice in a time and space where structural racism catches him and his mother in a double bind. Following six years in prison and the death of his mother, Allmon trains as a horse groom, and the two narratives converge when he is hired on Forge Run Farm by Henrietta. But this is not the first time their stories have overlapped: Allmon's ancestor is Scipio, a fugitive from slavery who was owned by Henrietta's ancestor Edward Forge in the 1820s. Scipio successfully escaped the estate, crossing the border into Ohio by swimming the Ohio River at night; his journey, and the illusory freedom it offers, is replicated by Allmon over 150 years later, when Henry tricks him into accepting a deal which leaves him far worse off than before.

The second novel this chapter will examine, Hari Kunzru's *White Tears* (2017), also cuts between different periods in America's history in order to highlight the reappearance – continuance, even – of institutional racist structures. It begins in the contemporary period, with two white college friends, Seth and Carter, bonding over their shared interest in music, Black music in particular. They start a recording studio with Carter's family money, and remix an old blues song and market it as their own, when in fact the song originated in the 1920s, sung by a young Black man named Charlie Shaw. Charlie had been on his way to a recording studio in Jackson, Mississippi when he was arrested for vagrancy and forced into hard labour under the system of convict leasing. Charlie reappears in hallucinatory form, forcing Seth to consider the links between Charlie's fate in the Jim Crow period and that of contemporary Black men, also picked up for minor infringements, subjected to police brutality, and handed disproportionate prison sentences. In this novel the Wallace family fortune, to which Carter is the heir, were the direct beneficiaries of convict leasing during Jim Crow, and they continue to generate vast revenue from prison construction in the twenty-first century. Seth's deliberate ignorance as to the source of his friend's wealth is destroyed when his own identity is conflated with the ghost of Charlie, giving him first-hand experience of the centuries-long history of violence and discrimination towards Black men.

This chapter considers the presentation of post-slavery experience in each of the novels – the ways in which racist structures of violence and control, although manifested through different 'means and modes', repeatedly 'fracture the present' (Sharpe 12, 9). It takes Morgan's novel first, examining the reappearance of images and circumstances that pertain to the Forge family's enslaver past, its ongoing involvement in racial violence from the antebellum period until the twenty-first century, and the impact of this on individual characters such as Filip and particularly Allmon. In particular it looks at the novel's comparison of Reconstruction-era violence in Kentucky with the white supremacist backlash to the civil rights movement in the 1950s; thereafter the chapter examines Morgan's suggestion of further temporal slippage, this time between the antebellum period and the present day, focusing in particular on the treatment of Scipio (in the 1820s), and his descendant Allmon (in the late-twentieth and early-twenty-first centuries). It also considers Allmon's impoverished upbringing in Cincinnati, the manifold ways these circumstances hold him back throughout his life, and the similarities between his situation and that of Black men during the Jim Crow period. This chapter will then turn to Kunzru's novel in order to explore the direct links between Jim Crow-era convict leasing and present-day policing, arrest, and sentencing. It looks at how discriminatory laws in place during the first half of the twentieth century are replicated in parts of America today as a way to generate revenue and to imprison vast numbers of Black men.

Drawing particularly (although by no means exclusively) on Saidiya V. Hartman's *Scenes of Subjection* (1997), Michelle Alexander's *The New Jim Crow* (2010) and Christina Sharpe's *In the Wake: On Blackness and Being* (2016), this chapter examines how in these two novels by Morgan and Kunzru, racist structures of violence and constraint continue, daily, to 'rupture the present' (Sharpe 9) in ways that range from the overt to the barely visible. In these novels white supremacist violence during Reconstruction resurfaces during the civil rights movement; limits on Black freedom and movement during the Jim Crow era re-emerge, in slightly altered form, during the War on Drugs; the conditions of antebellum servitude are replicated in twenty-first-century working conditions; systems of policing and mass incarceration in the early twentieth century continue to operate in the present day; and the racist backlash to civil liberties during the 1950s has its contemporary resonance in the era of Black Lives Matter. Sharpe describes this ongoing violence and subjection as 'the past that is not past' (9), and as 'Living in the wake', by which she means 'living the history and present of terror, from slavery to the present, as the ground of our everyday Black existence' (15). Her book, which draws on examples of Black suffering and death in her own family, as well as from literature, film, photography and historical records, emphasises the reconfiguration, rather than reduction, of racist attitudes and structures through time: while the context has shifted from the conditions of slavery to more contemporary forms of control, violence and exclusion nevertheless endures. Yet Sharpe proposes that 'wake work, wake theory' (20) is not just 'recognizing antiblackness as total climate' (21), but 'inhabiting' this 'blackened consciousness' to conceive of 'particular ways of re / seeing, re / inhabiting, and re / imagining the world' (22). Sharpe therefore moots the possibility of resistance through knowledge: wake work, she writes, is a process: 'a mode of inhabiting *and* rupturing this episteme with our known lived and un / imaginable lives' (18). Hartman, whose work Sharpe draws upon, uses the phrase 'nonevent of emancipation' to make the case that 'racial slavery was transformed rather than annulled' (116, 10). Hartman's book describes 'the still-unfolding narrative of captivity, dispossession, and domination that engenders the black subject in the Americas' as 'the history that hurts', but this is a pain which 'has been largely unspoken and unrecognized . . . due to the sheer denial of black sentience' (51). Both Morgan and Kunzru's novels track the ways in which slavery and its afterlives of 'subjection' and 'exclusion' (Sharpe 12, 14), which amount to 'an abiding legacy of black inferiority and subjugation' (Hartman 10), still shape Black experience in America, but these texts also contain moments of 'resistance' and 'rupture' to 'that imposition of non/being' (Sharpe 21, 22, 21), as characters become increasingly cognisant of the structural barriers placed in their way.

I.

Morgan's long opening section, covering Henry Forge's development from child to young adult, spans the period 1954 until 1965, making it exactly synonymous with the civil rights movement. His father, John Henry, is furious at the challenges to Jim Crow laws in the federal courts, and following the *Brown* v. *Board of Education* decision in the Supreme Court in 1954, he removes Henry from school altogether, keeping him at home and hiring a private tutor from New Jersey. John Henry is explicit about his rationale for taking his son out of the public education system: 'things are happening right now in the courts. There are changes in the air, changes I don't want you exposed to. I swear the Negroes are intent on delivering themselves to hell' (25). In reality these changes took years to enact, hampered by immense resistance on the part of local and state authorities, violence carried out by a revitalised Ku Klux Klan, and the hostility of White Citizens' Councils, made up of wealthy right-wing businessmen, professionals, and religious leaders opposed to desegregation. As a lawyer and rich landowner fiercely opposed to racial equality, John Henry would almost certainly have been a Council member, and he tells his son that 'The Klan and their ilk, for all their rabble-rousing, often have a keen sense of right and wrong undiluted by relativism, and they can carry out justice with alacrity. Rough justice, yes, but justice' (56). And like some of the real-life Council members, he is not unwilling to call on their services: his comment to Henry that 'the Klan comes in handy. They're more discreet these days than they used to be' (57) is retrospectively laden with malevolent meaning when on the following page we learn that Filip, his Black farmhand, vanished overnight, just after John Henry discovered he was having an affair with his wife, Lavinia.[1] The narrator offers a deliberately muted response to Filip's disappearance, leaving readers to interpret the situation for themselves: 'The next morning, Filip did not show up for work at the Forge house, nor did he appear any day thereafter, and the code on the white, silencing streets of Paris was that the man had simply left town' (58). But the narrator, here and elsewhere in this novel, is unable to maintain this complicit silence for long. There is a sardonic tone to subsequent remarks that 'After all, sometimes black men simply left a small, Southern town' and (following a list of several other public lynchings around the same time) 'this was the 1950s and Kentucky had stopped hanging its black laundry' (58, 59). Filip's own mother, who was 'born out of the foul pussy of slavery on a Jessamine County farm' (59), lived through Jim Crow and kept a long list of the Black men and women lynched in Kentucky during the 1930s, even lighting Advent candles for those killed around Christmas:

> December 23: Sloan Allen, George King, seven men together in Georgia, James Martin, Frank West, Mack Brown, Mr. Brown, and one unidentified man.
>
> December 24: Kinch Freeman, Eli Hilson, James Garden, five together in Virginia, and fourteen unidentified men in Meridian on this day (59–60).[2]

When the Forge's cook, Maryleen, also Black, returns from her Christmas break to discover that Filip apparently 'ran off' (64), she imagines a 'lynch mob' waiting for her too, and flees from the house and the state, leaving 'this bloody borderland behind' and moving to New York: 'by the time she was approaching the outskirts of town, sweating through her blouse, she could almost see Filip hanging from a tree right before her eyes, and her decision was made' (67).

Maryleen's fears – and Filip's probable murder – shows how dangerous Kentucky was for Black Americans in the decades before and during the civil rights era.[3] In fact that reference to the 'bloody borderland' suggests that there is a direct connection between this period in Kentucky (the 1950s) and the immediate aftermath of the Civil War nearly a hundred years earlier, when Kentucky was gripped by wave after wave of racial violence, with the Ku Klux Klan instilling fear across the state. John Henry, in 1954, describes Black Americans as 'monkeys' who 'never realize until they leave the cage that they were warm and well fed in the cage' (25), and he tells his son that

> there are not merely masters and slaves by happenstance, or overse-
> ers and laborers by happenstance . . . these divisions are inherent and
> unavoidable. God save the mark – there were slaves in the Republic,
> and these liberals would imagine themselves greater minds! (55)

John Henry wants to restore the system of slavery that had been outlawed long before he was born, echoing the sentiments of conservative Democrats in the 1860s hoping to return to a pre-Civil War social order. This expression of affinity with earlier stages in Kentucky's history is worth focusing on: during Reconstruction (1865–1877) the state was notoriously violent, and a lethal place for Black Americans. Its loyalties during the Civil War had never been entirely clear-cut, but it was generally regarded as a Union state: Anne E. Marshall puts the figures at between 66,000 and 76,000 white Kentuckians fighting for the Union, and between 25,000 and 40,000 on the Confederate side (20). After the war, however, many conservative white Kentuckians from the Union side found themselves struggling to celebrate Civil War victory when it was practically synonymous with 'black emancipation and Republican politics' (Marshall 93) and the state quickly gained a reputation for extreme lawlessness, with white Kentuckians engaging in 'loosely organized campaigns of intimidation, shooting, burning, ransacking, and lynching' in a bid to restore 'as much of the prewar social and racial order as possible' (56).[4] Kentucky's reputation for acute racial violence in the two decades following the Civil War meant that a state which had been largely Union during the conflict was now perceived as part of the former Confederacy. And Confederates in Kentucky actively promoted this image, constructing monuments to memorialise Confederate soldiers, publishing soldiers' memoirs, and taking up the Lost Cause ideology – thereby remarketing its lawless behaviour as being rooted in 'honor and chivalry' (Marshall 73), and working towards reconciliation with the North. But this promulgation of a supposedly more honourable rationale for the racial violence did not alter the fact that Kentucky was a lethally dangerous place.[5] And John Henry's impassioned call, nearly a century later, for a return to slavery, coupled with his advocation of racial hostility (and even murder), reveals that this chapter in Kentucky's history never in fact ended: his avenging of Filip's affair with his wife is an example of the 'personally sanctioned justice', or the 'southern code of honor' that Marshall suggests was characteristic of Kentucky both before and after the Civil War (75). The murder of Filip, and Maryleen's response to that death, is therefore part of what Sharpe terms the 'precarities of the afterlives of slavery': the 'disaster of Black subjection' which is both historical and 'deeply atemporal' (5), as that earlier stage of terror and violence is continually reconfigured through the multiple and varied atrocities that are still enacted against Black lives – murder, in Filip's case, and the fear of murder in Maryleen's.

Kentucky is a compelling example of how memory can be reconstructed for a particular purpose. National amnesia enabled Kentucky to remarket itself as a Confederate state driven by chivalric ideals. And John Henry's apparent nostalgia for the conditions of pre-emancipation Kentucky, and for the violence of Reconstruction, allies him with those proponents of the Lost Cause nearly a century earlier who similarly defended slavery as a necessary and benevolent institution. But this is not the only time John Henry offers a take on the past that deliberately glosses over the reality of racial violence. He promotes a particular narrative of Forge family history which emphasises its 'long, distinguished line' (22), traceable all the way back to Samuel Forge, who travelled from Virginia with an enslaved man in 1783. This lineage, John Henry believes, is what gives the family its pedigree, and this is the lesson he teaches Henry: 'All roads have led to you, Henry ... I'm a planter's son, and you're a planter's son. There is no need for improvement, Henry, only adherence to a line that has never altered, because it's never proven unsound' (51). Years later Henry gives a 'towering donation' to fund the Genealogical Museum of Central Kentucky; when he and his daughter attend the reception to mark its opening, the woman giving the toast explains that 'The Forge family is one of the crown jewels of the Bluegrass' and 'We wouldn't be – we couldn't be – who we are without men like John Henry and Henry Forge, men who preserve our past and guide us into a future where the past still matters' (359). But this particular version of Forge history conveniently overlooks the existence of enslaved people who were front and centre in running all aspects of the estate in the antebellum period – enslaved people built the house in the first place back in the 1780s, and thereafter carried out all farm work and domestic jobs for nearly a hundred years. Henrietta's inculcation in the 'dignity' of her family line is such that when, at the age of thirteen, she stumbles across a ledger from 1827 detailing Edward Forge's will, which includes a list of twelve enslaved people, including Scipio and his mother Prissey, she swiftly returns it to the shelf in her father's library:

> the heat of the thing was threatening to scorch her fingers. What to do with this remnant of another century still hot enough to burn? Put it away. Which is exactly what she did. The names, whispering repeatedly out of the flames, were dampered by the closing book and then the black ledger was returned to the shelf, where she would soon forget about it entirely, this page from the history her family had made (140).

Clearly only one version of the Forge family history has been officially recorded, and this is a whitewashed narrative, from which the parallel history of the enslaved people owned by successive generations of the family has been expunged. The Forges have remarketed themselves as founders of the Commonwealth, whose own blood and sweat built its foundations and supported it ever since.

That handwritten draft of a will from 1827 temporarily disrupts Henrietta's understanding of her family's past, as she discovers (but just as quickly forgets) that her own fortune was built on slavery. The ledger is swiftly returned to the shelf; the world of Thoroughbred breeding is her sole concern, and she is unwilling to accommodate this dark revelation. And in a similar fashion, Scipio's narrative of enslavement emerges in brief, rather impressionistic fragments which are always about to be swept aside, or overwhelmed, by the more dominant Forge storyline. This narrative hierarchy replicates the unacknowledged trauma of Black American experience, repressed and contested by a much more powerful white national discourse. But Scipio's harrowing experience as an enslaved man in the 1820s, however fleetingly rendered in the novel, is worth dwelling on here, not least because his escape across the Ohio River and his remaining years as an ostensibly free man in Bucktown, an African American neighbourhood in Cincinnati, foreshadows the various limitations placed on his descendant Allmon more than 150 years later, in the last few years of the twentieth century. Their yoked fates underlines Sharpe's thesis that Black Americans are 'living in the afterlives of that brutality that is not in the past' (99), as slavery 'changed over time' so that 'its duration expands into supposed emancipation and beyond' (106). In the novel Scipio is the product of rape: his mother Prissey, the Forge family cook, was raped by her master, Edward Forge. After Prissey's death Scipio makes a desperate bid for freedom, running at night towards the Ohio River. And when Allmon is first introduced in the narrative, he too is heading north across the border after the death of his own mother. He has been invited to live with a distant relative down in Lexington, Kentucky, but in the middle of his first night there, homesick and grief-stricken, he steals the woman's Cadillac and heads back north – only to be stopped by police while crossing the border and sentenced to ten years for possession of just five grams of crack cocaine. Scipio, too, found that the Ohio–Kentucky border offered a vision of freedom that was ultimately illusory: while on the run he encountered another escaped enslaved person, the heavily pregnant Abby, who begged Scipio to take her with him. While swimming across the river together he mistakenly kicked her, before leaving her to drown during his desperate scramble to reach the other side. Having reached literal freedom on the Ohio side of the river, so that 'His broad, white-latticed back is a curtain drawn on the crude festival of the South', his guilt over Abby's death created a sense of moral constraint: the narrator explains that Scipio 'found something worse than slavery' (305), and he hanged himself fifteen years later, finally overwhelmed by his own guilt. Consistent with Sharpe's point about the rhythms of repetition, Allmon, like Scipio, is also wracked by guilt after imagining himself suddenly free: he accepts a sham deal from Henry which promises him future earnings on a racehorse providing he cuts off all contact with Henrietta. But Henry then withdraws the horse from racing, tricking Allmon out of his money. Rather than being set up financially, Allmon is left with nothing, and at the same time he has unwittingly walked away from his pregnant girlfriend, and inadvertently allowed his baby son to be raised by Henry.

The falseness of Allmon's supposed 'choice' to make that deal to leave Forge Run Farm is exposed by Reuben, the Black jockey, who draws a direct parallel between Allmon's situation and that of an enslaved woman forcibly separated from her child:

> White lies don't add up to the truth! Your only choice was no choice!
> . . . You think little sister had any choice when Massah sold her baby
> off the auction block at Cheapside, not seventy miles away from this
> here horse track? They call their madness logic, but that don't make
> it logic! Your life or your child? You call that a choice? (514)

Reuben, unlike Allmon, operates from what Sharpe terms the 'position of the wake: from a position of deep hurt and of deep knowledge', having understood the way 'gratuitous violence . . . occurs at the level of a structure that constitutes the Black as the constitutive outside' (Sharpe 27, 28). He fully grasps the way Kentucky's violent history endures into the present day, warning Allmon to 'learn your history!', because 'This land right here under your clumsy-ass feet' is still the 'No-Man's-Land, the Borderland, the Dark and Bloody Ground, the In-Between, the Slaughterhouse, the Wild Frontier' (512), and 'fuckery and perversion' is still the 'cant of Kaintuckee!' (514). Allmon's entrapment at different stages of the novel is made worse because he is sold the illusion of choice: not just by signing his name to Henry's deal, but also before that, in juvenile detention, where he was repeatedly told there was an alternative path for him should he wish to take it: '*you have to choose to move beyond race. It's your choice. You want to be a victim forever?*' (269). Hartman uses the term 'burdened individuality' to describe the 'double bind of freedom', which equates to being technically self-determining while at the same time denied access to resources and opportunities that would allow one to capitalise on that freedom: 'being freed from slavery and free of resources, emancipated and subordinated, self-possessed and indebted, equal and inferior, liberated and encumbered, sovereign and dominated, citizen and subject' (117). This is the 'gap', Hartman explains, 'between the formal stipulation of rights and the legitimate exercise of them' (123). Even when Allmon is free, his life is circumscribed in countless ways: his poverty-stricken childhood in a tough part of Cincinnati, with an ill mother too sick to work but without health insurance, leaves him little choice but to sell drugs in order to support them both. That Allmon's fate is predetermined seems so obvious that even Henry is moved to acknowledge it: when asked where Allmon came from, he laughingly answers, 'From wherever they grow America's criminals' (339) – the implication being that Allmon's arrest and imprisonment was a direct, involuntary consequence of his early environment.

In the late-nineteenth-century context Hartman mainly focuses on, those restrictions on freedom included 'vagrancy, breach-of-contract, and antienticement laws' (141) – so-called 'Black Codes' which placed limits on employment and even movement; arrest for these and other crimes would likely lead to fines and thereafter forced labour under the system of convict leasing (145). She describes how the onus was nevertheless on the individual to become a self-supporting freed man in spite of these restrictions. He needed to prove himself a responsible citizen, worthy of his freedom. This led to self-imposed constraints on the freed man's conduct; any perceived shortcomings in discipline or productivity might suggest to outsiders that one's work ethic simply fell away without the threat of the overseer's whip. Hartman's context is the post-Civil War era, but these ideas map usefully onto Allmon's situation in the early 2000s.[6] Allmon was tricked into taking a deal with Henry which was presented as the only means to secure any type of future for himself; Henry also lied to him that Henrietta had had another man's baby. But when Allmon discovers the truth about the deal, his instinct is to blame himself: 'a sneaking thought: Forge lied, but I sold my child. My soul is as rotten as old fruit' (510). Allmon is similar to Hartman's freed man who was encouraged, by various conduct handbooks, to attribute any failure to support his family to his own idleness and moral ineptitude, rather than those far-reaching and punitive restrictions on his freedom: 'to be responsible', Hartman explains, 'was to be blameworthy' (125). Allmon has absorbed these lessons, believing himself entirely responsible for this failure to safeguard his child, rather than the practical barriers standing in his way such as poverty, lack of education and discriminatory treatment as an ex-convict.

As a teenager Allmon followed the same course as his enslaved ancestor Scipio, driving north across the border towards a longed-for freedom. And aspects of Allmon's situation after release also replicate some of the day-to-day conditions of slavery. Having been forced out of his position at Forge Run Farm and into a low-paid job with Mack, the family's horse trainer, his living conditions are hardly better than those of the enslaved people owned by the Forges in the antebellum period, and are actually worse than his prison cell at Bracken Penitentiary. Allmon sleeps in 'unventilated cinder-block dorms with dingy, mold-streaked walls and sputtering lights' alongside the Peruvian and Guatemalan migrants also working as grooms; the lack of an air conditioner means that he 'sweated in the swampy ninety-degree nights and watched the other grooms swoon and puke from the heat' (417). The narrative perspective enters Allmon's mind during a passage when he starts to imagine himself as somehow non-human: 'You drew flies like any other animal', he thinks to himself (417). Those appalling conditions under Mack's employment, of sleeping in humid conditions and working without a day off 'unless you were dying' (417), are Allmon's only option having been banished from Forge Run Farm following the discovery of his relationship with Henrietta. But of course, that dismissal also echoes the disappearance of Filip, back in the 1950s, when he was killed by Klansmen after John Henry found out about his wife's affair. The point to be made here is that Allmon's existence calls to mind various different aspects and moments of antebellum and post-slavery experience, with racial violence existing in diffuse ways which vary from the insidious to the flagrant. When Reuben suggests to Allmon that they 'Swap prison tales!' (426), he hints at the fact that although he has never been physically incarcerated, the modes of control affect him too; he later remarks that 'It's no longer the man but his very house' (432) – that is, the entire structure is to blame. Allmon's discovery of Filip's dire fate becomes a moment of illumination akin to Reuben's revelatory point that 'The man that stole your child is the same man that killed your mother, the man that put you behind bars, that's the same man that's been stringing up the black brother since time immemorial' (514). When he hears of Filip's murder, he finally realises that his own life has been hampered by a centuries-old system designed to constrain him:

> The Forges had murdered a man, the woman had said. Of course they had. Of course! He felt the righteousness of his vindication like a sun in his chest; it transformed and shined light on the guilt that had been torturing him. He had always known what the Forges were, but in Henrietta's deceiving arms, he'd allowed himself to ignore it! Of course, he'd known; he'd spent his whole life on the run from a fucking lynch mob (485–6).

Allmon reaches, in this late stage of the novel, what Sharpe terms a *'state of wakefulness; consciousness'* that his life – and Filip's before him – is lived in 'the wake of the unfinished project of emancipation' (Sharpe 4, 5). Reuben, who has known this for some time, has repeatedly warned Allmon that Kentucky's bloody history is still ongoing. But Allmon has tried to disregard these stories, to 'close [his] ears to time' (485), only to find, when it is altogether too late, that he cannot outrun the truth. 'Time told stories that busted your eardrums and made them bleed' (485), he thinks, as he recognises that aspects of his experience contain echoes of Filip's fate, and even of Scipio's some 200 years earlier.

This long history of exploitation and violence, which Allmon only latterly understands, has already been signalled to the reader in a more subtle way, through a set of racially-charged images that are loosely replicated within different temporal contexts – rematerialising in diverse ways across decades, and even centuries. This contributes to the novel's sense of historical sedimentation, and underlines what Henrietta, in a different context, considers the 'brittle veneer between past and present' (342). The Forge kitchen in particular repeatedly operates as a space of racial encounter in this novel, and in the first (1950s) section, the cook, Maryleen, hears Filip and Lavinia having sex in the pantry, just off the kitchen. When she goes to investigate, she sees 'Filip and the lady of the house, clutching at each other' and flees from the kitchen 'with the negative of their black and white scorching her eyes' (44). The direct upshot of this discovery is the murder of Filip. This scene is subtly evoked many years later when Henrietta interviews Allmon for the groom job: 'Has there ever been a black man in this kitchen before? In their house? Some memory was rattling around in her mind, but it wouldn't stand still' (185). Later, when Henrietta is having sex with Allmon, the pair are seen by Mack, the horse trainer. Before he too flees the scene undetected, he uses the same imagery as Maryleen as he considers what he has seen: 'the black guy moving over a white woman who had turned her face away . . . it stood out in his mind later with all the startling, upending stark of a photographic negative' (356). Very soon after, Allmon (in a less violent parallel with Filip) agrees to the deal that banishes him from the estate and bars him from any further contact with Henrietta. But these scenes in the kitchen, unbeknown to those involved in them, implicitly recall an even earlier moment, this time of sexual violence, which took place in the same room around the turn of the nineteenth century, when the cook, Prissey, is raped by her enslaver, Edward Forge: having forced some of the others to have sex at gunpoint, he 'charges through the kitchen door' to Prissey, and yanks her into the 'cornmeal and spice smell of his own pantry, where she is saying no no no no please no . . .' (484). Prissey, mother of Scipio, is Allmon's distant ancestor; this may be why Allmon 'instinctively' knows his way around the kitchen 'as if he'd been there before' (364).

Allmon's proximity to the conditions of enslavement is also signalled by Morgan during an earlier scene at a yearling sale, when the narrative temporarily confuses Allmon with the horses on sale:

> And like a barn cat, Allmon was everywhere. Even here – brown like a bay, Henry thought – at the yearling sale in the Keeneland pavilion. There were occasional glimpses of him in the parade of horses brought to the auction block, where the auctioneer presided ten feet high on the dais, flanked by his relay men, whispering and pointing, their eyes trained on the proceedings below. The auctionable flesh emerged stage right, passed to the black ringman in his coat and tie, the yearling striding to the center with a hip number trembling on its quarter, eyes bobbling with fear . . . (338–9).

Henry considers Allmon's skin colour in equine terms at the start of that passage, but the conflation of him and the horses becomes altogether more arresting with that phrase 'auctionable flesh', which seems at first to refer to Allmon. The subject of the sentence has switched, between sentences three and four, creating a narrative slippage that suggests, very briefly and before things are clarified with the mention of the 'yearling striding to the center', that it is Allmon who is being brought to the auction block. This momentary but disturbing confusion collapses the temporal distance between the present day and antebellum Kentucky, when enslaved people were routinely put up for auction. And while working for the Forges, Allmon feels constantly under siege; even with Henrietta, his body seems to be 'tied up in old rope' (346): he wishes to 'escape' (351), but her arms were 'like iron bands' (350) around him. Maryleen, back in 1954, thinks to herself that some of the kitchen equipment she is using 'probably dated from slavery days', but 'she'd bet fifty dollars if anyone actually cared' (42). In the early 2000s, the old whipping post is still standing in the garden, and the house has kept its enslaved persons staircase: tangible proof of the sedimented layers of racist violence and exploitation which continue into the present day, and which the Forges consistently refuse to acknowledge.

II.

There are important correlations between Allmon's situation in around 2006 and that of his ancestor Scipio in antebellum Kentucky, and of Filip during the civil rights movement in the 1950s. And Allmon's situation also evokes the treatment of Black Americans during the Jim Crow period, when hundreds of laws were passed to legalise racial segregation and restrict civil liberties. Allmon's entrance into the narrative is delayed until almost 200 pages of the novel have passed by, but the chapter detailing his troubled early life swells to nearly 100 pages, side-lining, for a time, the previously dominant Forge storyline which he subsequently enters when he is hired by Henrietta. In that long Allmon chapter, set in Cincinnati during the 1980s and '90s, Allmon and his mother Marie are trapped in a system which marginalises their struggles with poverty and ill-health, and punishes them when they try to find a way through. Marie is left to care for Allmon on her own after his father, Mike Shaughnessy, abandons them; with only one meagre income they move to a cheap apartment in Northside, a dangerous and almost exclusively Black neighbourhood: Marie is accused of being a 'race traitor' (203) because Allmon's father is white, and Allmon, aged nine, witnesses the suicide of a young Black girl whose 'pert ski-slope nose' was 'like a white girl's', and had 'made her a beloved pariah, as despised as she was envied' (222). When Marie collapses at work, having been sick with lupus for some time (a disease which disproportionately affects Black women, and gets little in the way of research), she is too poor to pay for an ambulance or proper medicine, but earns just too much to qualify for Medicaid – and her medical records mean she would be rejected for health insurance anyway. The doctor's apologetic remarks sum up the impossible situation: 'There's really nothing else to do but take steroids. We're all still following a script that was written fifty years ago' (257).[7] The situation reaches breaking point when Marie's food stamps are taken away after she is found guilty of defrauding the welfare system for owning a car she no longer drives. Summoned downtown to a 'pre-appeal disqualification hearing' (247) (the full implications of which are not made clear), she is not offered legal representation, and clumsily answers the panel's questions. Desperate, in great pain, and finally unable to feed her son, she exposes the hopeless agony of her double bind:

> I'm sick, and I can't do anything about it, because I'm broke, and I can't go to a specialist. I promise you, it's a fact . . . I'm so sick I can't hardly work, but I can't stop working or what – or what? What are we going to do? Does the world just want us to roll over and die? (249)

That speech calls to mind Hartman's point that 'Being emancipated without resources was no freedom at all', as she emphasises 'the absence of the material support that would have made substantial freedom ultimately realizable' (136). There are clear distinctions to be made between Marie's 1980s context and scenes taking place a century or more earlier, yet Marie and Allmon nevertheless experience a version of those 'exclusionary strategies' (Hartman 134) which render it inevitable, after they move again to the cheapest place they can find in the worst part of the city, and Marie becomes too ill to leave the house, that Allmon should start running drugs for a local dealer to pay for rent and a doctor. The swiftness with which Allmon tracks down the local drug dealer, Aesop, demonstrates how easy (but also how necessary) it is to slip into criminality. In a passage of free indirect style Allmon reflects on his new circumstances:

> he studied on Aesop (caps, glocks, swagger, wit, threat, diamond signet ring on his pinkie), who his mother didn't know a thing about, but then she didn't know anything about being a man, what it was to

be in your body, how you were born into obligation. A man's whole life was a haymaker. So he continued to run in the afternoons after school. Sure, you weren't supposed to lie, to cheat, to bribe, to hit, to sneak. But increasingly, the world of rules was being shown up for what it really was, a rigged system, a fixed game. You should be good, definitely – but only until you couldn't, until everything you loved was on the line. It just made him want to kill someone if he studied on that too hard. So the key was to not study on the truth – the madness in the center of everything that was called common sense in a white-ruled world (258–9).

This passage communicates several aspects of Allmon's state of mind at this point: firstly, his fetishization of gangster culture – the 'swagger' and 'wit' of Aesop, but also his gun, money, jewellery and clothes. These objects represent power and wealth, and signal it to outsiders. But there is more to the passage than that: the line about being 'born into obligation' and 'being a man' echoes the language used to drive home the 'responsibilities of independence' laid on formerly enslaved men after the Civil War, who were expected to work hard without complaint; the 'failure to meet this obligation', Hartman explains, 'at the very least, risked the loss of honor, status, and manhood' (135). Allmon evokes Hartman's self-regulating freed man at another stage of the novel (as we have already seen) when he instinctively blames himself for taking Henry's rigged deal. And even here, as a teenager, Allmon has a clear sense of his responsibilities: he is accountable for his family's success. But crucially he has also seen the barriers placed in his mother's way when she tries to make a reasonable living: her hours at work are cut, her welfare is stopped, and she cannot afford healthcare, nor risk falling into debt. Her work ethic has offered her no security and not enough money; those watchwords like 'industry' and 'diligence' (Hartman 135) – qualities which the freed man was encouraged to develop in order to become disciplined and ultimately self-policing – have not brought any reward. While Allmon therefore feels that same sense of obligation to support his family, he does so by circumnavigating the discriminatory and unlucrative workplace altogether, directing his energies towards making money through any means possible.

Allmon reacts with weary acceptance to his sentencing of two years in juvenile detention for arson, despite having no involvement in the riot: in fact, he was arrested in front of his grandfather's church, screaming as he watched it burn to the ground. And in the 'dingy courtroom' where he is first among dozens to be sentenced that day, they 'threw the book at him. But he didn't need to read it, he already knew all the words by heart' (267). Like his mother during her welfare hearing, Allmon 'never had the benefit of an attorney or even the offer of one', and therefore he 'couldn't pretend to be surprised when they sentenced him' (267). Michelle Alexander's book *The New Jim Crow* examines the mass incarceration of Black men in America, convicted of trumped-up drug charges, denied legal representation and handed disproportionate sentences for non-violent offences. It allows us to understand Allmon's trajectory – and particularly the inevitability of his arrest and imprisonment – as part of a broader social and political pattern. Alexander points out that the extraordinary rise in the prison population is a direct consequence of the War on Drugs launched by President Reagan in 1982, which licensed police to focus their efforts particularly on Black communities, to hand down vastly longer sentences for possession of crack cocaine (arrests for which tended to be majority-Black) than the powder version (predominantly white), and thereafter to operate a system of 'legalized discrimination' for ex-offenders, barring them from jobs, housing and welfare for the rest of their lives (7).[8] The upshot of this, Alexander explains, is that young Black men are 'part of a growing undercaste, permanently locked up and locked out of mainstream society' (7).

It is worth exploring some of the ways in which Alexander's findings correspond to Allmon's experiences in Cincinnati. During the riot, when Allmon is arrested for the first time, police have flooded the Black working-class neighbourhood of Over-the-Rhine, notorious for its high crime levels, in order to make hundreds of arrests. Alexander describes how the police are incentivised to 'round up' (17) as many drug criminals as possible, which means they tend to operate in poor communities of colour: 'decisions must be made regarding who should be targeted and where the drug war should be waged' (123), she explains, and 'So long as mass drug arrests are concentrated in impoverished urban areas, police chiefs have little reason to fear a political backlash, no matter how aggressive and warlike the efforts may be' (124). Allmon instinctively understands this: he hears the 'sirens looping out of the precinct house' and the sound 'jogged something': he senses that 'They'd all be rounded up, or there'd be blood, or both' (265). In fact, the police have already shot one of Aesop's friends 'in the motherfucking back' (263). Alexander uses the term 'ghetto communities' to describe poor, racially-segregated, inner-city areas which have high numbers of ex-offenders, because they have nowhere else to go after release (196). Allmon's grandfather prefers the even starker terms 'ghetto plantation' and 'Jim Crow prison' (217) to describe the progressively worse parts of Cincinnati where Allmon and his mother move, drawing a more explicit historical comparison with earlier systems of racial control.

Living in a dangerous and deprived urban area made Allmon's initial move into criminality already more likely, and after he is released from juvenile detention, his chances of finding gainful employment are slim. As an ex-offender, his best chance of a job would have been in construction or a large factory, but this once-viable option has disappeared as a result of deindustrialisation – Cincinnati is a Rust Belt city, hit hard by the decline of heavy industry, increased automation and the transfer of manufacturing overseas. Previously industrial parts of the city, which once employed large numbers of unskilled men, are now falling apart: when Marie loses her benefits they move to

> a noplace crumbling under the black shadow bands of the viaduct and I-74, where the houses were shambling, filthy, and few, over-shadowed by the behemoth brownfields looted of their industry, windows shattered by rocks and bullets, down into forgottenness where few families lived and the ones who did lived in decay, in the bowels of the city (250–1).

Allmon cannot travel far for work because he needs to report to his parole officer, and has no access to a car; he also needs to look after his mother. He is therefore trapped in a loop, and the novel describes how within five days 'He was back in it in every way – running, hanging with the crew, pocketing change, wearing a bomber Aesop gave him' (274). Allmon marvels that 'it's just crazy how you slip into your old gambling seat at the casino, start stacking chips like you never even went anywhere' (274). During his second arrest, this time for stealing a relative's car and driving north from Lexington back into Ohio, multiple charges are laid against him, including 'possession of five grams of crack cocaine', for which he is sentenced to ten years, and a further two for 'motor vehicle theft and possession of a weapon and resisting arrest' (289). The judge, having listened to Allmon's description of his circumstances ('Northside, juvie, your momma, her dying – no, wait, I was something else before all that, I promise'), declares himself 'tired' of the familiar 'sob story' he hears from 'identical young men who parade through these chambers and ask for leniency, day after day, year after year' (524).

After release, convicted offenders like Allmon continue to be discriminated against in what Alexander terms a 'parallel universe' where 'discrimination, stigma, and exclusion are perfectly legal, and privileges of citizenship such as voting and jury service are off-limits' (94). Once they 'check the box' marked 'felon' on job applications they are much less likely to find employment – this is the case for Black offenders in particular – and convicted criminals can also legally be refused public housing, making it more likely they will end up homeless, or in a shelter; in many states they will also be denied access to welfare (94). The right to vote is also withheld after release – in some states, for the rest of the offender's life. And even those legally entitled to vote tend not to register – either because they have been told, 'by parole and probation officers', that they are no longer eligible, or because they fear 'any contact with governmental authorities' (160). The reality of Allmon's situation is articulated in a passage of second person narration near the novel's end, in 2006:

> They say there's gonna be a black president someday. Maybe. Or maybe just black skin. Either way, you won't ever get to vote in Kentucky. Won't have a place to live, 'cause you won't qualify for Section Eight housing to get your feet on the ground, won't ever serve on a jury to keep a brother out of jail, won't ever get a good job once you X the little felony box, can't legally carry a gun to keep some crazy racist from killing you, and there was never any protection against the cops to begin with (530).

Allmon therefore recognises, too late, that the treatment of ex-offenders like him amounts to a form of state-sponsored control that replicates the legalised discrimination under Jim Crow: unable to vote (or serve on a jury), segregated in the worst areas of the city and discriminated against at every turn.

That quotation also brings into focus the specific context for this novel, which ends two years before Barack Obama's 2008 election victory. Allmon's prediction that Obama's presidency would have little impact on the lives of ordinary Black Americans like him was one that was frequently articulated in the months and years leading up to the election – prominent writers on race such as sociologist Eduardo Bonilla-Silva, together with Victor Ray, highlighted the incoming president's refusal to tackle (or even really discuss) the issue of racial inequality; his dissociating himself from civil rights activists (including, controversially, Reverend Jeremiah Wright, the pastor of his own former church); and his presentation of a 'post-racial persona and political stance', a '*strategic* move towards racelessness' which ensured he remained a viable proposition for white voters (178).[9] Obama was fully cognisant that to address racial inequality ran the risk of alienating large swathes of white voters by 'offending white innocence' (Coates 115), and stirring up an already rabid right-wing press who took any opportunity to focus on *his* Blackness and accuse him of representing only Black Americans, rather than the country as a whole. And as Ta-Nehisi Coates has described, this was made plain on those rare occasions when (during his presidency) he did comment publicly on race and policing: the backlash was fierce when (in 2009) he described the officer who arrested Henry Louis Gates in his own home as having 'acted stupidly', and stated (after Black teenager Trayvon Martin was shot dead by George Zimmerman in February 2012) that 'If I had a son, he'd look like Trayvon'.[10] For the most part, Obama avoided making contentious statements on race, pitching himself as a moderate, pro-business conservative who could be trusted to look after the economic interests of white Americans; and far from addressing those obstacles put in the way of Black Americans, his presidency made it even less likely that racist structures would be challenged, because those two election victories seemed to prove that those structures no longer existed.[11] White voters in particular after 2008 and 2012 could feel satisfied that the country no longer had a racism problem – after all, many of them voted in a Black president – despite the fact that housing and education remained (and still remain) largely segregated; that higher-level or managerial positions are still disproportionately white; and that prisons are still filled with Black men. Michelle Alexander makes this point towards the end of her book when she suggests that 'Black success stories [like Obama's] ... "prove" that race is no longer relevant' because they 'lend credence to the notion that anyone, no matter how poor or how black you may be, can make it to the top, if only you try hard enough' (248). These examples of Black excellence therefore 'legitimate a system that remains fraught with racial bias', because singling out particular examples of high-achieving Black Americans contributes to the continuation of discriminatory policies by suggesting to observers that those policies do not exist, and that the failure of other Black Americans to achieve successes of their own must therefore be their own fault – in this way, 'society is absolved of responsibility' (248). Obama himself seemed to underline this point during a commencement speech to students graduating from Morehouse College (an all-male HBCU and the alma mater of Dr Martin Luther King Jr) in May 2013: in comments which recall Hartman's 'burdened individuality' (117), he talked to students about their 'individual responsibilities', telling them that 'there's no longer any room for excuses' and 'nobody is going to give you anything that you have not earned', before reminding them 'to work twice as hard as anyone else if you want to get by'.[12] These cautioning remarks emphasised individual responsibility as the path to success – 'set[ting] a good example for that young brother coming up' – which was matched by his reluctance to enact specific policies to address the systemic barriers holding Black Americans back.[13] And in words which echo the judge's words to Allmon when sentencing him, Obama also warned the students that 'Nobody cares how tough your upbringing was. Nobody cares if you suffered some discrimination'. Obama's presidency post-dates Allmon's death in 2006, but by this stage he has already concluded that his circumstances are unlikely to change for the better: 'men like Forge had the keys to everything' (510), he reflects, and finding a path through the 'white fucking maze' (453) of contemporary America seems nigh-on impossible.

III.

Like Morgan's novel, Hari Kunzru's 2017 *White Tears* is also concerned with issues of racial incarceration, both historical and contemporary; also like *The Sport of Kings*, the opening section of this novel quickly establishes the wealth and privilege of its central white characters. Kunzru's novel begins in contemporary America, at a 'not-quite-Ivy school' where the narrator, Seth, first encounters Carter Wallace, a very rich fellow student and amateur DJ who enjoys 'quasi-celebrity status' (9) on campus. Carter has dreadlocks and a 'Blond beard plaited into a sort of fashionable rope, no shirt and a tattoo of Mexican *calaveras* on his chest' (8). Seth, on the other hand, is a self-declared 'loser', whose personal style seems to be that of a 'homeless computer scientist' (10). But Carter recognises that Seth shares his interest in music and in making his own recording devices, and invites him over to listen to old vinyl records on his expensive analogue equipment. Carter is also a serious collector, particularly of rare and undiscovered records, and is a music obsessive, listening 'exclusively to black music', which he feels is 'more intense and authentic than anything made by white people' (9). This music has to be both old and undiscovered: having already been through a hip hop period, and before that a phase of old house and techno, Carter's taste has settled on blues music from the late 1920s and early 1930s; Seth notes ruefully that 'An ever longer list of things was not real enough for him, tainted by the digital sins of modernity'

(19). After college the pair move to Brooklyn and set up a recording studio together (with Carter's family money), and Carter insists that all the equipment must be pre-digital:

> always with a history, everything at least forty years old, tube amps and sixties fuzzboxes and a desk certified to have once been installed at Fame studios in Muscle Shoals. Vocals went through a pair of nineteen-fifties AKG C12's that cost fifteen thousand dollars (25).

The boys' obsession – or fetishization – of Black music becomes harmful when Seth happens to record a chess player in Washington Square Park sing a line from a blues song. Carter mixes the song and brands it the work of Charlie Shaw, a name he apparently makes up on the spot. When the boys release the hoax record to various file-sharing sites, the response from other collectors is of feverish excitement, but also triggers a series of violent and unsettling events enacted on the two boys: the song, and Charlie Shaw, seem to possess a ghostly revenge motive originating in the Jim Crow era, when the real-life Charlie, a young musician from Mississippi, was arrested on his way to a recording studio in Jackson. The narrative cuts between Seth's first-hand testimony as progressively stranger things start happening to him (particularly when he takes a road trip to Mississippi with Carter's sister), and that of JumpJim, an elderly record collector who tells Seth the story of Chester Bly, a white blues aficionado from the 1950s who also took a trip South, using bullying and trick tactics to get hold of rare records sitting forgotten in people's homes.

Morgan's novel contained images and motifs which recurred across several periods. The Black body, that novel repeatedly showed, continues to be the site of violence and negation more than 150 years after the Thirteenth Amendment was ratified in 1865. But whereas Morgan's novel focused on the persistence of discriminatory structures which operate against successive generations of Black Americans from the antebellum period onwards, Kunzru's novel depicts the literal reappearance, albeit in ghostly form, of a young Black man who was arrested in the 1920s under Jim Crow laws, and later died in a labour camp. The system of convict leasing, which was perfectly legal under the Thirteenth Amendment, helped to rebuild the Southern economy after the Civil War, providing free, forced labour for mines and quarries. Charlie Shaw had been on the way to a recording studio in Mississippi in 1929 when he missed his train from Moorhead to Jackson and had to walk some of the way. He was picked up in a white neighbourhood, convicted of vagrancy and fined a hundred dollars. Unable to pay the fine, he was sent to work for a year – a sentence which was constantly being extended, as Charlie explains: 'always the fines for falling behind, talking back. Everything you do they add days or dollars. And you got no dollars so they add days. That's how they do. That's how they drive you down' (257). The judge sentencing Charlie and nine others that morning was related by blood to those he sent them to work for: 'Judge Wilbur, on behalf of the thrifty state of Mississippi, set us all to work for his brothers on the levee. Then he broke for lunch' (255).

Charlie is unable to pay the fine for the crime of 'vagrancy' – a law established after the Civil War in order to control and contain formerly enslaved people.[14] He is forced to labour under inhumane conditions, working all day in the heat, and chained together with other criminals at night. Charlie describes a man being beaten to death with a pick handle; others are shot in the head. In an interview following the publication of *White Tears* Kunzru spoke of 'the very direct structural connections between present-day policing in a lot of places in the US – one could say across the US – and techniques of social control that are associated with slavery', specifically 'the convict-leasing system that grew up after the formal end of slavery'. His novel identifies the many parallels between Charlie's fate in the 1920s of being fined for a trivial offence and sentenced for not being able to pay, and the contemporary practice among police officers of issuing as many fines as possible in order to generate income for the city budget. If the violators, the vast majority of whom are Black, find themselves unable to pay the fines, they often find themselves in court, which generates further fees. Those who fail to make their court appearance might be arrested and wind up in prison. Michelle Alexander lists some examples of 'preconviction service fees' such as 'jail book-in fees levied at the time of arrest', 'public defender application fees' for when a defender applies for 'court-appointed counsel', and a 'bail investigation fee', levied 'when the court determines the likelihood of the accused appearing at trial' (155). And while in prison, offenders continue to generate revenue, just as they did under the system of convict-leasing, working on farms or in factories for little or no money. This system has become normalised, as it was under Jim Crow: in the final pages of Kunzru's novel Charlie's ghost resurfaces in the twenty-first century at the same hotel where he had been booked to record his music ninety years earlier, only to discover that a conference is taking place there: banners in the lobby welcome visitors to the '*33rd Annual Congress of the American Federation of Incarceration Service Providers*' (259). A system which directly capitalises on thousands of Black men being removed from society has been rebranded under the most bland and euphemistic of corporate labels, and conference delegates wearing lanyards wander around trying to find the next panel session. Charlie also discovers (in another supernatural moment) that 'Time is flattened here' (263), as several generations of the Wallace family are present at the conference, including Judge Wilbur, who originally sentenced him to work on the family's farm back in 1929. In a back room filled with cigar smoke, the judge offers a brief, perfunctory remark to the relatives gathered there that 'A lot of things happened back then that – well, let's just say those were different times' (263), before launching into a boast which seems to contradict that assertion of progress:

> You don't have to work 'em anymore. You don't have to walk the line with a rifle. All you got to do is get them into the system. Don't matter how you do it. Speeding ticket. Public nuisance. Once they're in, your boot is on their neck. Fines, tickets, court fees. And if they can't pay, well. Days or dollars, one or the other. Either way, we get ours and they stay in their rightful place. Same as it ever was (263–4).

By looking across the two novels we can see how similar the systems of incarceration are. On the levee where Charlie works (under a man appropriately named Ferguson), whippings and even murder are routine, and the heat and smell of the fever-ridden camp renders conditions almost uninhabitable.[15] Charlie describes how 'They chained twenty of us bad ones together when we slept' which meant that

> You tied up and someone wants to cut you or fuck your ass, not a damn thing you can do. The knife blades working, making another dead man while I squeeze my eyes tight, hoping they don't come for me (257).

This closely resembles Allmon's description of prison in *The Sport of Kings*. At the end of that novel Allmon recalled seeing, in the cell opposite his, 'a big white monster fucking some skinny white dude up the ass' (526); heeding his cellmate's warning that 'You in the slaughterhouse now. Cut or get cut' (528), he wrapped a padlock in a sock and attacked one of the other prisoners in order to avoid being raped or beaten up himself. The two descriptions of incarceration relate to different time periods, but the dangers, and the means by which the prisoners are placed there, remain the same.

Kunzru's novel emphasises some of the parallels between convict leasing and present-day policing, arrest and sentencing. But the connections between these two systems of racialised mass incarceration are rendered even more explicit when we discover, in an ironic twist, that the labour Charlie is forced into, as a convict leased to Judge Wilbur's own brothers, is to build a levee in order to prepare the ground for prisons to be built. Charlie and his fellow convicts are inadvertently and forcibly building the physical structures to imprison incarcerated men of the future, most of whom are also likely to be Black, and to have been needlessly arrested and handed an excessive prison sentence. Nowadays, we are told, again rather euphemistically, that the 'Wallace family company' is a 'behemoth with tentacles in construction, logistics and energy [which] had expanded since 9/11, helping America prevail in the War on Terror' (10). Cornelius, Carter's older brother, celebrates being made 'VP of Correctional Services' and therefore 'in charge of the whole Walxr operation' (46); much later things are clarified a little when we learn that '*Walxr . . . is a leading provider of detention, correctional and community reentry services with 58 facilities, approximately 25,500 beds, and 8,000 employees around the globe*' (260). Among the services Walxr offer their '*clients*' are '*design, construction and financing of state and federal prisons, detention centers and community reentry facilities as well as the provision of community supervision services, using advanced networked monitoring technologies*' (260). Having sentenced Charlie (and many others), and then leased them to work for free to build more prisons during Jim Crow, the Wallace family continues to benefit from the large-scale detention of thousands of Black men today. Michelle Alexander points out that 'Prisons are big business and have become deeply entrenched in America's economic and political system', and 'Rich and powerful people . . . are deeply interested in expanding the market – increasing the supply of prisoners' rather than 'eliminating the pool of people who can be held captive for a profit' (230). Near the start of the novel Seth mentions in passing that Carter's father is 'a big Republican donor who appeared in news photographs with senators and members of the Bush clan' and 'Carter's dead aunt's name was on a new lecture theater, which, given his near-total lack of interest in academic work, may have been the price of his [college] admission' (10).

Although Seth happily benefits from the significant financial success of the Wallace Magnolia Group, he is remarkably uncurious about the roots of his friend's wealth: he explains that 'Money was Carter's invisible helper, a friendly ghost making things happen in the background' and admits that 'By the time we made the move to New York, I'd adopted a religious attitude towards the many benefits that came to me: bow your head, open your hands, silently give thanks' (24). This weak-minded and ultimately self-serving approach towards the Wallace family firm seems to be part of the reason why he is targeted by the ghost of Charlie Shaw alongside Carter and Leonie (the former is carjacked and left for dead; Leonie is killed). At the end of the novel Seth considers the 'invisible thread [that] connected Carter and Leonie to Charlie Shaw' and considers how this murky past was covered up:

> I remembered something Leonie had said, about grandpa somebody or other moving the family up to DC, so the firm could bid for Federal Government contracts. Already big by then, Wallace Construction became a money machine. Then, years later, the DC children took the next step and moved to New York, to convert all that capital into culture (248).

Douglas A. Blackmon's 2008 book *Slavery by Another Name* uncovered the extent to which major US corporations, some of them now obsolete, others having gone through 'mergers and acquisitions' and existing in a new 'incarnation', profited economically from the mass-scale forced labour of convicts (387). In Blackmon's epilogue he described tracking down the descendants of the company owners and officials who had generated fortunes through convict leasing, and found them either in denial about their predecessors' role in the practice, and their responsibility for deaths caused, or vehement that 'their company shouldn't be associated with it' (389) as 'it would be impossible to appropriately assign responsibility for any corporation's actions in so remote an era' (390).[16] In the novel Wallace Construction has been rebranded as the Wallace Magnolia Group – a name that slyly signals its whitewashing of history. And Leonie, Carter's sister, resents being asked to consider her family's role in Charlie's death, complaining that 'My whole creative life literally depends on me being contemporary. This whole scene, this dead musician, this record. It isn't what I should be focused on' (153). Seth, too, repeatedly absolves himself of any responsibility for the harm caused by his friend's family company, despite taking money from them. When he encounters Charlie's present-day incarnation in Mississippi, for instance, his first instinct is to claim that 'I am a good person. I have done nothing wrong' (174). Later, when Charlie's ghost seems to be following him around the streets of New York, he complains that 'It's not fair to blame me for things that took place long before I was even born' (237). And later still, when he takes the bus down to Jackson to look for the hotel where Charlie never appeared for his recording session, a woman in her sixties with 'A head wrap in red, black and green' and 'heavy wooden earrings' stops him from taking photographs of the area: 'Only two reasons people like you come down here. The blues or taking pictures of ruins. We're fascinating to you, as long as we're safely dead' (246). But he can only respond, once again, with the weak refrain that 'I'm not the one to blame' and 'I had nothing to do with whatever happened to your neighborhood' (246).

Seth had imagined (or perhaps merely hoped) that there is an impermeable boundary between past and present, so that acts of racial violence which took place years before his lifetime can now safely be forgotten. But the reappearance of Charlie Shaw signals that racialised state control cannot be dismissed as an historical crime because it never in fact went away. Charlie's treatment at the hands of the police and state in the 1920s is replicated over and over again in the novel's contemporary period. To take one example: when Charlie is arrested in 1929 for the crime of vagrancy he simply disappears from view. The producers waiting for him at the Saint James Hotel casually 'glance at their watches' before scratching out his name on the set list and moving onto the next artist (261). Charlie narrates his own dissolution: 'And just like that, I am gone. Never to be remembered. Never to be spoken of again' (261). But this systematic erasure of supposed criminals is not confined to the Jim Crow period; when Seth tries to discover what happened to the contemporary incarnation of Charlie Shaw, a violent figure accused of killing Leonie, he is told that

> The suspect was taken to a special unit, a place which did not participate in the usual police booking formalities. I tell him I don't understand. Participate? I thought it was the law. He tells me the place is an exception, a black site. It is exempt from scrutiny. There is no publicly available information about the special unit (226).

The term 'black site' denotes a place where the usual laws of justice do not apply, where the suspect simply disappears without trace – presumably either tortured or killed, or both. But there is a double meaning to that phrase which suggests that this building where the suspect died of 'Natural causes', having been found 'unresponsive in an interview room' (227), is used exclusively for the detainment of Black Americans.

When Seth is arrested for murdering Leonie, he is afforded first-hand experience of how Black suspects are treated. After he leaves the motel room he is sharing with Leonie to buy food and tequila for them to share, armed police force him to the floor, their knees and elbows across his neck, and their knuckles grinding into his temple.

When he tries to resist, they batter him with batons and fists and smash his head off a concrete block. At the police station his face is cleaned up for a mug shot and he is then handcuffed to the desk and a hood is placed over his head. Seth's identity has temporarily merged with Charlie, whose ghost has been stalking him for some time. The first sign of this is just before his arrest: he notices that along with the takeout, Sprite, and bottle of tequila Leonie sent him out for, he is also holding a box of records and the battered guitar case Charlie was arrested with in 1929. When he looks down at his hands, and then lifts up his shirt to see his stomach, he realises that 'I can't tell what color I am' (206). During the interrogation he is shown 'Black-and-white eight-by-tens of a woman, a female corpse' (204). She is wearing 'old-fashioned underwear', he notices, and a 'vintage shoe with a strap and a rounded toe' (204); the motel room in the photos is also different, because while the room he left Leonie in earlier that day had had 'plain magnolia' walls, 'She [the woman in the photos] was dead in an old room with rose pattern wallpaper' (205). Seth also notices changes in the interview room where he is repeatedly beaten by the police. When the hood is removed, he recalls that previously the policeman's coffee had been in a 'paper cup, with a plastic lid', whereas now the cup is 'A chipped white tin mug with a blue rim' (205). The policemen are also wearing period clothing: 'wingtip oxfords, highly polished' and 'Argyle socks, wide cuffs on suit pants' (205). These details combine to suggest that the time period has somehow shifted, and Seth is now experiencing something of Charlie's treatment after his arrest in 1929. Earlier in the novel Seth and Carter had felt that their fetishization of Black music bought them 'some right to blackness': Carter, Seth explained, 'spoke as if "white people" were the name of an army or a gang, some organization to which he didn't belong' (18, 9). They even expressed their disappointment with the 'actual black kids at our school' who 'seemed to us unsatisfactorily preppy or Christian or were basketball jocks doing business degrees' (17). Later, when Carter releases Charlie's song onto a file-sharing site, he boasts about having tricked fellow collectors: 'We made it, fools! We made that shit last week! So who's the expert now? Who knows the tradition? We do! We own that shit!' (61). And when they agree to produce an album for a 'famous white hip hop artist' (28) who wants every song 'to be a tribute to a particular period and style of African American music' (29), calling the album *My Past Lives*, Seth is enthusiastic about the idea. But what Seth slowly realises is that this perceived ownership (or appropriation) of Black experience takes no account of the racial discrimination that is endemic in American society. This occurs to him most forcefully following his treatment at the hands of the police having been mistaken for Charlie. His personal safety, he finally accepts, is bound up with his whiteness, so that after his release he 'stared down at my hands, their raw pink knuckles, the blue veins, terrified that I would see them begin to change, all my security slipping away' (213).

Seth's treatment under arrest has a lasting impact, just as Allmon's discrimination continued long after leaving prison. Seth is ordered by the Wallace family to vanish from their lives and not draw attention to himself in any way, so he drifts from town to town, often sleeping in bus terminals, feeling the 'stink of [his] abjection' cling to him (223). That word 'abjection' is used repeatedly by Christina Sharpe to describe the 'ongoing and quotidian atrocity' – 'the varied and various ways that . . . Black lives are lived under occupation' (20). Like Charlie he has been arrested, beaten by the police, and then stripped of all rights before disappearing entirely; on the novel's final page Seth reflects that

> You wanted the suffering you didn't have, the authority you thought it would bring. It scared you, but you thought of the swagger it would put in your walk, the admiring glances of your friends. Then came the terror when real darkness first seeped through the walls of your bedroom, the walls designed to keep you safe and dreaming (271).

The novel very deliberately signals the fact that Charlie's unwarranted arrest, and ultimately death, at the hands of the police and justice system in the 1920s has its parallel in the treatment of Black men by police in contemporary America. When Seth (whose identity has temporarily merged, by this stage, with Charlie) is arrested in the parking lot and dragged onto the ground, he is confused by the police order to 'Stop going for our guns!', before he realises, 'Through the kicks and punches', that 'they are setting a scene, erecting a legal framework within which I can be killed' and predicts, knowingly, that 'It will be quick, a justifiable homicide. Brave officers acting in self-defense. I flinch from the next thing, the bullet' (199). He assumes the footage is being recorded and will be examined after his death; the police are therefore fabricating his response to the arrest: 'You're resisting, they shout, for the benefit of some dash or chest cam. I am not resisting. I am just screaming' (199).[17] Just before that point, when the police surround him in the parking lot, he is forced to the ground: 'There is a knee on my neck. I can't breathe, I say' (187). That last phrase, 'I can't breathe', was said over and over again by George Floyd in May 2020 as Minneapolis police officer Derek Chauvin knelt on his neck for over nine minutes. That same phrase had also been said eleven times by Eric Garner in July 2014 when he was put in a chokehold by New York City Police Department (NYPD) officer Daniel Pantaleo after being suspected of selling single cigarettes. Garner's death was ruled a homicide, but Pantaleo was not indicted, despite the fact that the NYPD prohibits chokeholds; the footage was captured on a mobile phone by Garner's friend Ramsey Orta, and the phrase 'I can't breathe' became synonymous with the Black Lives Matter movement, which had begun in 2013, after George Zimmerman's acquittal for the death of unarmed Black teenager Trayvon Martin. The death of Garner was followed quickly by that of Michael Brown, another unarmed Black teenager who was shot dead by police, this time in Ferguson, Missouri on 9 August 2014. This was when Black Lives Matter (which began as a phrase, then a hashtag, then a movement) gathered steam. Brown was believed to have shouted the words 'Hands up, don't shoot' just before he was shot; this phrase, too, became 'a national rallying cry, the chief chorus of the dead boy's defenders' (Lowery 24). But just as the massive eruption of protests following the murder of George Floyd were designed to shed light on widespread racial profiling and police brutality, the 2014 rioting in Ferguson during the first few nights, and the peaceful protests that lasted much longer, were never simply about Brown's death: Wesley Lowery, a *Washington Post* journalist who reported from Ferguson for several months, describes how for residents

> Mike Brown [was] a symbol of their own oppression. In a city where, federal investigators would later conclude, traffic tickets and arrest warrants were used systematically to target impoverished black residents, Brown's death afforded an opportunity through protest for otherwise ignored voices to be heard (16).[18]

The deaths, in the months that followed, of other Black men (and in one case boy) by police, including Tamir Rice (aged just twelve), Walter Scott and Freddie Gray, led to further serious unrest in cities across the US, drawing into focus the breakdown of police and community relations as a result of racial profiling, 'zero tolerance' policing, multiple arrests for minor or non-existent infractions, police brutality and the failure to indict police officers who kill.[19]

Kunzru's novel makes a direct reference to the Black Lives Matter movement when Leonie mocks Carter's obsession with blues music.

She tells Seth that 'No one cares if you like black people' (152), and that listening to the music 'doesn't make them like you any better. It's theirs. They'd rather you left it to them. Even if you did something, I don't know, really selfless. Black lives matter or whatever. They still wouldn't like you' (152–3). This glib remark, offered as a knowing insight into contemporary racial politics, casually dismisses Black Lives Matter (that 'or whatever' is key), while reducing all Black Americans to a monolithic 'they', whose thoughts and feelings she claims to understand. But it is no great surprise that Wallace family members, direct and long-term beneficiaries of a predominantly white policing and judiciary system which firstly targets Black men for arrest, and then hands them disproportionate sentences for often minor offences, should have no particular interest in this activist movement. And Kunzru also connects these deaths with murders that took place near the start of the civil rights movement, many decades earlier, in the Jim Crow state of Mississippi. Chester Bly and JumpJim (both white) travelled around the Mississippi Delta during the 1950s looking for old blues records to buy; this particular time and place puts the reader in mind of fourteen-year-old Emmett Till, who was brutally murdered there in 1955 by two white men who were acquitted by an all-white jury. When Emmett Till's mother insisted on an open casket for her son and allowed photographers from *Jet* magazine to take photographs of her son's bloated and battered body, the shocking images generated widespread condemnation of the violence against Black Americans in Mississippi, and focused attention on the civil rights movement across the South. Till's murder and its aftermath has been identified as a point of comparison with Trayvon Martin's death nearly sixty years later: Lowery explains that after Zimmerman's acquittal, activists could no longer believe 'they had the luxury of working within the system, of coloring inside the lines ... those cries [for justice] had gone unheard' (169).[20] The response to Michael Brown's death, not long afterwards, further crystallised these sentiments, sparking an international movement which was widely reported in the media.

Those two periods of civil rights activism are not, of course, the same, yet in Kunzru's novel, white characters tend to respond to them in similar ways. JumpJim, an elderly record collector (whose name is a clear nod to 'Jump Jim Crow') describes to Seth how in the 1950s South they were 'Still killing Negro boys, despite the so-called advances', and 'Reckless eyeballing was the name of the crime, and it could get you hung or burned alive or tied to an engine block and thrown in the river' (138). But despite emphasising to Seth that

'I believed in civil rights' (139), he then recounts his failure to contradict Chester's reassurance to a police officer, during a routine stop in the Delta, that 'I stand with the white man, one hundred per cent' (156). And when the two men knock on doors to try to buy old blues records, JumpJim perceives the Black Mississippians he encounters as a homogenous group: 'All kinds of people opening doors, but only one kind of people. Black people' (147). Even before leaving New York for Mississippi, he had regarded the civil rights movement from a distance:

> I thought every man ought to be able to live his life. But handing out flyers and signing petitions didn't seem to make much difference. Sure, I spent all my time listening to the blues, but one of the reasons I liked those old songs, those disembodied voices rushing up out of the past, was because they were a refuge from the world. I didn't want them contaminated by current affairs (139).

Leonie, in the contemporary period, is similarly unresponsive to the charged political mood: when she and Seth happen to catch a news report of a police shooting, she makes no comment and goes straight to sleep; and when she tries to describe feeling threatened on the streets of New York, her remarks sound remarkably similar to JumpJim's, knocking on doors in the 1950s: 'I mean, they could be young or old, male, female. But they're all the same. They – none of them – shit, it's not easy to talk about this. What I'm saying is it's never white people' (162).

When Charlie is arrested, chained to five other men for a brief court appearance, and finally put to work on the levee, he predicts that this is the last anyone will hear of him: 'I was thrown into silence and darkness. Never to have my voice recorded. Never to be remembered, never known for who I was or how I could play' (255). After he dies, he is buried in an unmarked grave, and many decades later, at that conference in the hotel, he realises that his story has been erased altogether, and now eludes narration: 'What happened to me did not happen . . . When I speak I am not speaking. When I speak, it dies away into silence' (263). Charlie's silencing has its parallel in Morgan's novel when Mack, the horse trainer, advises Allmon never to speak about his time in prison: 'whatever you had to do to get by inside – leave it inside. Don't ever breathe a word of it to anyone' (317). This maps on to Michelle Alexander's point that 'silence . . . hovers over mass incarceration', a silence that is 'driven by stigma and fear of shame', making it almost impossible for those affected to consider their experiences within a larger pattern of racialised state control (169). Reuben's alternative proposal, that Allmon 'Throw open the doors of that prison!' and 'Tell the tale!' (514) of his life thus becomes an incendiary act, an incitement to resist the 'violence of abstraction' (Sharpe 131) by articulating his experiences. An early conversation between the two men had taken place in a chaotic 'shack' somewhere off the grid, 'filled to busting with grooms, hot-walkers, and a few slumming jocks' (427), bearing a striking resemblance to the Golden Day, the tavern in Ralph Ellison's *Invisible Man* (1952) where the narrator takes Mr Norton, the white founder of the college. In Ellison's anarchic scene a Black veteran attempts to make the narrator see that he is being tyrannised by white structures of authority, remarking to Mr Norton that 'He takes it in but he doesn't digest it . . . Already he's learned to repress not only his emotions but his humanity. He's invisible, a walking personification of the Negative' (81). Reuben likewise scolds Allmon that 'You're too busy trying to shit out prison instead of digesting it, letting it make you stronger! You got to build your blood, son!' (453). But when Allmon later seizes control of the story, and over ten pages of second person narration describes the terror and lethal violence of his time in prison, he suspects that 'I'm talking to nobody at all, am I? No one in the living world is listening. They kill your most precious thing, then close their ears to you' (524).

Notes

1. Manning Marable explains that 'In 1955–59, White Citizens' Councils were initiated in almost every southern city', and 'As the movement towards desegregation gained momentum, the measures employed by the white supremacists and terrorists became more violent' (42). Stephanie R. Rolph notes that while the Citizens' Councils were officially opposed to violence, they nevertheless engaged in intimidation tactics, propaganda, and 'Economic pressure' – for instance Black Mississippians who signed petitions in support of school desegregation would have their names printed in the local newspaper, and many of them 'lost their jobs and received threatening phone calls', while 'Wholesale distributors denied deliveries to black store owners' (43). Meanwhile the Klan was also enjoying a reprisal in the 1950s: Marable describes how it 'reasserted itself as a powerful secret organization, committing a series of castrations, killings, and the bombing of black homes and churches' (42).
2. Although the novel ends in 2006, the reader will register a deliberate foreshadowing in that list of Black men killed in the 1930s, with those

killed by police over the last few years, including Eric Garner, Michael Brown, John Crawford, Tamir Rice, Walter Scott, Freddie Gray and George Floyd.

3. Kentucky was comparatively progressive when it came to civil liberties, particularly in industrial cities like Louisville, which had a large and vibrant Black community, and where voting was largely unrestricted. Nevertheless, segregation was still the norm across the state, and Black Kentuckians had restricted access to housing, jobs, and public spaces such as libraries, parks and theatres. There was also major resistance, across the state, to school integration following the 1954 *Brown* v. *Board* ruling. And a fault line in the state's racial politics was exposed that same year, when a Black couple, Andrew and Charlotte Wade, purchased a house in the white Louisville suburb of Shively with the help of a white activist couple, Anne and Carl Braden, who secured the mortgage and then signed the deeds over to the Wades. After moving in, the Wades were subjected to threats and violence, and when a bomb ripped through half of the property, it was Carl Braden who was convicted of sedition, by an all-white jury, of planting the bomb in order to incite a race war – a verdict that was only overturned after he had spent seven months in prison. For a detailed discussion of this incident and its wider political significance, see Fosl 135–73 and K'Meyer 61–76.

4. Allen W. Trelease explains that 'Kentucky was the only state outside the former Confederacy where the Klan found any significant lodgment' (89), with the area of southwestern Kentucky 'from Bowling Green to the Mississippi River' the site of 'Systematic terrorism' in the summer of 1868 (90). This took many forms, including lynchings, beatings, threats leading to exile and the burning-down of homes, churches and schools.

5. George C. Wright explains that this white violence tended to be directed at former enslaved people, and the worst period for lynchings was from 1865 to 1874, when 117 people were killed by lynch mobs, 87 of them Black (71). David W. Blight puts this figure higher: he records one estimate that 'in Kentucky alone . . . in the first ten years after the war, at least three hundred people, mostly black, perished at the hands of lynch mobs, and that during the period 1867–71 in rural counties of central Kentucky, as many as twenty-five lynchings occurred per year' (114). But even these estimates are likely to be lower than the reality: determining an exact figure is difficult because some of the lynchings went unrecorded.

6. Michelle Alexander makes a similar point about the 'politics of responsibility': she explains that 'When black youth . . . fail, stumble, and make mistakes, as all humans do – shame and blame is heaped upon them. If only they had made different choices, they're told sternly, they wouldn't be sitting in a jail cell; they'd be graduating from college' (215). Of course, this completely overlooks the fact that they are more

likely to be arrested for minor misdemeanours, and be given long sentences (far longer than white youths) that are disproportionate to the crime.

7. This has been well-documented: Sharpe makes the point that 'recent studies . . . show again and again that Black people in the United States receive inferior health care because they are believed to feel less pain' (50).

8. Alexander puts these prison numbers at 300,000 in 1980, rising to over 2 million in 2000 (6).

9. Michael Tesler has also discussed Obama's 'deracialization strategies' (47–8) during the 2008 campaign such as 'ads [that] overwhelmingly featured white imagery' in order to overcome the 'prevalent fear about black political leadership' that 'African American politicians will disproportionately favor the black community's interests over that of whites' (47).

10. See Coates 68–9, 115–16, and 119–25. Obama made the first comment during a news conference on 22 July 2009, when asked by a reporter 'What does that incident say to you and what does it say about race relations in America?' The full transcript can be found at: https://obamawhitehouse.archives.gov/realitycheck/the_press_office/News-Conference-by-the-President-July-22-2009. He made the second during a press conference in the Rose Garden on 23 March 2012: https://obamawhitehouse.archives.gov/the-press-office/2012/03/23/remarks-president-nomination-dr-jim-kim-world-bank-president

11. In the 5th edition of Bonilla-Silva's book *Racism without Racists*, published in 2018, he suggested that there was reasonable evidence to support his 'major prediction' about the effect of Obama's presidency: that 'the voices of those who contend that race fractures America profoundly would be silenced', because 'Obama's blackness' would be used as proof that 'race was no longer a big deal in America' (213).

12. A full transcript of the Morehouse College speech, which took place on 19 May 2013, is available online at: https://obamawhitehouse.archives.gov/the-press-office/2013/05/19/remarks-president-morehouse-college-commencement-ceremony. Coates, a long-standing admirer of Obama, was nevertheless critical of Obama's tendency towards 'black self-hectoring, railing against the perceived failings of black culture' (135). These lecturing speeches, versions of which were given to all types of Black audiences, cautioned them not to renege on their responsibilities, and not to blame white people for their problems.

13. Bonilla-Silva also wrote that 'sadly', many of his 'predictions and arguments about Obama . . . became a reality. Obama was clearly not a stealth progressive, but a centrist, pro-market, traditional politician with a *quasi*-color-blind-view about race matters in America' (219).

14. Douglas A. Blackmon defines vagrancy as 'the offense of a person not being able to prove at a given moment that he or she is employed' (1).

15. Ferguson is the city in Missouri where Black teenager Michael Brown was shot by white police officer Darren Wilson in 2014, leading to protesting and riots for several weeks afterwards, and a spotlight being shone on police discrimination and violence against Black citizens.

16. One exception to this was Wachovia Bank, in North Carolina, which revealed in 2005 that its predecessor banks 'owned or held as collateral at least 691 slaves before the Civil War' and 'formally apologized to "all Americans and especially to African Americans and people of African descent", established scholarship funds for minorities, and promoted a broad discussion of racial issues inside the company' (Blackmon 391).

17. In Wesley Lowery's 2016 book about the Black Lives Matter movement, *They Can't Kill Us All*, he describes being arrested while reporting on events in Ferguson. Despite putting up no resistance, and with his hands behind his back, the police accuse him of struggling: '"No, you're resisting, stop resisting", an officer barked back at me, before I was led out of the building' (7).

18. St. Louis has a long history of racist governmental policies; for a detailed exploration of the city's history of segregation, see Richard Rothstein's 2014 article 'The Making of Ferguson: Public Polices at the Root of Its Troubles'.

19. Lowery refers to the findings of his colleagues Kimberly Kindy and Kimbriell Kelly, in their research into the conditions that needed to be in place before an officer would be indicted: 'there had to be video, evidence of a cover-up (perhaps a missing or planted weapon), or fellow officers needed to have turned on the shooter and contradicted his or her story' (113).

20. See for instance the article by Angela Onwuachi-Willig; also Clayton 450 and 456–7; and Lowery 169. For an extensive comparison of the two social activist movements, see Dewey M. Clayton's article 'Black Lives Matter and the Civil Rights Movement: A Comparative Analysis of Two Social Movements in the United States', particularly pages 457–72.

Chapter 2

Ben Lerner and Literary Antecedents of the City

Ben Lerner's 2014 novel *10:04* offers us a strikingly contemporary depiction of New York: the narrative begins and ends with the hurricanes Irene and Sandy, which hit the city in August 2011 and October 2012 respectively. And near the start the narrator, also called Ben, allows an Occupy Wall Street protestor he connected with via the classifieds website craigslist to use his shower and washing machine. Ben also ruminates on the ethical implications of co-operative food stores in gentrified Brooklyn, and he and his best friend Alex go for drinks in a hipster bar complete with 'Edison bulb sconces' and 'carefully selected ephemera on the walls [which] dated from before the Civil War' (136, 135). The novel itself also fits squarely within the genre of autofiction, which while not a new form, has certainly become more prevalent within the past decade or so.[1] Yet while such motifs from the twenty-first century are scattered throughout *10:04*, the novel's central thematic concerns date back much further, as it grapples with issues that were a particular preoccupation for twentieth-century modernist writers: the 'extraordinary discrepancy' Virginia Woolf famously outlined between clock time and 'time in the mind' (*Orlando* 68); the alienating effect of urban spaces; and, at the level of form, fragmentation and discordant images. Ben's repeated retreats into his own imagination, and his privileging of narrative time (films, literature, personal histories) lead to frequent bouts of temporal confusion – absences from conventional routine which amount to a 'falling out of time' (Lerner 166). The lines from Woolf, T. S. Eliot, Ezra Pound and Wallace Stevens which punctuate the novel serve to underline the isolation Ben experiences himself and notices all around him: connections are hard-won in this version of New York which (if those storms are any indication) is moving swiftly towards an impending apocalypse while under the grip of global capitalism. These feelings of estrangement are reflected in the novel's dislocated structure: the frequent juxtaposition of unrelated scenes (and even lines) creates a sense of discombobulation both for Ben and also for the reader, who is sometimes unsure how the parts connect together, or even which character is speaking. But the novel also subtly interrogates Ben's angle of vision: his recourse to modernist writing as a means to conceptualise the contemporary moment suggests a frame of reference that is anachronistic, a sterile and inappropriate commentary on the pressures of neoliberalism. A better and more redemptive literary alternative to this 'Unreal City' is afforded by Walt Whitman, as Ben later discovers. Whitman's conception of the urban sublime and his faith in the emerging demos as a model of unity was set out most famously in his 1856 poem 'Crossing Brooklyn Ferry'. That poem rejoices in the crowded, raucous city streets, and the friendship with others that urban spaces both establish and accommodate. Ben turns to Whitman as a remedy for his feelings of urban and temporal dislocation, and this awakens his perception of New York as a 'communal body' (Lerner 108–9) or 'collective person' which exists across time, and 'to whom all the arts, even in their most intimate registers, were . . . addressed' (108).

This chapter begins by examining how the triggering of particular memories negates, for Ben, the authority of clock time, allowing him to be transported back into the past; thereafter it considers his repeated resistance to objective structures of time in favour of narrative – films, literature, other people's stories – and the role of Whitman as a stimulus and an example in this effort. In the second half of the chapter focus shifts more directly to Ben's experience of living in the city, the novel's return to modernist writers at points of crisis represented by Occupy Wall Street, and finally the competing visions of urban life presented by Eliot and Whitman, and the spiritual redemption offered by the latter's conception of the urban sublime.

I.

The novel's preoccupation with the unconventional passing of time is clear from the title, a nod to the 1985 film *Back to the Future*, which Ben watches with Alex during the first storm.[2] And from the outset Ben feels as though he exists in an alternative temporal zone, where the normal process of ageing does not take place. This is first apparent in an early scene at the hospital where he is being diagnosed for Marfan syndrome, a 'genetic disorder of the connective tissue' which causes the aorta to dilate, and if not operated on, to rupture (4). Because the disorder is usually diagnosed in early childhood, Ben's appointment is in the paediatric wing, and he waits in a 'red plastic chair designed for a kindergartner' in a room painted with a mural of a sea scene: 'an octopus and starfish and various gill-bearing aquatic craniate animals' (5, 4). Alex, meanwhile, takes on the parental role, sitting in the 'lone adult chair', and with a notebook to write down what the doctor says, since, in childlike fashion, Ben 'had proved unable to leave a doctor's office with even the most basic recollection of whatever information had been imparted to me there' (5). The three doctors, when they arrive, are all younger than him, a fact he finds unnerving because rather than standing in 'benevolent paternal relation to my body', recognising their 'past immaturity', instead they see in him only 'their own future decline'; nevertheless, he still finds himself 'infantilized' by them (6). The scene's temporal confusion is compounded by the sense that his own beating heart – the thing that allows him to continue living – may also, through every contraction, be causing the expansion of the 'overly flexible tubing of my heart' (7), and therefore his death. He senses his 'future collapsing' in upon him, and feels like a temporal anomaly as a result: 'Including myself, I was older and younger than everyone in the room' (7).

This sense of being 'out of time' occurs at various moments in the novel: the direction of time feels unpredictable, with Ben's own memories proving so powerful that he can feel physically transported into the past. The act of walking around the elementary school of a boy he is tutoring triggers such strong memories that he finds himself suddenly back in his own classroom, more than twenty-five years earlier:

> I pass through Mrs. Greiner's door and find my desk, the chair no longer small for me, Pluto among the planets in the Styrofoam mobile suspended from the ceiling. My parents are at the Meninger Clinic; my older brother is in a classroom directly above mine (15).

This transportation back into the past occurs time and again in modernist narrative.[3] But these earlier moments cannot be experienced exactly as they were originally, because the future of these past memories – which is of course the present – fundamentally alters the tone of them, as Ben realises:

It is sad work to build a diorama of the future with a boy you know will hang himself for whatever complex of reasons in his parents' basement at nineteen, but that work has been assigned, Mrs. Greiner standing over us to check our progress, the synthetic coconut odor of her lotion intermingling with the smell of rubber cement (15).

Ben's involuntary capacity to be transported back in time through his memories alerts him to the ways in which past events can be altered or even 'retrospectively erased' (24); following this to its logical end, his experience of present-day events must be regarded as provisional, likely to be reshaped in the future by the perspective he brings to bear on them.[4] The conditional nature of the present is expressed by Lerner at the level of style: Ben uses phrases such as 'I am kidding and I am not kidding', 'to a lesser or greater degree', 'was or was not', and 'rightly or wrongly' (3, 108, 108, 168), a semantic flexibility that arms him for possible future contradiction. Sentences also drift on as though uncertain of their own conclusion: consider the second sentence of the novel, for instance, about the baby octopuses Ben and his agent order at an expensive restaurant in Chelsea: 'We had ingested the impossibly tender things entire, the first intact head I had ever consumed, let alone of an animal that decorates its lair, has been observed at complicated play' (3). That last clause feels tacked on, as though the narrator has pushed the sentence past its own expected ending, unwilling to allow it any formal closure when his own understanding of temporality reveals that all experiences may be revised, subject to re-formulation, at a future time.

But the almost tortuous construction of this and other sentences in *10:04*, with their seemingly redundant added clauses and excessive length, also shows the degree to which Ben's consciousness runs up against ordinary temporal structures. The meandering style spurns efficiency: the unconventional syntactical arrangement is semantically unproductive. In Ben's day-to-day life in New York, he repeatedly finds himself in conflict with 'clock time', and finding an alternative in the form of narrative duration. This opposition is particularly palpable in a scene where he and Alex attend *The Clock*, an art installation at the Lincoln Center. *The Clock*, created by Christian Marclay, is a

twenty-four-hour montage of thousands of scenes from movies and a few from TV edited together so as to be shown in real time; each scene indicates the time with a shot of a timepiece or its mention in dialogue; time in and outside of the film is synchronized (52).

Ben and Alex get to their seats at 11:37 at night, and stay for three hours; during that time Ben is struck by the reappearance of particular characters: a young woman is attempting to seduce a boy at 11:57, and at 1:19 'they reappear, sleeping in separate beds' (53). Here, unusually, the time that passes within the story (those events that might have happened to these characters between 11:57 and 1:19) has been afforded the same amount of time in real life: time in the film, and time in reality, is now one and the same. But a little later on Ben is reminded of the distinction that remains between narrative time and clock time, and of his own propensity to privilege the former. This occurs sometime after midnight, during their second hour watching the installation. Noticing that Alex is asleep, Ben 'surreptitiously checked the time on [his] phone' (53) before realising that this is a nonsensical move given that each scene of the montage matches the ticking of the clock in real life. Forgetting this for the second time half an hour later, he checks his phone again. This highlights Ben's resistance, however unintentional, to clock time: the fragments of stories taking place in hundreds of different scenes draw him in, so he focuses more on the unfolding of the various narratives ('some kind of zombie woman emerged from a grandfather clock'; 'a young girl awakes from a nightmare' and is 'comforted by her father' (52)) than on what they point to in the real world. This involuntary valorising of fiction, or the world of the imagination, over the reality of clock time, is a concern Ben shares with a number of modernist writers: in *Mrs Dalloway* Clarissa's memories and sensations persistently flood the narrative, triggered by various sights and sensations over the course of one day in London, June 1923; clock time is temporarily abandoned with the powerful influx of thoughts and past associations. The inevitable intrusion of 'the clocks of Harley Street' (Woolf 87) and 'the hour, irrevocable' (4) announced by Big Ben is painful for Clarissa, bringing into sharp relief the tension between this 'Shredding and slicing, dividing and subdividing' (87) of objectively marked time and interior, subjective time, including memory and the unimpeded flow of thought. That there are two concepts of time – one official, the other intuitive – becomes apparent to Ben when he checks his phone during the installation in spite of the fact that clock time is being accurately portrayed on the cinema screen in front of him. For Ben, this new temporal equivalence between narrative and reality does not hold; he is still convinced that 'a distance remained between art and the mundane', which triggers his immediate decision to 'write more fiction' (54) – in other words, to retreat more into the mind.

The discrepancy Ben perceives between the subjective perception of time and clock time becomes a central thematic concern in *10:04*. At his monthly shift at the Park Slope Food Coop, he finds himself working alongside Noor, with whom he is friendly, and when she hesitates to begin a long story about her family, he convinces her this is a useful way to fill the time: '"We have more than two hours," I exclaimed with mock desperation' (99). When she has completed her absorbing rumination on her childhood, her late Lebanese father, and her own racial self-identity – a story by which Ben has been utterly gripped – he is disappointed to discover that although it seemed as though 'Noor had been speaking for hours', in fact 'only forty-five minutes of our shift had passed' (107). Under the grip of narrative Ben had been afforded a temporary escape from the stultifying impact of clock time, but this reprieve cannot last: after Noor leaves to take over on the checkout, he spends the remainder of the shift 'bagging dates and trying not to look at the clock' (107) – the reassertion of objectively marked time rendered more tedious by the repetitive nature of his task.

This particular moment speaks to a broader, related set of concerns throughout the novel relating to how capitalist systems of production are perceived by Ben. The Brooklyn co-op of course differs from industrial labour or factory work in that here 'nobody is extracting profit' (95), and it is designed as a force for social good: 'The co-op helped run a soup kitchen. When a homeless shelter in the neighborhood burned down, "we" – at orientation they taught you to utilize the first-person plural while talking about the co-op – donated the money to rebuild it' (96). But leaving these benevolent intentions to one side for a moment, the organisation still runs (albeit inefficiently) along similar lines to a system of rationalised production, and Ben is fully aware that its altruistic ethos makes no impact on that economic model: 'Complaining indicated you weren't foolish enough to believe that belonging to the co-op made you meaningfully less of a node in a capitalist network' (95). As Ben explains it, each shift worker (or 'member') is assigned to a section, each of which carries with it a fairly basic set of tasks. He is allocated the role of 'food processing' for one night a month:

> In general the work was simple: the boxes of bulk food were organized on shelves in the basement. If dried mangoes were needed upstairs, you found the ten-pound box, opened it with a box cutter, and portioned the fruit into small plastic bags you then tied and weighed on a scale that printed the individual labels. Then you took the food upstairs and restocked the shelves on the shopping floor (96–7).

This is unskilled work, and we might also note the limited knowledge each 'employee' has of any other tasks involved in the operation. Ben is not trained for the checkout, for instance, and when he is forced to go upstairs in order to deposit some of the bagged mangoes, he feels 'embarrassed to emerge into the semipublic space of the shopping floor with a bandanna in my hair and sporting a pastel apron' (101). Although he is reasonably capable working within his one section, he is uncomfortable (for a variety of reasons including self-consciousness but also apparent incompetence) when temporarily repositioned. Clearly the organisation runs according to a mild and relaxed form of Taylorism, with individuals acting as willing, middle-class cogs within the machine of the co-op. In 1923 Georg Lukács described how in this system 'the process of labour is progressively broken down into abstract, rational, specialised operations so that the worker loses contact with the finished product and his work is reduced to the mechanical repetition of a specialised set of actions' (88). He then explained the adverse effect of this on the worker's experience of time, which 'sheds its qualitative, variable, flowing nature' and 'freezes into an exactly delimited, quantifiable continuum filled with quantifiable "things"' (90). The repetition of tasks Lukács identified, coupled with a heightened awareness of rationalised time as 'exactly measurable' (Lukács 90) and therefore restrictive, is consistent with Ben's experience in the co-op, as he tries not to mark off the minutes until the end of his shift. Yet here and elsewhere, these 'quantifiable' units of time are counterbalanced by diversions into narrative and the imagination: Noor's story has temporarily distracted Ben from the tedious nature of the work, just as the films patched together in the Lincoln Center allowed him to focus more on the stories being told than on the real-life clock time they display. We might regard these welcome flights into narrative as part of what Fredric Jameson termed, in his discussion of modernism in *The Political Unconscious*, 'Utopian compensation for everything reification brings with it' (225). The 'increasing dehumanization' and 'rationalizing desacralization' in the 'world of daily life' (Jameson 27) that clock time both symbolises and facilitates is partly endured (and at times even neutralised) by Ben through recourse to the 'sheer color and intensity' (Jameson 225) of the imagination in the form of narrative, memory and individual consciousness.

But Ben's description of the co-op draws into focus a subtle but pronounced problem with his angle of vision that will become progressively more urgent as the novel develops. The co-op's subdivision of tasks replicates the structure of a modernist-era assembly line: material labour is being harnessed in the production of tangible product, and the work is tedious and repetitive, making his monthly shift of two hours and forty-five minutes feel much longer than it actually is. Yet this reasonably straightforward economic model also marks the co-op out as an aberration: it sits uncomfortably among the dizzyingly complex strategies of finance we see elsewhere in the novel. Its economic structure therefore represents a much earlier stage of capitalist industrialisation, epitomised by what Mark Fisher calls the '"rigidity" of the Fordist production line', as opposed to the 'flexibility' of post-Fordism which 'both required and emerged from an increased cybernetization of the working environment' (33). The Fordist co-op is out of place in a world of finance capitalism char- acterised by 'deterritorialization' and 'dematerialization' (Jameson, 'Culture', 260), and Ben registers this dislocation when he describes, wryly, the group of wealthy 'zealots' whose extreme commitment to the co-op system slightly runs up against their desire to send their children to private school, 'while probably holding investments in Monsanto or Archer Daniels Midland in their 401(k)'s' (96). Some of them, he suggests, even dispatch their nannies to do their shifts. While the co-op's economic model seems fair ('labor [is] shared and visible'), it is also anachronistic, and possibly even irrelevant, within the broader context of global capitalism: 'you could usually trust [it] to carry products that weren't the issue of openly evil conglomerates' (96). In an analogous fashion, Ben's references to modernism also start feeling inadequate, or out of place, when he applies them to his experience of living in a fast-moving, twenty-four-hour city. When he distinguishes between official time and narrative, as he does at this stage of the novel, his modernist forebears do not seem inappro- priate: his various flights into memory and narrative do offer some reprieve from the clock. But as the novel develops, he falls 'out of time' in another, unexpected respect, in that these literary reference points from earlier writers start failing to hit the target. He would do well to take account of the point made by Jameson, in his 1997 essay 'Culture and Finance Capital', that the 'radically new forms of abstraction' that characterise the 'new logic of finance capital' are 'sharply to be distinguished from those of modernism' (260). This is not to say that literary antecedents in general serve no purpose (they seem adequate here, and we will also trace the usefulness of Whitman's urban vision), but that Ben's recourse to specifically mod- ernist expression for so much of the novel will gradually reveal some of the limitations of his conceptual vision.

In the novel's early stages, however, Ben's modernist lens helps him to articulate his particular receptivity to what he terms the 'strange duration of the literary' (34). This is further underlined when he spends time with Bernard and Natali, his great friends and literary mentors. They seem (to Ben) to be immune to the ordinary passing of time: Natali 'always seemed the same age to me', and although Bernard is probably around eighty, Ben 'could never imagine [him] actually aging . . . his bodily fragility never seemed, in any particular present, real to me' (34). The couple are the products of a sort of 'temporal exception' that renders their impressively long and productive careers somehow 'anachronistic' (34). Ben also perceives their house in Providence to be 'exempt from time': 'their days were not structured conventionally; the house was not subject to quotidian rhythms' (34). The explanation for this comes when Ben introduces the reader to Natali as a 'literary hero of mine', while Bernard is 'for me an equally important figure' (32): they represent for him all forms of literary activity – poetry, translation, 'experimental writing' (34), and so on. Their metonymic relation to narrative accounts for their existing in a different 'temporal medium' (33) beyond the constraints of objectively marked time – because they represent the world of narrative ('reading and writing' (34), 'otherworldly learnedness' (33), 'stories the import of which would often only occur to me years later' (35)), they are therefore resistant (at least until Bernard is admitted to hospital after a fall) to 'biological time' (40).

Bernard and Natali are for Ben unbound by ordinary temporal rhythms, but he too has periods of evading the clock altogether, when pure consciousness – in the form of hallucinations and daydreams – take precedence, however involuntarily, over the conventional passing of time. This occurs most forcefully when Ben leaves the city. Towards the end of the novel, he leaves for a five-week residency in Marfa, Texas, arriving there in the late afternoon, and immediately going to sleep, 'not waking until a little before midnight' (163). He then goes for a drive around Marfa in the dark, before buying some food and coffee at a gas station to eat back at the house, where he writes until daybreak and then goes back to bed. This has a disorientating effect, akin to jetlag:

> It was 5:00p.m. when I woke and, because I'd already woken in the bed once the previous day, it felt like the morning of my second full day, not the late afternoon of the first; I was already falling out of time (166).

When he 'trie[s] to remember the light snow that morning in New York' (163–4), he discovers that his 'life in Brooklyn eighteen hours in the past' is now 'receding' (165). Rather than make any effort to realign his body clock, Ben decides to embrace this new routine, and the pattern is quickly set: 'Days passed like this: turning in around sunrise, waking a couple of hours before sunset, my only contact with other humans the few words I exchanged with the attendant at the gas station where I continued to buy groceries' (169). But this period of Ben's life is not just notable for his adopting an alternative routine, reversing the usual pattern of day and night; he also spends the bulk of his waking hours reading Walt Whitman's 1882 autobiography *Specimen Days*, abandoning the project he had planned for the residency, and instead writing 'a weird meditative lyric in which I was sometimes Whitman, and in which the strangeness of the residency itself was the theme' (170). This is a period when Ben ceases to operate within normal temporal structures, as we have seen, and this unusual experience of time is also a notable feature of *Specimen Days*. In the first few pages of that book Whitman describes his motivation for publishing these fragments of memoranda as being to 'symbolize two or three specimen interiors, personal and other, out of the myriads of my time, the middle range of the Nineteenth century in the New World' – which he describes as 'a strange, unloosen'd, wondrous time' (24). The apparent 'strangeness' of this particular period of history is underlined by Whitman's unusual approach to structuring his autobiography. Betsy Erkkila notes that Whitman eliminates certain periods, such as 'the period of Reconstruction and the public and private dis-ease associated with those years'; this allows him to move the narrative 'directly from the tragedy of the war to the restoration of an eternalized nature that bears no sign of political struggle and the wounds of history' (295). Many of the very short chapters that make up *Specimen Days* are given dates, but the sections devoted to the period he spent at Timber Creek in the New Jersey countryside recovering from a stroke feel ahistorical or Edenic, removed from time altogether; Ben's remark (in an obvious nod to 'Song of Myself') that 'Whitman is always "loafing", always taking his ease' (168) is a perceptive one, and recognises the very languid, restorative tone of the nature passages which constitute that third quarter of the book. Whitman's indifference to some of the historical details that mark the period and the emphasis instead on timeless moments spent in the countryside is exemplified in the following representative passage from *Specimen Days*, spatially and temporally distanced from the destruction of 1870s America:

Not a human being, and hardly the evidence of one, in sight. After my brief semi-daily bath, I sit here for a bit, the brook musically brawling, to the chromatic tones of a fretful cat-bird somewhere off in the bushes. On my walk hither two hours since, through fields and the old lane, I stopt to view, now the sky, now the mile-off woods on the hill, and now the apple orchards. What a contrast from New York's or Philadelphia's streets! Everywhere great patches of dingy-blossom'd horse-mint wafting a spicy odor though the air, (especially evenings.) Everywhere the flowering boneset, and the rose-bloom of the wild bean (Whitman, *Specimen* 146).

In his reading of *Specimen Days* Ben focuses particularly on the Civil War chapters, which sit at the heart of Whitman's book. The book is for Ben an 'interesting failure', as he criticises Whitman for the perceived 'delight he took in the willingness of young men to die for the union whose epic bard he felt he was destined to be' (168), and the 'kind of ecstasy' he seemed to feel when visiting thousands of sick and wounded soldiers during the early 1860s (169). But we might note the similarities between Whitman's autobiography and Ben's narrative arc in *10:04*. William Aarnes has described *Specimen Days* as presenting 'a period of intense involvement, a period of withdrawal, and a period of reinvolvement', which is revealing of 'Whitman's ambiguous relationship with American society' (402). Broadly speaking, *10:04* follows a similar pattern, with Ben's middle period of withdrawal in Marfa seeing him carve out for himself an atemporal space where the flow of his imagination is unconstrained – comparable to Whitman's retreat into the countryside for a period of recuperation.

This analogous pattern of engagement and isolation is not, however, the full extent of Whitman's presence in this part of the novel. We saw earlier that immersion in narrative facilitates Ben's escape from clock time, and this occurs again here, when his total absorption in *Specimen Days* prompts him to 'fall out of time': while reading Whitman's autobiography he works through the night, stops shaving, and conflates his own present time at the residency with Whitman's Civil War years. The excerpts from the lyric poem Ben is supposedly writing in Marfa (which are reproduced in the novel) are taken from a much longer poem published by Lerner as 'The Dark Threw Patches Down Upon Me Also'. The title is from a line in 'Crossing Brooklyn Ferry', and the narrator of Lerner's poem travels back and forth between twenty-first-century Texas and the soldier hospitals in Washington and Virginia during the Civil War, while his identity slowly merges with Whitman:

moths around streetlights
obscuring the casualty lists I'm trying to read
aloud to citizens in formal dress, address,
attempting to stay cool and extant.
I don't make any sense in the high desert (Lerner, 'The Dark', 257,
   lines 22–26).

In this longer version of the poem Lerner describes his purpose in
Marfa as being

'to chat with the dying or dead, / to let them lay a pale hand on my
   knee / if they still have hands' ('The Dark', 260, lines 124–6).

This is a deliberation invocation of Whitman's daily visits to injured
and dying soldiers during the Civil War. Back in the novel, the conflation of Ben's personality with Whitman's encourages him to take
care of a young intern who has taken too many drugs at a party.
Ben walks him inside the house like 'a parody of Whitman, the
poet-nurse, and his wounded charge' (188), before putting him to
bed and talking to him until he falls asleep. Again, the correspondence between this scene and Whitman's account of army hospitals
is clear – when the intern begs Ben not to leave him lying there, he
sounds like a wounded soldier: 'I saw all these things. I'm fucked
up. I feel like if I shut my eyes I'm going to die' (189). When Ben
smooths back his hair he considers that 'Whitman would have kissed
him' (190); after he has fallen asleep to the sound of Ben describing
the construction of Brooklyn Bridge (another reference to Whitman,
this time his poem 'Crossing Brooklyn Ferry'), he kisses him on the
forehead before heading back upstairs to where the others are sitting.
In *Specimen Days* Whitman described how 'Once in a while some
youngster holds on to me convulsively, and I do what I can for him;
at any rate, stop with him and sit near him for hours, if he wishes it'
(45). Several times he also mentioned kissing injured soldiers during
his bedside visits. Whitman is a forerunner and symbol for Ben's own
sense of timelessness – that is, his temporary escape from conventional temporal patterns. But as we see in that scene with the intern,
his emulation of the Whitman in *Specimen Days* during his Marfa
residency also ushers in a more caring vision of social conduct, and
this is at odds with his hostile encounters on the streets of New York.
   This period of 'ghostly rhythm', where Ben writes his long poem
about Whitman, the poet Robert Creeley (who died in Marfa), and
the residency, is eventually broken by the sound of Mexican labourers
working on the roof – the hammering which starts up one morning

prevents Ben from sleeping through the day, forcing him into a more conventional routine: 'I decided to make coffee and walk a little – for the first time in broad daylight since I'd arrived' (172). He imagines how the workers must perceive him and his fellow writers: as 'residents whose labor could be hard to tell apart from leisure, from loafing, people who kept strange hours if they kept them at all' (172). The interruption of his own dreamlike spell of creative energy by the entrance of normal rhythms – people who work during the day and sleep at night – encourages him to set aside the 'heat wave of the poem' where his self-identity has blended with Whitman, and instead 're-enter time' (174), venturing out to a bookshop now feeling 'at least semihuman and diurnal' (176) although still 'socially disoriented' (177). Ben's period outside New York has facilitated an immersive and intensely subjective experience of time passing, shaped chiefly by his own thoughts and imagination. However, these weeks of almost total solitude have also rendered his self-identity newly unstable. This becomes apparent when he meets some acquaintances from New York and is cajoled into joining them at an exhibition and then dinner. At the restaurant he notices that when 'trying to make conversation as we waited for our drinks, I felt like a character actor trying to return to an old role' (180–1), and at a party later that night he is aware of behaving oddly towards the intern he had only met that day:

> I hugged him as if he were an old friend I was thrilled to see after an interval of years – a kind of humor totally out of character for me – and everyone laughed and was at ease. How many out-of-character things did I need to do, I wondered, before the world rearranged itself around me? (182)

While the period 'out of time' in Marfa has been completely absorbing for Ben on an imaginative level, he comes to realise that he needs other people around him to provide the framework for a coherent and stable sense of self. He remarks in passing that 'I had gone more than two weeks without really speaking to anyone, a period of silence with no precedent in my life' (176); his own identity is partly formulated through his interactions with other people, and the complete absence of social contact has led to a severe weakening of his personality, and a temporary loss of proprioception.

The absence of other people in Marfa results in the near-dissolution of Ben's personality; in New York he is surrounded by people, yet despite his best efforts still finds himself unable to forge meaningful human connections. He is 'alarmed', for instance, by Alena's 'dissimulation' when they see each other again shortly after having sex:

Here I was, still flush from our coition, my senses and the city vibrat-
ing at one frequency, wanting nothing so much as to possess and be
possessed by her again, while she looked at me with a detachment so
total I felt as if I were the jealous ex she'd hoped to avoid (29).

Earlier he had noted her 'nonchalance' (26), and the 'shadowed
eyes' which seem to express 'perfect indifference' (28) and which he
attempts to mimic. This feeling of isolation and estrangement when
around other people is familiar from modernist literature: in Woolf's
Mrs Dalloway, Rezia Smith's desperation at her husband Septimus's
shellshock is set against the busy London streets where she knows
practically no one, and where passers-by go about their business,
oblivious to her distress: 'Help, help! she wanted to cry out to butch-
ers' boys and women. Help!' (Woolf 13). Hemingway's 1926 novel
The Sun Also Rises presents Paris as a post-war wasteland: narrator Jake Barnes socialises with friends and acquaintances (including his ex-lover Brett Ashley), yet these chaotic nights of drinking
and dancing only underline his own jealousy and acute loneliness.
Examples of urban isolation abound in modernist literature more
generally: these include Leopold Bloom; the eponymous protagonist in Wyndham Lewis's *Tarr* (1918); Franz Biberkopf, the hero of
Alfred Döblin's *Berlin Alexanderplatz* (1929); the unnamed young
man from the prologue to John Dos Passos's trilogy *U.S.A.* (1938);
Sasha Jansen in Jean Rhys's *Good Morning, Midnight* (1939); and
Ulrich from Robert Musil's *The Man Without Qualities* (1930–43).
These novels also contain series of transitory, fragmented impressions that create a collage-type effect: a way of replicating, at the
level of style and structure, how it feels to live in a noisy and fast-
moving modern city. To show that Ben is permanently conscious of
these earlier paradigms, Lerner employs the same technique in *10:04*.
After Ben attends Alena's exhibition, he goes to a bar with his friend
Sharon, before the two of them get on the subway to go home. As
the pair travel underground and then emerge again on Manhattan
Bridge, the reader is presented with a series of apparent non-
sequiturs – advertising slogans, subway announcements, fragments
from strangers' conversations, music spilling out of headphones,
and, right there among them, a line from *The Waste Land*:

'Stand clear of the closing doors, please'.
'We helped edit a film on bonobos for the BBC; they're our closest
    relative and have no concept of sexual exclusivity'.
'They say monogamy is an effect of agriculture. Paternity only
    started to matter with the transmission of property'.

'Get tested for HIV today,' said the poster on the D.
'But they do eat the young of other primate species'.
'So why did you get married if you don't want kids?' We emerged
   onto the Manhattan Bridge; almost everyone checked e-mail,
   texts.
'You left without saying goodbye', Alex's said.
'Shine bright like a diamond', Rihanna sang through the earbuds of
   the girl beside me, whose fingernails were painted with stars (31).

The effect of this linguistic chaos is one of discombobulation: like
Döblin's Berlin or Joyce's Dublin (or Eliot's London), Ben experiences New York as a series of clashing 'broken images' artificially
pushed together to create a sense of discord. As with all of these
earlier texts, *10:04* also moves from scene to scene in a disjointed
manner: the incident described above when Ben works his shift at the
co-op is followed, without any introduction or link, by a long quoted
monologue – which we only subsequently learn is Ben's speech to an
audience during a writers' panel at Columbia's School of the Arts. In
another unexpected shift, the next section begins with the contents
of an e-mail Ben is writing in the style of Robert Creeley, as part of
his project to create a false archive of letters from famous authors.

II.

Ben's articulation of the contemporary city repeatedly relies on a
modernist frame of reference. Just before Ben and Sharon step on
the subway he quotes a line from *Mrs Dalloway* ('A match burning a
crocus; an inner meaning almost expressed'), but his voice does not
carry, the words 'lost in the noise of the approaching train' (30–1,
31). And before bed that same evening, he texts (and then regrets
texting) Alena the line 'The little shower of embers' (32), taken
from an earlier version of Ezra Pound's *The Cantos*, which Ben has
recently been reading. Much of the time these allusions to modernist writing do not seem altogether jarring, given that Ben's concerns
largely relate to the pressures of clock time and his impression of
New York as alienating and chaotic – issues which also preoccupied
many of these earlier authors. Nevertheless, Ben's attempts to apply
the writing and ideas that emerged with greatest force in the decade
after World War One, to a neoliberal twenty-first-century context,
do run up against moments of resistance. In one of the novel's early
scenes, he allows an Occupy Wall Street protestor to use his shower
and wash a bag of dirty clothes. He also cooks him a meal, and the

two men get on well for the short period they spend together: when they part company Ben tells him to text if he or a friend need to use the apartment again. This short episode draws into focus the specific context for Lerner's novel, which takes place over just more than a year, from August 2011 to October 2012. This covers the period of the Occupy demonstrations, which began on 17 September 2011 (although of course preparations had been going on for several months prior to that date), when protestors converged on Zuccotti Park, close to Wall Street. Although that particular occupation was closed down at the end of 2011, the movement had already spread to more than 800 different cities both within the US and across the globe. The media had initially been largely indifferent to the protests, but they quickly took notice – particularly after more than 700 protestors were arrested while marching across Brooklyn Bridge on 1 October. Thereafter Occupy Wall Street became a major worldwide media story, with journalists choosing to focus not just on the protests themselves but on the issues driving them, such as income inequality, high levels of unemployment, the 2008 crash and bailing out of 'too big to fail' financial institutions, rising student debt, corporate power over politics and (connectedly) financial aid and tax cuts for major banks and corporations. But even journalists without any knowledge of the issues at stake could easily take as their angle the many unprovoked acts of police violence towards protestors. As Todd Gitlin notes, 'The police kept coming to Occupy's rescue' (32), as journalists filmed and reported on the 'violence perpetrated by police against demonstrators', including pepper spraying and rubber bullets (52). Social media and catchy slogans (most famously, 'We are the 99%') also allowed the Occupy message to spread nationwide. Gitlin describes how the movement 'spawned mantras, rituals, symbols, imagery galore – a riot of pastiche and contagion' (74). The terms 'occupy' and '99%' in particular became ubiquitous, shorthand for the movement and its manifold grievances. (An early concern among protestors was whether to clarify the aims of the movement by focusing on a single issue.) But broadly speaking, Occupy aimed to shine a spotlight on the connection between wealth and political power; on the perceived greed and irresponsibility of financial institutions and their culpability in the crash of 2008; and to debate radical alternatives to the political and economic systems currently in place.

For Ben, rather eccentrically, there are some important parallels to be drawn between this twenty-first-century focus on the inequalities created by what David Graeber terms the 'financialization of capitalism' (xix), and the discontent voiced by modernist writers regarding the physical and psychological impact of oppressive new industrial processes in the early decades of the twentieth century.[5] D. H. Lawrence's 1920 novel *Women in Love* contains a famous description of the impact of capitalist rationalisation on individuals like Gerald Crich, who becomes increasingly machine-like himself having taken over from his father as head of mine. In the chapter 'The Industrial Magnate', Gerald's radical overhaul of the business leads to greater efficiency but also renders him cruel and inhuman, devoid of any 'emotional qualms' when firing older workers (229). Lawrence describes the 'incarnation of [Gerald's] power' as 'a great and perfect machine, a system, an activity of pure order, pure mechanical repetition, repetition ad infinitum' (228). His workers are 'reduced to mere mechanical instruments': this is 'the substitution of the mechanical principle for the organic' (230, 231). One also thinks of the typist in Eliot's *The Waste Land*, who 'smooths her hair with automatic hand' (line 255); the same image is used in Eliot's 1911 poem 'Rhapsody on a Windy Night', which describes the 'hand of the child, automatic' (line 38). This rendering of people as machine-like parts was a literary device designed to reveal the impact of economic conditions during a particular stage of capitalism, as Randall Stevenson explains: 'making people interchangeable with things ... clearly exposes the denaturing, reifying conditions of modern industrial labour' (80). Yet for Ben, these earlier authors' concerns about the effects of capitalism provide a useful lens through which to negotiate the *contemporary* context of financial deregulation, bailouts and protest. This is clear during Ben's lunch with his agent when he realises that, due to the particular logic of the neoliberal market system, his as-yet unwritten (and therefore 'virtual') second novel is worth more than it will be when published. Having made this calculation, Ben's mind quickly turns to Wallace Stevens. He is enjoying 'yuzu frozen soufflé' (158) and 'sake-based cocktails' in a restaurant filled with 'Investment bankers or market analysts in their twenties' (156), yet he suddenly thinks of the (slightly adapted) line 'Money was a kind of poetry' (158), from Stevens's 1957 *Opus Posthumous*. Ben's reversion to Stevens as the means to conceptualise, or at least communicate, his ambivalent relationship to twenty-first-century systems of finance seems quaintly naïve, if not entirely specious. Ben's New York is under the grip of neoliberalism, which is so far removed from the capitalism of the modernist period as to seem unrecognisable. Mark Fisher's 2009 *Capitalist Realism* functions as an interrogative intertext for Lerner's novel in this respect:

Fisher argues that the era of 'capitalist realism' has taken 'the vanquishing of modernism for granted: modernism is now something that can periodically return, but only as a frozen aesthetic style, never as an ideal for living' (8). Ben's recourse to modernist diction here therefore seems dated and inapt, his fixation with these writers exposing his limitation, his second-hand quality – in other words, to signal authorial criticism of his angle of vision, thereby preparing the ground for Whitman, a more redemptive and adaptable interpreter of urban life.

The fact that many of the ideas and images from Eliot, Woolf and Stevens that are included in *10:04* tend towards the obvious and generic seems to be another strategy by which Lerner subtly points out the imprecision of his narrator's commentary. That line from Stevens is a well-known one, as are the lines Ben quotes from *The Waste Land*; his allusions to these poems therefore hardly indicate a particularly comprehensive or complex understanding of the period and its literature. Given this potentially superficial engagement with modernism, the reader therefore needs to be on guard against blithely accepting that these writers can offer a useful angle on the contemporary city. And further complications arise from the fact that Ben's supposedly ambivalent relationship to neoliberalism does not preclude him from revelling in some of the benefits it affords him personally. In the novel's opening scene (which is repeated much later on) he has just enjoyed an 'outrageously expensive celebratory meal' (3) with his agent at a Chelsea restaurant after having secured a '"strong six-figure" advance' for his second novel following a 'competitive auction among the major New York houses' (4). The financial system has served Ben well here: like stock traders, those publishers are speculating on the future value of his novel. His art has become an expensive commodity, and by selling it he can purchase material items to make his life more pleasant; he even imagines paying for other people's labour:

> After my agent's percentage and taxes (including New York City taxes, she had reminded me), I would clear something like two hundred and seventy thousand dollars. Or fifty-four IUIs. Or around four Hummer H2 SUVs. Or the two first editions on the market of *Leaves of Grass*. Or about twenty-five years of a Mexican migrant's labor, seven of Alex's in her current job (155).

Ben's delight at this unexpected financial boost – generated through the 'rise and fall of art commodities and tradable futures' (156) – suggests that his hosting of the Occupy Wall Street protester is nothing more than a gesture. When the protester arrives at Ben's apartment Ben finds himself 'embarrassed by the luxury' of the 'small washer-and-dryer unit in the closet' (45), yet the encounter is unlikely to change his mind about the current economic model, since that same system works to his advantage.

Elsewhere, however, Ben seems more persuaded that an alternative to the current financial system might be worth considering. Around halfway through the novel he visits the 'Institute for Totaled Art', an enterprise created by his girlfriend, Alena. She has contacted the country's largest art insurer and persuaded them to donate to her institute a gallery's worth of artworks that have been damaged, and either cannot be restored at all, or the restoration would exceed the cost of the insurance claim. In purely legal terms these works are regarded as having 'zero value' (129), and therefore languish in a warehouse on Long Island. Ben marvels at being so close to works by famous artists: Alena tells him to shut his eyes before placing in his hands 'the pieces of a shattered Jeff Koons balloon dog sculpture, an early red one' (131). But other works are less obviously damaged. A Cartier-Bresson print has no visible marks or tears, and it is this which highlights, for Ben, the ludicrousness of a system where the value of an object changes for no discernible reason: 'It [the print] had transitioned from being a repository of immense financial value to being declared of zero value without undergoing what was to me any perceptible material transformation – it was the same, only totally different' (133). Ben seems awed by these artworks, suggesting they represent a 'utopian readymade' now that 'the market's soul had fled' from them (134). We might compare this with his enthusiasm elsewhere for that same 'market', or financial system, when it came up with a generous valuation of his second novel.[6]

One of the novel's final scenes reiterates this negative take on neoliberalism, with Ben instinctively reverting to an image from modernism as the means to conceptualise it. That series of supposedly random phrases heard on the subway contains an altered version of Eliot's line 'What you get married for if you don't want children?', from 'A Game of Chess', the second section of *The Waste Land*. And another image from Eliot's poem appears at the novel's climax, when Ben and Alex are forced to make their way from Manhattan back to Brooklyn after the power has gone down. No taxi will take them down to Brooklyn, and the buses are all full. Increasingly desperate (Alex is pregnant, and Ben is keen that she should take it easy), and in dark streets that are running on candlelight, the city starts to feel chaotic and dangerous: on Lafayette and Canal 'two men

approached us, at least one of them drunk, and asked for money',
but Ben's disorientation is so thorough, as though mirroring this
'absence of streetlights and established order', that he struggles to
read the social cues: 'I couldn't tell if they were begging or threatening to rob us, making a demand' (236). The city again feels isolating,
and even a policeman refuses to help them:

> I asked a cop on the corner of Broadway and Fifteenth how we could
> get back to Brooklyn, and he just shrugged dismissively; to my sur-
> prise, I felt a surge of rage, fantasized about striking him, and only
> then realized how many contradictory emotions were colliding and
> recombining within me (235).

The city's chaos is reflected in the form, with a jumble of discordant
images:

> my voice sounded weird in the lightless streets – loud, conspicuous,
> although there was plenty of other noise: somebody was hammering
> something nearby; I could hear, but not see, a helicopter; the slow,
> high-pitched braking of a large truck in the near distance sounded
> submarine, like whale song. A cab surprised us as we turned onto
> Park Place (237).

Noises are disconnected from the machines making them, and inani-
mate objects have come to life. One thinks here of Septimus Smith
in London in 1923: Woolf describes how 'In the street, vans roared
past him; brutality blared out on placards' (76). Closer to home,
Ben's evening calls to mind Dos Passos's descriptions of New York in
Manhattan Transfer (1925), for instance when Bud is standing at a
street corner while the elevated train 'thundered overhead', and then
'A black shiny cab drawn by two black shinyrumped horses turned
the corner sharp in front of him with a rasp on the cobblestones of red
shiny wheels suddenly braked' (64). These resemblances suggest that
Ben is not completely misguided in drawing certain parallels between
the two periods; this continual tension between his often persuasive
modernist vision and Lerner's implied judgement of this preoccupation is never quite resolved in the novel, frustrating attempts to
locate the authorial position with any degree of confidence.

    As Ben and Alex continue walking in the cold and dark, even
basic rates of exchange have stopped functioning: a bodega 'weakly
illuminated by a generator' (237) has every item priced at ten dollars
– a bottle of water, torches, even matches. This is the city at its most
unfriendly and exploitative: people see the blackout as an opportunity to make money, rather than to help. Even (or perhaps especially)

at this moment of crisis New Yorkers are 'market actors' (Brown 36), jostling for a competitive edge over their fellow citizens. Ben feels that 'along with power, we'd lost a kind of social proprioception' (236) – that is, an awareness of one's relation to other people; the urban crowd's quasi-intuitive sense of itself as a collective has gone astray. Wendy Brown suggests that neoliberalism has led to the 'economization of everything and every sphere', which translates as an attack 'on public goods and the very idea of a public, including citizenship beyond membership' (40, 39). She describes how 'The replacement of citizenship defined as concern with the public good by citizenship reduced to the citizen as *homo oeconomicus* . . . eliminates the very idea of a people, a demos asserting its collective political sovereignty' (39). This describes the situation towards the end of *10:04*, where the social contract has finally dissolved with the flood of human capital. When Ben and Alex finally reach Brooklyn Bridge, having walked more than seven miles, Ben is confronted with the following scene:

> A steady current of people attired in the usual costumes was entering the walkway onto the bridge and there was a strange energy crackling among us; part parade, part flight, part protest. Each woman I imagined as pregnant, then I imagined all of us were dead, flowing over London Bridge. What I mean is that our faceless presences were flickering, every one disintegrated, yet part of the scheme (238).

It is worth focusing on how Ben alters, or qualifies, his description – that passage pivots with the phrase 'What I mean is' at the beginning of the last sentence, which allows him to change direction from Eliot's alienated crowd in post-war London to the much more affirmative vision of the urban (New York) landscape in Whitman's 'Crossing Brooklyn Ferry', which describes the 'Crowds of men and women attired in the usual costumes' who together formed a 'simple, compact, well-join'd scheme' (129, lines 3, 7). These competing visions of the city have been held in balance throughout the novel, and here it is Whitman's description that finally dominates: during and after Ben and Alex's crossing of the bridge, human connections are suddenly easily forged – seemingly refreshed by the people around them, they are newly cognisant of what Whitman terms 'the ties between me and them . . . the life, love, sight, hearing of others' ('Crossing', 129, lines 11–12). Whitman here presents the possibility of resistance to neoliberal domination through an affective, 'bodily' (W. Sharpe 69) mode of being. Simple acts of kindness become effortless, and crucially they do not rely on any kind of return on the investment: Ben offers his seat on the bus to an old lady, who in turn intuits that Alex is pregnant; Alex suggests dedicating Ben's novel to a woman killed on her bicycle. This confirms what Ben had previously suspected about the city's Whitmanic capacity to foster new and unexpected connections. After his conversation with Noor at the co-op much earlier in the novel, he had taken a long walk through Brooklyn, before sitting down on a bench to gaze over at Manhattan. The view provoked in him an 'urban experience of the sublime' (108) whereby he 'tried to take in the skyline' but 'instead was taken in by it', and felt 'a fullness indistinguishable from being emptied, my personality dissolving into a personhood so abstract that every atom belonging to me as good belonged to Noor, the fiction of the world rearranging itself around her' (109). This is of course a nod to the opening lines of 'Song of Myself', and Ben becomes increasingly Whitman-like as he considers his relationship to the city. In *Leaves of Grass,* feelings of sublimity are stirred in the speaker by his conception of America's vastness and limitless potential, while he simultaneously identifies himself as its representative; his democratic instinct is to be both overwhelmed and captivated by the equal greatness of all things, but also attentive to his own position as an embodiment of the nation.[7] As Rob Wilson writes, 'Whitman becomes the great sublime he draws' (146).[8] In *10:04*, Ben registers the 'small thrill' he always feels when looking out at 'Manhattan's skyline and the innumerable illuminated windows and the liquid sapphire and ruby of traffic on the FDR Drive and the present absence of the towers' (108), mindful of his relative insignificance. But by the end of the novel, he is also able to stand outside and above this individual moment, subsuming it within his commanding, universal perspective of the city. The novel ends with the following lines, where Ben fuses with the Whitman of 'Crossing Brooklyn Ferry':

> at the time of writing, as I lean against the chain-link fence intended to stop jumpers, I am looking back at the totaled city in the second person plural. I know it's hard to understand / I am with you, and I know how it is (240).

This gets to the heart of why Whitman's vision eventually supplants that of Eliot in this novel: while *The Waste Land* seems to replicate Ben's feeling of urban alienation, it fails to offer an alternative. Whitman presents a way of seeing that manages to be both consolatory and affirmative.

Lerner's quotation from 'Crossing Brooklyn Ferry' underscores the prominent role afforded to Whitman throughout *10:04*, and their shared focus on the urban atmosphere in particular repays closer attention. Whitman's poem appeared in the second edition of *Leaves of Grass* under the title 'Sun-Down Poem', and takes as its ostensible subject the ferry journey from Manhattan over to Brooklyn. But it also presents Whitman's most vibrant, pulsing depiction of the city: noisy, utopian, uninhibited and centred on the ethos of commonality and friendship. While the poem does acknowledge New York's darker undertones (such as the 'foundry chimneys' that burn 'high and glaringly into the night' (131, line 47)), it also celebrates the energy of the crowded, bustling pavements, and the coming together with others that urban spaces can provoke. In the poem, this democratic union is felt with the people Whitman meets on the streets of mid-nineteenth-century New York, but also with the 'men and women . . . ever so many generations hence' to whom the poem is addressed (130, line 21). Wendy Brown suggests that in neoliberalism the 'demos' has been 'discursively disintegrated' (44): economic competition saturates every domain, meaning that 'everything is capital' (38). Lerner invokes Whitman to remind readers that an alternative to this used to exist, and parts of it might perhaps again. In Werner Hamacher's influential reading of Walter Benjamin's 'Theses on the Philosophy of History', he describes the '*weak* messianic force' as 'the expectation of others towards us, the undischarged remains of possibility that are transferred from former generations to the future ones' (165). The 'missed possibilities of the past' call on us 'not to miss them a second time, but to perceive them in every sense: cognisingly to seize and to actualise them' (165). This sense of historical time, whereby the past is 'possible happiness' that 'demands actualisation' (165), offers a way of thinking about Whitman's bid for spiritual recuperation in the reader's present-day New York.

Of equal importance is the poem's suggestion that the city comes to life through the poet's experience. William Sharpe has noted that 'city life does not exist apart from his [Whitman's] perception of it' (98), and 'Crossing Brooklyn Ferry' is packed with sensory words, emphasising above all else the poet's own response to the crowds and sights: 'Throb, baffled and curious brain!' and 'Sound out, voices of young men! loudly and musically call me by my nighest name!' (133, lines 106, 109). This tendency to regard the city as being created at the very moment he perceives it has its parallel in Lerner's novel. During their frequent strolls around New York, Alex and Ben feel themselves to be assembling the city scene as it unfurls in front of them. Ben explains that in the galleries as on our walks our gazes were parallel, directed in front of us at canvas and not at each other, a condition of our most intimate exchanges; we would work out our views as we coconstructed the literal view before us (8).

This reimagining of the city is a joint endeavour, a 'coconstruction' which forges a bond, allowing them to talk much more openly than they would when sitting across from each other. Ben is talking directly to the reader when he writes,

> You might have seen us walking on Atlantic, tears streaming down her face, my arm around her shoulders, but our gazes straight ahead; or perhaps you've seen me during one of my own increasingly lacrimal events being comforted in kind while we moved across the Brooklyn Bridge, less a couple than conjoined (8).

Walking through the city is a necessary condition for these moments of tenderness, fostering a level of intimacy out of reach to them within other contexts:

> We did not avoid each other's eyes and I admired the overcast-sky quality of hers, dark epithelium and clear stroma, but we tended to fall quiet when they met. Which meant we'd eat a lunch in silence or idle talk, only for me to learn on the subsequent walk home that her mother had been diagnosed in a late stage (8).

The bond between Alex and Ben, reaffirmed on their walks through the city, calls to mind Whitman's hopes for connection with his future readers. The detail and energy that goes into Whitman's city scenes emboldens those readers to use the vivid descriptions to imaginatively construct the city for themselves; he makes this task easier for them by including impressions of New York that are so broad they will seem familiar to practically anyone who has lived in a city. For example, in the lines 'Just as you feel when you look on the river and sky, so I felt, / Just as any of you is one of a living crowd, I was one of a crowd' (130, lines 22–23), the sensations are non-specific enough to accommodate any interpretation that the reader might bring to bear.[9] Whitman's expectation that the future reader would apply the descriptions in his poem to their own surroundings, and thereby join in his 'urban construction' (W. Sharpe 89), was a way of drawing the reader closer to him: as Sharpe describes, 'the circuit of sight' between Whitman and his reader is 'completed indirectly by the landscape they both look upon, separately yet together' (96). At the start of section five of 'Crossing Brooklyn Ferry' Whitman asks,

'What is it then between us?' (131, line 54), and while this can be understood as a reference to the 'scores or hundreds of years' (131, line 55) that divides him from his future readers, it can also be read in the sense of, what do we hold in common; what do we share? An earlier line in the poem has already confirmed this assumed connection with his readers, with the confident line 'It avails not, time nor place – distance avails not' (130, line 20). And near the end of the poem in section eight, Whitman and his readers are now welded together:

> What is more subtle than this which ties me to the woman or man that looks in my face? / Which fuses into you now, and pours my meaning into you? (133, lines 96–7)

James E. Miller has described this as the 'climax' of 'Crossing Brooklyn Ferry', when Whitman 'works his way into the very being of the reader' (82). Poet and future reader are now bonded by their common experience of urban life; the relationship between past and present has become one of continuity and identification.

But Whitman's sense of self is never fixed in this poem: alongside that 'fusion' with the reader, he also signals that his poetic identity is indistinguishable from the city itself (just as in 'Song of Myself' he *becomes* America, in all its enormity, multiplicity and wonder).[10] The line from 'Crossing Brooklyn Ferry' quoted by Lerner about the 'simple, compact, well-join'd scheme, myself disintegrated ... yet part of the scheme' points to Whitman's absorption by the 'flood-tide' and the 'living crowd' (129, line 7; 130, lines 19, 23), but as we saw earlier (and in a circular motion so characteristic of this poem), the city itself is also fashioned through his contemplative gaze. William Pannapacker has described the 'urban writer' (such as Whitman) as a 'subjective interpreter of the city as a "text"' (58). Whitman rewrites the city in a manner that appears universalising – that is, applicable to all – but parts of this vision are also very personal: alongside those rather generic descriptions of urban life, he includes details about New York that hold particular resonance for him on the assumption (but not guarantee) that future readers will share in it:

> I too many and many a time cross'd the river of old,
> Watched the Twelfth-month sea-gulls, saw them high in the air
>   floating with motionless wings, oscillating their bodies,
> Saw how the glistening yellow lit up parts of their bodies and left
>   the rest in strong shadow (130, lines 28–30).[11]

Back in the novel Ben, too, sketches an alternative, subjective map of the city marked with meaningful events in his own life:

> Place a thumbtack on the wall or drop a flag on Google Maps at Lincoln Center, where, beside the fountain, I took a call from Jon informing me that, for whatever complex of reasons, a friend had shot himself; mark the Noguchi Museum in Long Island City, where I read the message ('Apologies for the mass e-mail. . .') a close cousin sent out describing the dire condition of her newborn; waiting in line at the post office on Atlantic, the *adhan* issuing from the crackling speakers of the adjacent mosque, I received your wedding announcement and was shocked to be shocked, crushed, and started a frightening multiweek descent, worse for being embarrassingly clichéd; while in the bathroom of the SoHo Crate and Barrel – the finest semipublic restroom in lower Manhattan – I'd learned I'd been awarded a grant that would take me overseas for a summer, and so came to associate the corner of Broadway and Houston with all that transpired in Morocco; at Zuccotti Park I heard that my then-girlfriend was not – as she'd been convinced – pregnant; while buying discounted dress socks at the Century 21 Department Store across from Ground Zero, I was informed by text that a friend in Oakland had been hospitalized after the police had broken his ribs (33).

New York is reinterpreted here in accordance with Ben's memories, and these continue to shape how he thinks about its various streets and landmarks. Both he and Whitman therefore offer up their subjective mappings of the city, although they differ in one important respect: whereas Ben recognises that those memories are his alone, with 'the news and an echo of its attendant affect' waiting 'in situ' for *his* return to the same area (33), Whitman regards his experiences as universal, and interwoven with the city itself, therefore accessible to every one of his future readers.

Consistent with Whitman's role throughout *10:04*, 'Crossing Brooklyn Ferry' also presents an alternative to the conventional understanding of time. The poem's speaker communicates directly with readers far into the future, whose experience of New York he assumes will echo and repeat his own. That claim that the 'count of the scores or hundreds of years' between him and these readers 'avails not' is an assurance that the passing of time does not operate in a normal manner, and this is designed to eradicate the feeling of separation from past events and people (131, lines 55, 56). In Texas Ben was able to move back and forth between the Civil War and his own present time; in the longer version of the poem he writes at the residency (which is published elsewhere by Lerner), he notes that in the last stanza of 'Crossing Brooklyn Ferry' the speaker is 'emptied of history so he can ferry across it' (Lerner, 'The Dark' 264). For Ben there is no longer a sense of moving forwards, inexorably; his is a circular, recurring understanding of time akin to the sun's 'slow-wheeling circles' (130, line 30) seen by Whitman in New York. It was noted at the start of this chapter that in *10:04* Lerner paints for us an image of New York that feels both contemporary and apocalyptic. One of the tasks for his narrator is to find a way to inhabit this neoliberal city while still maintaining faith in empathy, the imagination, and genuine human connection. There is a larger irony here regarding Ben's apparent resistance to the structures of global capitalism, given that the novel we are reading is supposedly the one he writes in order to hold on to his six-figure advance. He is not therefore immune to the advantages of the system. But Ben's identification of a literary predecessor whose vision of the city is both redemptive and capacious (allowing it to be applied to the present moment), as well as *bodily*, represents a significant turning point in the novel. Ben follows Whitman in carving out pockets of time where community and sincerity can still flourish, and where one can see oneself as part of a larger and benign collective that also transcends time, crossing between the mid-nineteenth century and the present day. The hurricanes that begin and end *10:04* do not prove to be devastating for either Ben or Alex, but the threat of a more catastrophic outcome hovers at the edges of the novel. One of Ben's students reminds him that 'the sky is falling, if you know what I mean – that's no longer just a phrase' (217). The solution is therefore to look backwards to a literary predecessor such as Whitman, whose urban vision represents the possibility of redemption through connecting with others across space and time.

Notes

1. Prominent examples include Karl Ove Knausgaard's multivolume series *My Struggle* (2009–11); Lerner's own first novel, *Leaving the Atocha Station* (2011); Teju Cole's *Open City* (2011); Sheila Heti's *How Should a Person Be?* (2012) and *Motherhood* (2018); Édouard Louis's *The End of Eddy* (2014) and *The History of Violence* (2016); Rachel Cusk's trilogy *Outline* (2014), *Transit* (2016) and *Kudos* (2018); Maggie Nelson's *The Argonauts* (2015); Olivia Laing's *Crudo* (2018); and Ocean Vuong's *On Earth We're Briefly Gorgeous* (2019).
2. In the film, the town's clock tower has been frozen on 10:04 ever since it was struck by lightning at that exact time on 12 November 1955.

3. This occurs throughout Marcel Proust's *À la recherche du temps perdu* (1913–27), most famously when Marcel tastes a piece of madeleine soaked in lime-blossom tea and is transported back to an identical moment in his childhood. Other famous examples from modernist fiction include Virginia Woolf's *To the Lighthouse* (1927), when Lily Briscoe's return to an incomplete painting triggers her sense that she is sitting beside Mrs Ramsay on the beach many years after her death. In *Mrs Dalloway* (1925) both Clarissa and Septimus Smith are repeatedly transported back into the past during a single day in June 1923. And in *Ulysses* (1922) Bloom's mind ranges freely back into moments from the past, while in the final chapter Molly seems to inhabit multiple temporal planes at once – Dublin in 1904, but also Bloom's proposal to her sixteen years earlier, as well as her childhood in Gibraltar.

4. Walter Benjamin's concept of '*weak* Messianic time' (as outlined in his 'Theses on the Philosophy of History') is a possible way to consider these moments in the novel. In Werner Hamacher's reading of Benjamin, he suggests that the 'messianic force' is 'the postulate of fulfilability' and 'redeemability' in 'each missed possibility' of the past (165). This mirrors Ben's feeling that his own present experiences might one day be reconsidered from a future standpoint. The novel turns to Benjamin at several key moments, not least its epigraph, which is from a story attributed to Benjamin, quoted in Giorgio Agamben's *The Coming Community*. And Paul Klee's *Angelus Novus* is reproduced on page 25 of the novel and referenced throughout: the 'back to the future' pun of the title clearly references the 'angel of history', as well as the 1985 film starring Michael J. Fox. Pieter Vermeulen's article on the novel draws particular attention to the Angel having his '*back to the future*' (660) to make the point that *10:04*'s project 'is to redeem the present from a future that only diminishes it' (661). For Vermeulen the novel wishes to 'cancel its dependence on the future' (661): he suggests that 'the status of present experiences as the objects of future memories is . . . what robs them of their significance', therefore 'only experiences that remain unremembered can claim the intensity and vitality that *10:04* wants to capture' (671). Events in the narrative that fail to take place as expected, and experiences which are immediately forgotten, manage to 'escape the anticipation of their own future remembrance, and so become fully meaningful in themselves' (671).

5. Graeber is referring here to the collusion between government and Wall Street, but also the notion of 'neoliberalism as a political project' where capitalism is presented as 'the only viable economic system' (280) – a view created and sustained in recent years, he argues, by media-led propaganda; the vast sums spent on 'security systems' despite the lack of 'any major rival' (280); the destruction of unions through precarious work contracts; and the 'imposition of an apparatus of hopelessness, designed to squelch any sense of an alternative future': the containment

of 'the imagination, desire, individual liberation' to 'the domain of consumerism, or perhaps in the virtual realities of the Internet' (281).

6. Arne De Boever focuses on this scene in Alena's institute within his broader discussion of *10:04*'s engagement with neoliberal financialization, which he feels is most palpable in the context of the novel Ben is supposedly writing. As De Boever notes, that future novel exists as a 'financial instrument' that generates 'speculative value' (in the form of a hefty advance) before it is written, and this will almost certainly dwarf its actual worth (either aesthetically or in monetary terms, in the form of sales) after Ben has completed it (158). Pieter Vermeulen argues persuasively that in this scene 'the totaling of art ... fully liberates the object from the cash nexus: totaled art works are officially withdrawn from circulation, and can never again acquire monetary value' (669–70). This frees the objects up to take on a different meaning or significance, as he also goes on to explain: rather than being a 'mere placeholder of future or potential gain' (as is usually the case), 'totaled art again becomes a contingent, material, vulnerable actuality that paradoxically possesses a broader range of potential futures' (670).

7. This is not to overlook the fact that Whitman is always also aware of those moments of radical inequality that threaten the vision he would like to bring into being – most obviously the passages on slavery in sections 10 and 33 of *Leaves of Grass*.

8. In Wilson's analysis of 'Song of Myself' he suggests that the poem's 'democratic sublimity' (152) is achieved through its simple, unadorned language, and through the everyday sights which provoke the poet's 'self-regenerative *wonder*' at the 'American life-world' (148). Wilson describes how Whitman presents his 'sublime empowerment' through the 'awe-struck ego-identity of a common man who has earned this ecstasy through a defiantly *physical* union with the vastness of God and America' (148); by doing so the poet-speaker shows that his experience of the sublime is available to all, but also that those modest sights and sounds are equally worthy of contemplation: 'Song of Myself' manages 'not only to proclaim the Godlike potential of any consciousness, or huge things, but also to elevate the "mossy scabs of the worm fence, heap'd stones, elder, mullein and poke-weed" as small-but-equal items of wonder within his American sublime' (150–1).

9. Ben makes the same observation but applied to *Specimen Days* when he points out that 'many of his memories are general enough to be anyone's memory: how he took his ease under a flowering tree or whatever' (168). And in that longer version of the poem Ben writes in Marfa (which Lerner published in *No Art*), he includes the following lines about 'Crossing Brooklyn Ferry': 'tide, wake, barge, flag, foundry are things / anyone could see, but no one in particular, / less things than examples of things, which once / meant a public meeting place, assembly. / Words are the promise he can't make / in words without render-

ing them determinate / and thereby breaking the promise because / only when empty can we imagine assembling, / not as ourselves, but as representatives / of the selves he has asked us to dissolve: / dumb ministers' (265, lines 265–75).

10. Wilson argues that Whitman in that poem 'identifies with and represents this American immensity' (137), presenting a capacious, inclusive, and awestruck vision of America at the same time as stressing his poet-speaker's 'absorption' of, and 'mastery' (150) over everything he describes: '"Song of Myself" embodies, on a grand scale of Emersonian self-intoxication, this attempt to represent sublime space by remaking the ego into a selfhood capable of blessing place and globe like a shamanized Columbus fusing "America" into an India of his own imperial design' (137). Wilson puts this in more straightforward terms later in the same chapter when he describes Whitman 'subsuming American forms into the bragging song of himself' (156).

11. Sharpe hints at the possibility that Whitman and his future readers will have contrasting (or at least not identical) experiences of New York when he writes that 'In place of the delocalized encounter usual in lyric poetry, Whitman situates the reader as part of a specific urban landscape, the poet's own. As it develops, their bond will depend increasingly on their common experience of the scene they share, each inseparable from the harbor and its sights' (93). For Sharpe, Whitman attempts to overcome this potential disparity by alluding to 'the fellowship of shared emotions', even if by doing so he 'cleverly assigns to the reader habits that actually belong to the poet' (95).

Chapter 3

Dana Spiotta and Political Commitment

The first character we encounter in Dana Spiotta's 2006 novel *Eat the Document* is Mary Whittaker, a young woman who has just turned fugitive after planting a bomb in a property she believed to be empty, accidentally killing the housekeeper. The bombing was politically motivated: this opening sequence is set in 1972, and Mary was targeting the home of a board member whose company was developing a type of poison gas used in Vietnam. Mary is a member of the notorious Weatherman collective (which later changed its name to the Weather Underground, and eventually to the Weather Underground Organization), a militant splinter group of the Students for a Democratic Society (SDS), formed after the latter organisation's implosion in 1969. The Weather Underground (whose original name comes from a line in Bob Dylan's song Subterranean Homesick Blues) were responsible for planting bombs in corporate and government buildings to protest the intensifying US military involvement in Vietnam.[1] Spiotta's novel spans the decades after the explosion, when Mary lives under a fake identity; this takes us up to the year 2000. The novel explores the lasting impact of 1970s New Left activism: it considers the effect of militant protest on the individuals involved in politically-motivated violence, but also traces how some of the radical motives and deeds from that period are reworked into a tamer and more cynical response to economic and social injustice twenty-five years later. Another plot strand takes place in Seattle during the late 1990s, where a bookshop selling fringe texts called Prairie Fire Books (named after the Weather Underground's 1974 book *Prairie Fire: The Politics of Revolutionary Anti-Imperialism*) becomes a central meeting point for adolescent left-wing groups, most of whom never carry out any acts of resistance. Spiotta's novels more generally can be defined as works of historical archaeology: reworkings or reconsiderations of particular moments in America's recent past – cultural, societal or political – in order to explore how this historical material asserts itself on the present day. *Innocents and Others*, published in 2016, is Spiotta's fourth novel, and centres on the friendship between two women, Meadow Mori and Carrie Wexler. Friends since they attended the same private arts high school in Santa Monica in the 1970s, they both go on to become filmmakers – Carrie going down the more mainstream route with a series of popular comedies, while Meadow, always the more earnest of the two, makes serious documentaries which set out to re-evaluate events such as the Kent State shooting, the Dirty War in Argentina and the dropping of the second atom bomb over Nagasaki. But *Eat the Document* and *Innocents and Others* are additionally preoccupied with notions of authenticity, of what goes into constructing a plausible identity, and the psychological damage (dissociation, isolation, loneliness) caused by decades of lying: *Eat the Document* takes as its main protagonist a fugitive criminal activist who takes on a series of false identities, while *Innocents and Others* includes a character named Jelly (also known as Nicole) whose hobby during the 1970s was to cold-call Hollywood executives and begin relationships with them over the telephone. When she falls in love with one of these men, Jack, and realises that for the relationship to continue they will have to meet, she cuts it off without warning, refusing to expose herself as a fraud.

Spiotta is attentive to the notion of authenticity in the context of New Left politics, too: as noted above, a central concern in *Eat the Document* is to compare the strategies of two different generations in responding to corporate and governmental decision-making, as she contrasts the violent yet apparently sincere radicalism of the 1970s with the less daring exploits of late-1990s left-wing adolescents. The question of earnest commitment, whether in politics or art, unites these two novels, with Spiotta encouraging us to measure the gains of a hard-line approach to filmmaking and radical protest, and then weigh this against the various degrees of devastation caused by such an uncompromising style. This chapter will begin by outlining the search for authenticity within youth protest movements in the 1950s and '60s, before exploring the politics of the New Left and the tactics of the Weather Underground. Thereafter it will examine, within *Eat the Document*, the profound personal impact on Mary of cutting all ties with her previous life and adopting a new identity that renders her existence inauthentic. The chapter will then compare the militant tactics of 1970s political radicals (such as Mary, but also her then-boyfriend Bobby Desoto) with the more quirky acts of public protest co-ordinated by Seattle teenagers twenty-five years later. And finally, this chapter will turn to *Innocents and Others*, exploring that novel's concern with the effects of adopting a false identity, and thereafter on Meadow Mori's committed approach to filmmaking and its devastating after-effects.

The notion of 'authenticity', which rose to particular prominence in 1950s- and '60s-era left-wing activism, is a central concern in *Eat the Document*, but the generality of the term means it demands careful definition before being applied to the novel. In the context of the New Left, and for the purposes of this chapter, authenticity is taken to mean commitment in a twofold sense – in the first instance, commitment to a personal ethical code. To be personally authentic the individual must adopt a standard of behaviour which corresponds with sincerely held ideals, so the manner in which they conduct and express themselves in public is as close as possible to what they privately believe. In this sense authenticity becomes performative: it is not sufficient simply to be true to one's ethical code; one has to demonstrate this through a series of public gestures, responding through words and behaviour to whatever situation is encountered. Jean-Paul Sartre's discussion of authenticity in *Being and Nothingness* (1943; translated in 1956) is constructive here, not least because his ideas of commitment and authenticity (along with those of Albert Camus) became the motors of existential thinking within the New Left.[2] Sartre proposes that there are elements of an individual's life that cannot be changed. The term he uses here is 'facticity', within which category we might include race, height, one's past, and the inevitability of death. But rather than allowing these ineradicable realities to define and circumscribe one's existence, the individual has the choice to behave in an active, agentive way towards them. Sartre termed this 'transcendence': when the individual acknowledges that they have freedom to adopt a particular attitude towards these elements of facticity and to conceive of alternatives. As Steven Crowell explains it,

> To speak of 'transcendence' here is to indicate that the agent 'goes beyond' what simply is toward what can be: the factual – including the agent's own properties – always emerges in light of the possible, where the possible is not a function of anonymous forces (third-person or logical possibility) but a function of the agent's *choice* and *decision*.

For members of the New Left, many of whom were readers of Sartre and Camus, the refusal to passively accept that one's entire situation has been predefined was a crucial step towards authenticity: instead, the individual could choose, and thereafter commit to, 'a certain course of action, a certain way of being in the world' (Crowell), shaping and maintaining a consciously-chosen mode of self-identity. This constitutes personal commitment. The second, connected aspect of commitment upon which authenticity relies is commitment in a political sense. Again following the existentialist philosophy of Sartre, this means engaging with one's broader context and working towards changing it for the better through social or political action. This political commitment is connected to the first, individual notion of commitment because one key way to take responsibility for upholding one's values (having understood and acknowledged that these are freely chosen) is to join together with others to alter society in such a way that it will better sustain those values. And again, just as Sartre's 'transcendence' depends on recognising that aspects of one's own existence can be shaped by taking an active stance towards them, political authenticity is premised on the understanding that society, too, can be remade if there is proper dedication to analysing the historical or economic situation and identifying which aspects may be changed. This second, politically-motivated aspect of authenticity is also performative: one must signal one's commitment; the political protest must be visible.

These ideas were central to left-wing activism in the 1950s and '60s. In Doug Rossinow's *The Politics of Authenticity* (1998) he describes how the unsatisfactory 'social and political arrangements' in that period such as racial segregation, class struggle and the war in Vietnam combined to leave 'new radicals' with the feeling of 'alienation', seemingly powerless to assert and maintain their personal system of values within a social environment that seemed profoundly hostile to these ideals (4).[3] Although many of these youths were middle class and drawn from America's student body, they nevertheless felt themselves to be existing within a society which did not reflect their own views; university campuses therefore became important, disruptive sites of political protest throughout the period. The means to overcome this personal and political alienation was commitment to 'radical social change' (4), joining together with tens of thousands of other similarly disaffected youths in order to mend social ills, rather than passively (or fatalistically) accepting the injustices of the world as immovable and ineradicable. This explains the appeal of large-scale protest movements such as the

SDS, the antiwar march on Washington in 1965, and the notorious protests outside the Democratic National Convention in August 1968. Rossinow emphasises that the 'search for authenticity lay at the heart of the new left' (4), and the point of its politics was to be both 'effective and morally honest' (10), in that its 'ultimate aim was to alter social arrangements so as to allow as many people as possible to pursue that goal [of authenticity]' (5).[4] The SDS's 1962 political manifesto the *Port Huron Statement*, written by Tom Hayden (one of the founders of the movement), reflected on this existential crisis, describing the 'felt powerlessness of ordinary people, the resignation before the enormity of events', and connecting this 'subjective apathy' to the '*objective* American situation – the actual structural separation of people from power, from relevant knowledge, from the pinnacles of decision-making' (Students 12). The *Port Huron Statement* listed the numerous ways in which this exclusion from power manifested itself, such as the disenfranchisement of certain groups (including 'Negroes in the South' and 'migrant workers'), and politicians repeatedly appealing to the welfare of 'the sovereign public' while engaged solely in representing business interests and fortifying their own position (13). A system of 'participatory democracy' (7) was seen as a potential remedy for the individual's alienation from the decisions affecting his or her life.[5] Opening up all kinds of policy decisions to a much wider array of people would enable each person to take responsibility for 'determining the quality and direction of his life' – thereby forging and actively maintaining a social context that sustains one's values, as a way to achieve a 'personally authentic' existence (Students 7, 6–7).

The SDS was, by the mid-1960s, the main conduit for New Left politics, with the war in Vietnam its focal point. This issue became more urgent as the decade wore on. In March 1965 President Johnson began 'Operation Rolling Thunder', an air assault over North Vietnam which continued until November 1968. US combat deployment also began in earnest: by the end of 1965 close to 200,000 troops were sent to Vietnam, a figure that would rise exponentially as the war intensified, seemingly without end. As a result, Johnson also battled public opinion at home, with influential newspapers including the *New York Times* and *Life* magazine openly declaring their opposition to the conflict.[6] The humiliation of the Tet Offensive in January 1968 brought home the precariousness of the US military position.[7] In early 1965 Johnson's positive approval ratings had been at 70%, with nearly 80% of Americans believing that withdrawing from the conflict 'would open Southeast Asia to

Communist domination', and the same percentage backing 'U.S. combat troop commitment' to prevent this from happening (Karnow 414). By the end of 1968, however, more than 30,000 Americans had been killed in a conflict which no longer seemed winnable, and antiwar sentiment was escalating. The assassinations that year of two prominent antiwar figures, Martin Luther King Jr (in April), and Robert F. Kennedy (in June), added to the prevailing public mood of anger and despair. The SDS was now vast, with 25,000 people attending its march on Washington in April 1965 – at that stage one of the largest antiwar demonstrations ever seen in the US. The SDS was also at the centre of innumerable antiwar teach-ins and campus demonstrations throughout the late 1960s, and by November 1968 its membership was estimated to be close to 100,000. This period of prominence for the SDS was relatively short-lived, however, and it largely dissolved after its 1969 National Convention, when the Weatherman, the radicalised wing of the SDS, seized leadership of the New Left. Because Spiotta's main protagonists in *Eat the Document* are fictional members of the Weatherman, it will prove constructive to briefly outline the group's objectives and actions, before turning to the novel and examining its function in the narrative.

The Weatherman was a militant protest group advocating street-fighting tactics in a bid to bring about meaningful systemic change and trigger a violent anti-capitalist revolution in America. It wrested control of the SDS during the highly fractious Convention, when policy disagreements between the SDS and its Progressive Labor faction provided the opening for the Weatherman's Bill Ayers, Jeff Jones and Mark Rudd to take over the national office.[8] Their first act was to call for a week of protests in Chicago in October, where the Chicago Eight were on trial following the violent protests at the Democratic convention in August. Local Weather collectives across the US attempted to recruit hundreds of thousands of youths to converge on the city to fight the police, in what was termed the 'Days of Rage', comprising several days of violent clashes between police and protesters, hundreds of arrests, and multiple federal investigations into Weatherman activities. By the end of that year the decision had been made to move underground; further notoriety came in March 1970 when a bomb went off accidentally in a house in Greenwich Village, killing several members of the cell who were hiding there. Within months the Weather Underground, as they were now called, had published a 'declaration of a state of war' to encourage more young people to join the fight against police and government. The trademark strategy of the Weather Underground was to plant a bomb in a government or corporate building, warn any occupants of the building to evacuate before the explosion, and follow this up with a communiqué to the press outlining the specific government action that had prompted the attack. This highlights two key features of their approach: they were intent on avoiding lethal violence, and they were determined, through strategic bombings, to provide direct, unambiguous condemnation of the US government on matters of foreign policy (particularly Vietnam) and civil rights.

I.

The Weather Underground was not the only left-wing movement advocating armed struggle at this time, but they were certainly the most notorious.[9] Spiotta made her two main protagonists in *Eat the Document* fugitive members of the group; this allows her to explore the personal and ethical consequences of the turn towards politically-motivated violence, and assess whether passivity and conformism can be defeated through a commitment to authenticity. Following the explosion at the house, which killed the housekeeper, Mary Whittaker is staying in a motel room in the middle of the country, experimenting with hair dye while choosing a 'hidden, modest, meek name' (9) for her new life. This dramatic personal transformation is at the root of the feelings of estrangement that plague Mary for the next several decades: she settles into her new identity (or identities) but in doing so becomes increasingly distanced from her true self. Her actions were a bid for authenticity: planting the bomb was a violent protest against the corporations that dictate economic policy and maintain the status quo, and Mary carried this out in order to force an alternative situation that was more responsive to her personal stance on Vietnam. Importantly, her actions were also performative: she wanted her commitment to the antiwar cause to be visible, to make the headlines. Some months later she describes her motivation for the bombing to her new friend Berry: 'I had to do something, I had to put myself at risk, personally. I had to meet the enormity of what they were doing with something equal to it' (189). But this radicalised protest (or political commitment) has failed to offer a way out of individual alienation through the forging of alternative social conditions; instead, Mary's actions have forced her into a position of silence and despair. Not only is her political resistance less visible and less feasible when living as a fugitive, but the necessary adoption of an alternative identity means that her personality becomes a series of falsehoods. She is unable to articulate and thereafter sustain her personal ethical code; her every action is now insincere, detached from her ideals. This foregrounds the personal risks of political commitment: Mary's attempt to achieve authenticity through the violent destruction of an unsatisfactory and unwilling social environment has the paradoxical effect of rendering her inauthentic, compelled to suppress her emotions, attitudes and memories in order to fully maintain a false identity. Her inauthenticity is now twofold: she experiences a loss of selfhood by being unable to express the values she had previously chosen to shape her existence (Sartre's 'transcendence'), instead adopting new, false attitudes that do not reflect her inner feelings; and she is no longer able to commit herself to a political cause, having cut herself off from the wider world by going into hiding. Her marginalisation is also now self-imposed rather than systemic, as it had been previously: while it was the case during the 1950s and '60s that individuals on the left such as Mary felt themselves to be cut off from the policy decisions affecting their personal circumstances (a situation that the participatory democracy espoused by the New Left set out to address), she has made this rupture much more tangible and decisive. She must remain largely 'off the grid' to avoid detection, drifting from one dead-end job to the next, entirely severed from all of the institutional structures that can form a bridge between the individual and wider society – such as family, friends, a home and a steady job.

In order for Mary to preserve a new identity, her appearance suddenly becomes the most important thing about her. By the time she has been underground for two days, she looks 'decidedly different': a new hair colour and style, big round sunglasses instead of her old glasses, and more makeup than she is used to – in her previous life as Mary Whittaker she had regarded 'overt makeup' as 'plastic, frivolous and shallow'; as Caroline Sherman 'she put on some coral lipstick and felt unrecognizably safe' (95). This careful overhaul of her own appearance causes her to pay much more attention to the people around her: she notices that whereas her new friend Mel 'held herself stiffly', Berry 'always seemed to be touching herself, and it made her appear suggestive and sybaritic' (104). As though more attuned to the particular motives that drive people to present themselves in a certain way, Mary also recognises about Berry's behaviour that 'it wasn't for show, it wasn't a display. It was just her, and the way she felt free to enjoy the thousand tiny soft delights of her own body' (104). Mary's own plainness, by contrast, becomes an advantage to her in her new role as Caroline:

> It meant she could move somewhere new and go to the store or apply for a job and people wouldn't feel threatened or aroused. She knew she could go unnoticed. She could not recall her own face if she wasn't staring in a mirror. This smeary obscurity that had caused her pain her whole life became an asset now, her anonymity her saving attribute (13).

That Mary has forgotten how she looks highlights the demarcation between her 'real' inner self and her adopted persona: the two components of her identity do not correlate in any way, so that

> for a while it would be impossible not to be confused and self-conscious during even the most mundane exchanges. Do you drink coffee? And she would have to think, Well, I always have, but now, well, maybe I don't. And she would reply, 'No, I never touch the stuff'. And the extra step of comparing the present with the past would keep her in a constant state of reaction (10).

But rather than regarding the journey towards gaining a watertight identity, when she will no longer have to hesitate before answering these types of questions, as a 'rebirth' (17), she can only think of it with dread. As the novel moves towards the present day it tracks the psychological damage enacted by decades of withholding. Early on in her new life she already feels barely human, 'A pallid suggestion of a person' (17). By the end of the novel (in the year 2000) she seems entirely removed from what is going on around her, regarding 'everything and everyone from a distance, both ephemeral and abstract' (224). Her adolescent son Jason notices that by drinking white wine and club soda solidly throughout the evening, she becomes 'increasingly placid and a bit dulled by bedtime' (23). But even sober 'She is generally so creepily guarded and cryptic in odd, sunny ways. Like she isn't really entirely sure she is in the right house or the right life. Like she's a guest here' (24). Her smile is 'vague, receding' (89), and her son thinks of her as 'a stranger. And she is strange. I am not sure at all what she thinks or feels about anything' (211). The permanent adoption of a new identity has ruptured Mary from her own sense of selfhood: unable (due to the threat of arrest) to choose a particular way of being in the world that feels to her active and sincere – in other words, *authentic* – she passively accepts that her situation is unalterable, and this submission leaves her with an identity that seems two-dimensional, only half-formed.[10]

As Mary comes to understand, personal memories are integral to the construction of a stable sense of identity, facilitating continuity between past events and the present remembering self. Active, conscious forgetting – the repression of memory – is thus an important step in the creation of an alternative identity. Spiotta's novel explores these ideas during Mary's 'Caroline' phase in the mid-1970s, when she abandons a commune in upstate New York (anxious that the FBI might have tracked her down there) and hitchhikes west. One of the men who offers her a lift also rapes her before leaving her by the side of the road without her bag or belongings. As the car drives off, Mary wills herself to forget what has just taken place:

> *It never happened.* She would never speak of it, or let herself think of it, ever. She was quite certain that you could change your past, change the facts, by will alone. Only memory makes it real. So eliminate the memory (195).

This active repression of the traumatic event is essential to her self-preservation, and she makes every effort to dissociate herself from the person who experienced the rape. And even while the attack is taking place, she resolves to remove herself at a conscious level from the assault on her body:

> She didn't struggle and lay there at a distance from the moment; it happened, and she was as absent as she could be . . . She did think for a moment of the girl watching in the rearview mirror, and it made her gasp. Then she regained herself and willed herself immobile and totally withdrawn. It worked (194).

That she seems able to eradicate (however temporarily) the experience and the memory of this attack is down to her well-honed proficiency at repressing great swathes of her own past, essential to the task of constructing her new identity as Caroline. But it also demonstrates that she is still conscious of her freedom to choose how she reacts to ineradicable facts about herself, and this complicates the notion that she is living an inauthentic existence in a Sartrean sense. In fact she actively chooses what mode of response to take, and although her range of choices are now more circumscribed than they would have been before (it would be unthinkable, for instance, for her to report this crime to the police), she still exercises her freedom of choice by wilfully forgetting the attack.

Mary's response to the rape serves a practical function, in allowing her to carry on without immediate distress, but her repression of personal experiences and memories throughout her life as a fugitive will become another source of trauma. By eliminating her past, she enacts a split from something resembling 'wholeness' to an identity that is partial and provisional.[11] Michel Foucault famously, in

The Archaeology of Knowledge (1969) suggested that 'Continuous history is the indispensable correlative of the founding function of the subject' (12). Because Mary has sought to eradicate the personal memories that allow her to express or comprehend a 'continuous' narrative of her life, her new identity seems unanchored, wholly insubstantial and liable to recede altogether: while living as Caroline, for instance, the novel states that she 'began to understand she could just not say anything, and people would make up their own lies for her. She just had to remember to say less and less' (111). This fading of selfhood is also enacted at a literal, physical level: in Los Angeles, armed with her final new identity of Louise Barrot, Mary becomes invisible to the people around her:

> On one occasion a man coming from the opposite direction walked straight into her. He didn't stop but kept walking. His nonreaction to their collision bewildered her. She stood there, unmoving, staring at his back as he walked away. And then, maybe a week later, the same thing happened again. A woman walked toward her on the sidewalk in front of Ralph's supermarket. She had the sort of unseeing stare that people wear in public. She didn't sidestep when she got to Louise but walked into her, smacking her shoulder. Again, the woman didn't stop walking or say anything to her. She kept going. This time Louise felt less disturbed. She almost laughed instead. Louise thought, It's finally happened. I'm invisible (201).

This incident appears to be a rewriting of the opening passage of Ralph Ellison's *Invisible Man* (1952), when the narrator has also gone 'underground', having escaped down a hole. His 'invisibility' is partly metaphorical, the result of not being seen by other people because he is Black: he explains in the Prologue that

> That invisibility to which I refer occurs because of a particular disposition of the eyes of those with whom I come in contact. A matter of the construction of their *inner* eyes, those eyes with which they look through their physical eyes upon reality (7).

By jumping down the hole, he has made himself literally invisible, a position he finds advantageous as it offers a temporary reprieve from the dangers he faces above ground. In Spiotta's novel, Mary becomes 'invisible' after she has taken on an identity that is completely secure. On arriving in Los Angeles, she had set about looking for the record of a baby who had died in order to obtain a copy of the birth certificate, and thereafter start building a file of official documents, including passport and Social Security number. The fact that her new identity is now 'safe, airtight' (200) signals a successful repression of her past, and this deliberate psychical loss of selfhood is enacted on the body, which promptly disappears from view. This absence exists at the level of voice, too: throughout the novel Mary is presented in the third person, and though we are privy to her thoughts and motives, our most direct perspective on her comes from her teenage son Jason, who is wary of her and records his suspicions in his diary. She is therefore powerless to articulate herself in her own words, but also knows that talking brings its own dangers: back at that commune, she had told Berry about her secret past after a few drinks, and this had placed them both in danger and forced her back on the run. The identity she was using then, Caroline, was clearly inadequate since the relaxants of beer and pot were enough to cause her past experiences to re-emerge, and her recognition of that fact leads her to Los Angeles, and the construction of a final unassailable identity.

It was noted above that what Rossinow terms the 'quest for authenticity' through 'political activism' (19) within the New Left was triggered by a sense of individual alienation, the consequence of discovering that one's social and political context appeared to be irreconcilable with one's inner feelings or values. A means to overcome this was through committed action aimed at changing the negative framework, and members of the New Left sought urgent redress for societal ills such as systemic racism, corporate irresponsibility and US imperialism – particularly the Vietnam War. This is of course the context for Mary's actions just before the novel begins: her dangerous tactics as a member of the Weather Underground are in direct protest at the development of lethal toxins used against the Vietnamese. But the deadly effect of this radicalised articulation of her political commitment (the death of the housekeeper) means that she is forced her to withdraw to a position where her choices seem even more limited, and it is no longer feasible to act on her personal principles. Ellison's narrator comes to feel that while his period of 'hibernation' (9) is free of danger, this is a threshold position which lacks commitment: towards the end of the novel (which circles back to that scene in the hole), he wonders if 'that's my greatest social crime, I've overstayed my hibernation, since there's a possibility that even an invisible man has a socially responsible role to play' (468). He suggests that 'A hibernation is a covert preparation for a more overt action' (15), the implication being that he plans to return above ground. In Spiotta's novel, by contrast, Mary never returns to political protest; her retreat into a condition of near-invisibility is permanent, and she remains a cipher even to those closest to her.

The novel also suggests that the more general 1960s crisis of alienation to which Mary is responding has its (much less extreme) modern counterpart in the ennui of late-1990s suburbia. Jason's journal entries from 1998 detail his 'loneliness' and 'isolation' (76) which have become so firmly entrenched that he now feels more comfortable when totally alone. He writes about his new neighbour and fellow music collector that

> Even someone like Gage (who is someone with whom admittedly I have a lot in common, a person with whom you might think I would enjoy keeping company) doesn't alleviate my feelings of loneliness. The effort it required just to be around him and tolerate him made me even more lonely. I am at home only in *my own personal* loneliness (76).

Jason is directionless and mired in his isolation, a state of mind that could plausibly derive from an instinctive lack of sociability and an obsessive interest in collecting music, but he wonders if he might also resemble his mother in this respect:

> Lately I find I wonder about my mother's loneliness. Is it like mine? Does she feel comfortable there? And if I am comfortable with it, sort of, why do I still call it loneliness? Because – and I think somehow she would understand this – you can have and recognize a sadness in your alienation and in other people's alienation and still not long to be around anyone (76–7).

That word 'alienation', as we have seen, is key to our understanding of the New Left. Jason's use of the term here suggests that those feelings of powerlessness are still very much present, but without the flipside of reaching for a collective political response, as thousands of leftist young Americans had done during the 1960s. Authenticity, another term Jason uses, has also taken on a different, apolitical meaning for him: it refers simply to having a sincere response to music, and to the Beach Boys in particular. His reaction to hearing an unreleased solo album by Dennis Wilson is to start crying: 'I found it [the album] operatic, a complete expression of a tortured, not-too-bright, not-too-gifted, weary guy. But here is the thing, say what you will about skill, technique, control, brilliance: this stuff is truly moving. To me anyway' (81). Jason's version of authenticity is a private emotion that expressly precludes others; there is a bathetic quality to this descent from authenticity as self-determination and political commitment, to its association here with listening to pop music.

II.

Part of the reason for Jason's seemingly unperturbed existence is down to his ability to indulge in this obsessive music collecting. He describes trawling websites for 'bonus tracks, alternate versions, reissues, demos, bootlegs. Cover versions. Obscure European or Japanese reissues in 180-gram vinyl. Or original issue, original packaging. Authenticity' (72). He along with other collectors worry that the 'best, coolest stuff is being withheld from us. In other words: there is never enough information. There is always more stuff to be had' (72). This reference to 'stuff' underlines the fact that Jason is above all else a consumer: it is not enough simply to listen to records; he has to own them. He is also aware how fortunate he is to be the advertising industry's target market, 'the center of America' (123). In his journal he boasts that

> Middle-aged men and women scurry for my attention. What Internet sites I visit. What I buy. What my desires are. What movies I watch. What and who I want; when and how I want it. People get paid a lot of money to think of how to get to me and mine.
>
> Everything is geared to me. When you see those herky-jerky close-ups in action movies, where the camera jumps and chops its way in rather hyperly to the close-up of the hero, that is not for anyone but me (123).

Conformity offers Jason power and authority: society is geared towards him and his desires, and his privileged position as a middle-class white male accounts for his general inertia – because all of his needs are met, he has no yearning to push for change. Jason lives in an updated version of the suburban existence that 1960s young radicals found to be empty and alienating, where the only escape from their parents' middle-class conformity was through individual rebellion and a commitment to societal change.[12] But Jason instead opts for the status quo, content to live in an environment of financial stability and where no demands are made on his time. He describes suburbia as

> A place where you can listen to your LPs for hours on end. You can live in your room, your own rent-free corner of the universe, and create a world of pleasure and interest entirely centered on yourself

and your interior aesthetic and logic ... You can burn CDs and
download music, catalog and repeat, buy and trade, all sitting on
your ass in the rec room. The recreation room – in suburbia there are
whole rooms dedicated to leisure and play and recreation. There is
space and time here, and comfort and ease. Just look at me. Just look
at Gage (73–4).

The complacency and self-absorption accommodated by Jason's
middle-class life offers a useful contrast with his mother's feeling of
being hemmed in by her circumscribed existence in suburbia. After
marrying Augie and becoming pregnant with Jason in the early 1980s
the family moved to Washington State, to an unremarkable development that 'could've been in any state from California to Connecticut':
the house was on a cul-de-sac 'In a development with other very
similar houses. The streets were clean and empty. The house had
lots of room, and nothing was broken. It was a clean, safe place'
(230). But for Mary the atmosphere is suffocating in its drabness and
monotony – far removed from her nervy fugitive existence, but also
from the fiercely-held values that led her there, which were in opposition to corporate governance and the status quo as epitomised by
private property, the family unit, and other emblems of modern capitalism. As a member of the Weather Underground she had planted
a bomb in a house 'built to resemble a Victorian shingle-style beach
bungalow' (285) with a stone path and courtyard; as a wife and
mother she lives in a more modest version of this suburban model.

Jason's music collection is the one area of his life where he is
prepared to show commitment. Hours each day are dedicated to
playing the rare, bootleg or recently discovered albums he has in his
collection. But he also admits that his responses to music can verge
towards the insincere. For instance, he draws attention to the fact
that describing the production on a track as 'airless' is a 'bullshit'
remark: just his way of dismissing an album that is 'not flying my
flag right now' (75). And he casts a rather sardonic eye over the tendency amongst his friendship group – 'what few friends I have' – to
argue about the superiority of various versions of a particular track:
'it is cool to ask the question because it proves you know there are
two versions and you are conversant with both' (71). Jason even
doubts that his various music obsessions are anything more than
'just random manifestations of my loneliness or isolation', musing
to himself that 'Maybe I infuse ordinary experience with a kind of
sacred aura to mitigate the spiritual vapidity of my life. But, then
again, maybe not' (76). This wariness about his own motivations for

listening to music (that it might after all be no more than a temporary distraction) is complicated by the ambivalence that accompanies
such an apparently clear-eyed assessment – as evinced by that final
sentence 'But, then again, maybe not'. His uncertainty provides a
striking contrast to Bobby Desoto, Mary's boyfriend back in the
1970s and a fellow member of the Weather Underground. Mary
recounts to her friend Berry that 'he had incredible confidence in his
opinions . . . Like Dylan was great *because* he went electric. Or my
Beach Boys records were shallow or even reactionary' (110). Bobby
is more assured about where aesthetic value resides: he is clear, 'confident' about what is worth listening to. And this conviction carries
over into the other more dangerous aspects of his life, drawing
Jason's rather indolent mode into sharp relief.

The contrast between the ennui and cynicism of the generation
coming of age around 2000 and the radical fervour of 1970s activists is at its most striking in the Seattle sections of the novel, where
the fugitive Bobby (now called Nash, and in his late forties) establishes Prairie Fire Books, named after the Weather Underground
book *Prairie Fire: The Politics of Revolutionary Anti-Imperialism*,
published in 1974. Importantly in this context, *Prairie Fire* offered a
reconsideration of the group's earlier guerrilla tactics. Jeremy Varon
notes that the book 'stressed the need for political education and
conventional organizing and embraced a range of progressive initiatives' (292). In a distinct moderating of tone, the book's authors
Bernardine Dohrn, Bill Ayers, Jeff Jones and Celia Sojourn called on
the New Left to work together towards the common cause of anti-
imperialism. This Weather Underground trajectory, from uncompromising armed warfare to collectivism and discussion, mirrors Nash's
own narrative during the past twenty-odd years. On the day he first
met Mary they broke into the Valence Chemical building and set fire
to a stack of files; before long he had drawn up a list of bombing
targets. In the book's present, however, he is content to create a hub
for Seattle's adolescent 'misfits and scragglers' (35), where they can
meet up and discuss their rather benign protest plans. Nash hopes
the young customers (and even the shoplifters among them) will
'see the store as part of their space' (27), and it is deemed harmless
by the rest of the community. Nash, for his part, tries to remain 'off
the grid' (34): he wears thrift store clothes and has neither a bank
account, health insurance, nor even a telephone. Like Mary he has
been a fugitive for decades, and as he describes it to his friend (and
financial backer for the store) Henry, his life now is 'Pretty fucking
modest. Humble, plain. In every way imaginable' (33).

The shop puts Nash in touch with numerous protest groups going under some bizarre names, including the SAP (Strategic Aggravation Players and/or Satyagraha by Antinomic Praxis); Re (Resist, Reclaim, and Rebel); the 'K' Nation; and the Scavengers Against Flat Effrontery (SAFE).[13] Although Nash facilitates many of the meetings, he is clear about the limitations of these young protest groups, speculating that they came out in opposition 'often to a seemingly arbitrary object, as much, perhaps, for opposition's own sake and energy as for a desire for social change' (36). He also regards them as 'entitled in this very dumb and tedious way', possessed of an 'ungenerous righteousness, as if merely being young was somehow to your credit' (36, 37). And while he likes some of the individuals who come into the shop, many of whom are 'funny and smart' and 'idealistic and angry' (37), he notes disapprovingly that 'for all their sarcasm and easy, shallow irony, there was still not enough self-reference . . . not enough wit' (36–7). There is 'self-obsession, yes, self-consciousness, sure', yet 'no concern with self-implication' (37). These teenagers are unable to conceive of themselves as part of the system they supposedly reject, and there is no indication that individual discontent will be channelled into a committed collective response designed to overhaul corporate or government structures. These adolescent groups are clearly meant to put the reader in mind of the 1999 World Trade Organisation (WTO) protests in Seattle, when up to 50,000 global justice protesters converged on the city to draw attention to a broad and amorphous set of causes, from labour rights and the environment to the dominance of multinational corporations.[14] Lesley J. Wood notes that the Direct Action Network (which was responsible for coordinating the action in Seattle) was an emphatically multi-issue enterprise, bringing together 'anarchist, environmental, antinuclear, feminist, anti-sweatshop, queer, community arts, and other networks' (31). Yet the vast majority of these protesters were from white and middle-class backgrounds: an influential critique of the Seattle protests, by Elizabeth Martínez, noted that 'people of color from the U.S. totalled only about five to seven per cent' of the estimated 50,000 protesters, citing fears over police brutality, lack of funds for travel, and a 'legacy of distrust about working with progressive whites as equals' (11). But the clearest reason for the small number of Black, Latino and Asian Americans at the protests, Martínez explained, was the fact that they had 'little knowledge about the WTO and how it affects U.S. communities of color' (11). This perception of the Seattle protests as primarily composed of white, middle-class youths is very similar to the image we have of the Weatherman, whose members were also drawn from comfortable backgrounds. But the similarities largely end there: unlike the Weatherman, the majority of the Seattle protesters were avowed pacifists, with favoured tactics including rallies, teach-ins and 'soft blocks' (groups of protesters locked arms, blocking WTO delegates from entering buildings to attend meetings); banners were also hung from buildings in the city, and there was music and giant puppets – both to create a street party-type atmosphere and as a non-violent way to block off the streets.[15] Spiotta's fictional groups seem to emulate this style of protest, and the novel implicitly compares this with the Weatherman, who reverted to aggressive tactics in a bid to overthrow the system. During the October 1969 'Days of Rage' in Chicago, which was carried out by the Weatherman, the damage to city property included the smashing-up of buildings, shop windows, cars and apartments, and the destruction of a commemorative police statue. Ron Jacobs puts the number of arrests at 284, '40 of them on felony charges', and 'Fifty-seven police were hospitalized' (64). In the months that followed, the Weatherman was placed under federal investigation and near-constant surveillance by the police; further damage was caused when members of the Boston collective fired at a Cambridge police station in November, while the murder by police of Black Panthers Mark Clark and Fred Hampton in Chicago on 4 December confirmed the level of state resistance to radical protests. This last event was chief among the reasons for the Weatherman's decision to go underground, adopting false identities and organised into small cells of members across the country; from these positions they planted numerous bombs at corporate and government buildings – banks, police stations, state offices, the US Capitol building in 1971 and the Pentagon the following year.

The primary targets of the fictional Seattle groups in Spiotta's novel, by contrast, are companies that had started in the Northwest before expanding into 'horrendous global ubiquity' (Spiotta, *Eat* 42). Nash reflects that the focus of youth anger has shifted from imperialism to commercial dominance: whereas 'It used to be you had to make munitions to piss people off', now being 'large, global and successful' was sufficient (43). He suspects that the fury towards Nike, Starbucks and Gap is rooted in the fact that the teenagers 'still loved and desired the products on some level', while hating that they had 'exploded' into major corporations (42–3, 42). The companies are no longer local, and it is this betrayal of their Seattle roots that appears to be at the root of the collective anger. It is significant that Spiotta should mention the targeting of originally Pacific Northwest corporations: in the real-life Seattle protests a black bloc minority, wearing black bandannas over their faces, targeted Starbucks and Nike premises, smashing windows in a bid to increase the 'costs of doing business' (Wood 93). Other, non-violent forms of protest, they argued, were simply ineffective. This property destruction triggered a police crackdown, with hundreds arrested, and photographs of demonstrators being beaten and teargassed appearing on newspaper front pages across the world. These destructive tactics were already divisive during the protest planning stage, with other, peaceful protesters keen to distance themselves from the violence. The Direct Action Network was opposed to property destruction, and during the protests some of the non-violent demonstrators even handed anarchists into the police when they saw windows being smashed. But it was these confrontational tactics which made the headlines, with fears over public rioting and delegate safety, and the growing sense that there were insufficient numbers of police to deal with that level of disruption. The teenagers in Spiotta's novel weigh into this debate about property destruction: when Miranda suggests (during a meeting of the Brand and Logo Devaluation Front in Nash's shop) that they might interfere with the labels on Nike shirts, the idea is quickly dismissed by another teenager because 'product tampering is like a major felony' (42), and few (if any) of them are willing to break the law. Instead, they plan (although importantly do not carry out) non-violent, rather quirky acts of public display: putting on impromptu plays in shopping malls and dressing up in business suits and handing out dollar bills – just as the real-life pacifist protesters used giant puppets and street theatre to block the streets.

Unlike the real events in Seattle, however, Spiotta's teenagers carry out very little in the way of protest, violent or otherwise. The deliberation process, which has been identified as a key component in successful protest planning, here represents almost the total sum of activity.[16] The groups discuss possible tactics, but rarely (with one or two exceptions) move on from that supposedly preparatory stage. When added to the regular petty shoplifting at Prairie Fire Books, and the rather sneering, complacent tone in which many of their discussions are conducted, these groups come to seem trivial and self-absorbed. But it is unclear whether the novel wishes to entirely condemn their reluctance to engage in militant protest, particularly when measured against the destruction wreaked by the Weather Underground. In a brief, impressionistic flashback to 1972, Mary is shown tricking the housekeeper into allowing her to plant a bomb in the bathroom; by this stage we already know that the house-keeper will be killed in the explosion. Spiotta positions this episode directly after a scene where Nash, in the year 2000, goes to destroy a billboard advertising Nepenthex, which made the drugs whose side-effects killed his friend Henry. As Nash approaches, he notices it has already been defaced by the SAFE collective, which meets at his shop: the ad is now covered with a huge skull and crossbones and the words 'Who is Responsible?' have been spelt out with cut-out letters. Nash stands back to admire this 'Perfectly done' vandalism (284). Juxtaposing this less destructive (and ultimately much more legible) act with that fatal Weather Underground bombing forces us to reappraise the creative adolescent response when compared with the messy and deadly tactics of 1970s radicals.

But the more general failure of Spiotta's fictional groups to act can be put down to the fact that they are too embedded in the cultural and corporate structures they are apparently protesting against. Miranda, for instance, repeatedly berates Nash for drinking Coca-Cola, claiming that to buy it is 'like totally underwriting American corporate hegemony' (138). Use of the word 'like' there – an adolescent verbal tic, semantically unnecessary – emphasises that she is still a teenager. And her ideas are also still unformed, or at least inconsistent: she will smoke Marlboro cigarettes, eat McDonald's burgers, and take 'big, luxurious wads of toilet paper and inches of Kleenex at a time' (134). Her apparent hypocrisy – criticising others for buying products made by multi-billion-dollar companies, but then doing the same herself, only with different items – is complicated by the earnestness of her stance. In a passage of free indirect style, we learn that she often throws items away instead of recycling them:

> she couldn't help it, she just did it and felt guilty about it. That was part of why she talked to Nash in the first place. Because she saw him there, at the meetings, drinking a Coca-Cola.
> And finally she wanted to tell him that the world offered horrendous terms, a terrible, huge price was paid in actual suffering, and if you didn't try to change that or mitigate that, your life was indefensible, wasn't it? (134).

Miranda is helpless in the face of corporate domination: while her feelings about wishing to change an unfair system where 'there are people with no homes and no food' (133) are genuine, she is also too enmeshed in that system (tempted by hamburgers and cigarettes). Moreover, any action she might take seems negligible: her vow at the age of twelve 'never to feel comfortable in the face of things obviously unfair and not right' (133) is not quite the same as pledging to fight that injustice.

III.

The Seattle protests in November 1999 were considered by activists to have been a success: delegate meetings were disrupted, there was global media coverage of the chaos, and the summit was forced to finish a day early. The feat led other organisations, particularly networks based in North America, to adopt some of the tactics which had proved effective in Seattle.[17] This was during the initial wave of enthusiasm in the months afterwards, as activist groups across the country (some of them predating Seattle, others established soon afterwards) felt the WTO protests represented a significant turning point, evidence that coordinated activism could offer real resistance to the spread of globalisation.[18] Yet various factors, not least 9/11 and the militarised policing introduced quickly afterwards, contributed to a subsequent decline in the enthusiasm for, and effectiveness of, social movement activism. The Occupy movement in 2011, which began in New York before spreading to move than 800 cities worldwide, seemed at the time another watershed moment in the backlash against neoliberalism.[19] But after the Zuccotti Park occupation was shut down by police in December 2011, the movement seemed to fall apart altogether, and in the longer term it is almost impossible to imagine that global justice activism will have an enduring impact on the way global corporations operate.[20] Spiotta's novel considers the unfeasibility of putting up an effective defence against multi-national corporations in the chapters which detail Josh's career with Allegecom. This corporation owns, among other assets, the pharmaceutical company which makes Nepenthex, a drug for treating the 'combat-related post-traumatic stress disorder' (163) which was caused by Allegecom in the first place: 'They put dioxin in Agent Orange and kept it in for years even when they knew it affected humans', Henry explains, and 'they make the antidepressant that was prescribed for me specifically for the depression I have due to dioxin and combat trauma' (206). That the drugs used to treat a set of symptoms are produced by the same company responsible for the illness carefully underlines the insidious reach of major corporations. And these same drugs are also fatal: Henry is prescribed Nepenthex for 'proxy memories' (163) but after his death the drug is revealed to cause cancer. Yet the issue of culpability for corporate malfeasance is rendered more complicated when it is intimated that by taking Nepenthex in the first place (and thereby 'buying into' the Allegecom corporation, however unwittingly), Henry has somehow authorised that corporation to invade his nervous system. Henry never fought in Vietnam, yet his financial support for a company that created deadly chemicals to use there more than thirty years ago has made him complicit in the devastation these chemicals caused, therefore his hallucinations consist of him flying the planes that dropped 'white phosphorus and napalm bombs' during the war, as he explains to Nash: 'I can see it – smell it burning through skin. My skin, too' (162). The invasion by Allegecom of Henry's body (through PTSD-related asthma and rashes) and mind (through the night terrors caused by the Nepenthex taken for those physical symptoms) is posited as the logical endpoint of not rejecting corporate products, or by neglecting to take account of their full range of assets, and there is an implicit warning here for Miranda given her inconsistent handling of exactly this issue.

Allegecom, of course, has numerous other business interests, among which is Alphadelphia, an artificially constructed, environmentally-conscious community of exactly 5,000 people: 'Just enough people to keep you from going stir-crazy and inbred but not so many that you don't feel surrounded by familiar faces' (157). Alphadelphia is on a list of companies being targeted by anarchist groups, and Miranda's boyfriend Josh manages to hijack their website through an 'elaborate parasite', so that the site automatically redirects the user to negative stories about the corporation:

> If users clicked on the little red wagon icon, which was where Allegecom discussed its community service projects, they were directed to a link about a lawsuit that a community of ten thousand in Central America was bringing against the biotech arm of the company (158).

Josh dresses preppily, but has a tattoo of the sabot cat, which is 'the anarchist symbol for sabotage' (154), and this reassures Miranda of his commitment. The furore over this website hacking leads to a profile of Josh in the *New York Times*, yet for all his arrogance about understanding how the world works ('That is lesson number one. You control what people believe to be true about you. All of it is subject to manipulation. You can avoid interference very easily' (153–4)), Allegecom is much savvier, and offers to fly him out to New York to discuss their new community project. Josh's insistence that 'This is a great opportunity to see Allegecom from the inside' is naïve: he is quickly seduced into working for the company and then put in charge of their next constructed community, an entirely cynical endeavour which is designed to 'make money on certain back-to-the-earth desires . . . We can take that spirit and exploit it for a franchisable experience' (160, 237). Josh is entirely converted to their worldview, and he starts lecturing to Miranda about 'the purity of capitalism', 'its elasticity, its lack of moral need, its honesty. It is the great leveler – all can be and will be commodified' (258). The fact that an intelligent and apparently staunch 'hacktivist' can so easily be manipulated by the corporation he had been railing against merely underlines the company's vast reach and its impressive powers of persuasion – as one might expect of an institution so reliant on careful advertising and on 'selling' its different products to various unwary sets of consumers. In Aliki Varvogli's discussion of this novel she describes how

> In Josh's character, Spiotta offers a marked contrast between 1960s and 1970s activism, where the lines of opposition were fairly clear, and the far murkier world of the late twentieth century, where corporate capitalism is able to contain or assimilate its enemies, and still fool them into thinking that they are the enemy (670).

But Josh is not the only one to underestimate the power of advertising to change minds, and Nash notices with a fair degree of horror that the adolescents gathering at Prairie Fire Books treat the media simply as a benign tool, rather than anything more sinister, and they are unfailingly impressed with anyone who works in the industry. In a twenty-first-century context, of course, the suggestion that one might have an uncritical view on the media seems almost quaintly naïve. It is also similar to Jason's self-satisfied remark that 'People get paid a lot of money to think of how to get to me and mine' (123). Attitudes such as these offer a stark contrast to Nash's much more nuanced engagement with broadcast media as an underground filmmaker in the late '60s, when he juxtaposed clips from films, army recruitment tapes and the news to create subversive political commentary where 'you are never sure if the extreme didacticism is being satirized or espoused' because 'It is both' (215). Back in 2000, his friend Henry takes a more direct approach, climbing up the side of buildings in order to cut down billboards advertising Nepenthex. His ill-health is testament to what the company is capable of, and it is therefore important that he completely destroys these advertisements. Josh, with no first-hand experience of Allegecom's dangers, is more interested in demonstrating his own cleverness, slickly rewording the corporation website and turning himself into the story.

Eat the Document takes corporate dominance as one of its governing themes – time and again it highlights the ability of conglomerates to assimilate oppositional interests into its own structure for financial gain. When Josh is working full-time for Allegecom he and Miranda wander into a shop called Suburban Guerrilla which sells t-shirts, patches, a calendar with a 'different Situationist graffito' for each month, coffee-table anthologies of anarchist movements, a diary with a photo of Weather Underground founding member Bernardine Dohrn on the front and even the 'triangle-shaped black scarves' worn by the 'anarchist blac bloc kids . . . when they busted windows at Niketown and Starbucks last year' (257). The cynicism of turning these symbols of rebellion into items to be bought is palpable – particularly when Josh takes out his gold corporate American Express card, given to him by Allegecom, in order to buy a pack of 'New Left Series' playing cards, featuring a different anarchist's photo on the front and their biography on the back. In other words, he purchases with corporate money (the corporation that was directly responsible for putting dioxin in Agent Orange) a pack of cards featuring Mark Rudd, Abbie Hoffman, Dave Dellinger and Mario Savio, each of whom had been active in protesting against the Vietnam War. Josh starts out by thinking he can 'subvert the system from within', but it is far too pervasive, and he lacked the necessary commitment to begin with (Varvogli 670). He is blind to corporate power to not merely ignore, but to integrate those who dissent from its capitalist worldview – such as Miranda, as we saw, who for all her earnestness is still willing to buy their products; or indeed those 1970s radicals, who are turned into a physical product priced at $19.95.

The women's commune just north of New York where Mary and her friend Berry move to in 1973 seems at first the polar opposite of Alphadelphia in the 1990s. Rather than a project to make money by constructing a 'nostalgic, knowingly referenced community experience' (237), Mother Goose's community is a women-only experiment, to test, among other things, 'what women were like without men' (177). And whereas this earlier commune requires that everyone take part in the work wheel, with jobs such as cleaning and cooking allocated in a democratic fashion, Alphadelphia (which is built on the same site near New Harmony) instead promises something much more approaching the status quo: this would be 'Communal, but not really. No elimination of private property, for God's sake. No shared lawn mowers or water heaters' (237). Communes such as

Mother Goose's settlement flourished in the late 1960s and early '70s, an alternative for those who felt disillusioned and excluded by the patriarchal structure of the New Left and its emphasis on single-issue politics which left it reluctant to address topics such as poverty or gender roles.[21] In the Weatherman manifesto 'You Don't Need a Weatherman to Know Which Way the Wind Blows', which was published in *New Left Notes* during the SDS National Convention in June 1969, the role of women and feminism in the revolutionary youth movement was almost entirely elided. Meanwhile the leadership of the Weatherman was tightly controlled, and the national leaders were ruthless about restricting power to only a small group of members who proved they would toe the party line.[22] The communes, by contrast, aimed towards decentralisation in terms of structure and decision-making, and were concerned with broader issues such as environmentalism, education and the fair allocation of labour and goods. The gender ethos of these communities was for the most part based not on women gaining influence (or even power) in a male-dominated society, but instead on emphasising supposedly 'natural' female characteristics such as serenity and the instinct to nurture. Many of those living at Mother Goose's commune have retreated from mainstream society, presumably disillusioned with the patriarchal structures that govern its institutions. Mary learns that 'most of the women had dropped out from the Harvard Classics Department, where Mother G used to teach. Others were design and architecture heads from MIT' (176). When Mary and Berry first arrive at the commune they encounter Jill, who describes the 'Self-consciously primitive, Rousseauian idealists' living there (173).

But as so often throughout this novel, Spiotta does not revisit these 1970s contexts in order simply to highlight the degeneration in sensibility and motive that has taken place in the decades since, as we move from an ethos of political commitment driven by fiercely-held values to a much more cynical, depthless environment; in fact several features of Mother Goose's community appear to directly foreshadow its contemporary incarnation of Allegecom-owned Alphadelphia. Although half the members of Mother Goose's scheme 'cook and wash in one common space and share everything' while living in 'simple modest shelters, such as tepees, corrugated-tin sheds and mud huts', the other half are fully connected to the modern world: Jill is among the group of 'tech-yeses' (173) and her house incorporates the latest design technology. Jill proudly explains to Mary and Berry that she is 'tied in to the grid with electricity', connected using 'fiberglass insulation, PVC pipe. Plastic sealants'

(171). The similarity to Allegecom is striking: just as Alphadelphia vows that there will be 'Nothing primitive' (237) about the new village, Jill, in 1973, insisted that 'I am no primitivist' (171). And Allegecom declares that 'Technology allows a postsuburban environment. Let's call it a radiant posturbia . . . We are wired' (238), just as Jill, on the same patch of land over twenty-five years earlier, had stated that technology was there to 'eliminate drudgery' and to 'set you free' (171). Permanent residents back in the 1970s were required to build their own homes, but they had to be out of sight of all the others, just as the modern Alphadelphia prioritises private property. Moreover, despite the bucolic atmosphere Mother Goose created (baking pies, growing vegetables, collecting eggs), Mary and Berry still found themselves (like Miranda in the late 1990s) craving hamburgers, cigarettes, beer, TV, candy bars and newspapers – in other words, exactly the type of manufactured goods they were supposed to have left behind.

IV.

Both of these communities – Mother Goose's commune and Alphadelphia – are too heavily aligned with capitalist structures (such as private property, land ownership, possession of personal wealth) to represent a radical alternative to mainstream society. Throughout *Eat the Document,* as we have seen, Spiotta compares ideas taking shape at the very end of the twentieth century with analogous formulations in the 1970s, subtly eliding the differences between the two periods. Spiotta's fourth novel *Innocents and Others* is less directly political, although it too is preoccupied with how our perception of events in America's recent past is shaped by the particular contemporary lens we choose to apply. This novel also shares with *Eat the Document* a concern about the impact on an individual of adopting a false identity; these two issues come together in the work of filmmaker Meadow Mori, the central focus of *Innocents and Others.* We are accorded direct access to Meadow's thoughts and motivations, while an intimate but external perspective on her is provided by Carrie Wexler, her best friend and fellow filmmaker. Like *Eat the Document*, this novel moves back and forth between the early 1970s and the present day, as well as points in between. It opens with a (fictional) article written by Meadow for the magazine *Women and Film* in 2014. There she recounts her early interest in films while a high school student, and how this led to a nine-month relationship with a very famous but at that stage ageing and washed-out film director, whom we assume is Orson Welles. Aspects of this autobiographical essay – in particular the relationship with Welles – have been made up: details about his house and the date of his death are incorrect, and we later discover that none of it took place. From the outset, therefore, the novel's focus is on how individuals present themselves to the world, particularly when this identity seems to be constructed out of a series of falsehoods; and, connectedly, what can be achieved by revisiting particular individuals and episodes from recent history.

One of Meadow's film projects is titled *Inward Operator* and takes the real-life story of Jelly (real name Amy, but she also calls herself Nicole), who worked in a call centre in the 1970s selling timeshares in North Carolina. These are not cold calls: Jelly is given notes for each of the customers, detailing their contact history with the company along with data on their financial circumstances. Jelly relishes the brief but intimate encounters these phone calls allow. As part of her pitch, she asks them to describe their ideal vacation, and her ability to listen quietly to these accounts forges a connection based on trust and shared impulses: she reciprocates with an emotive story of her own, and their brooding discussion of ambition and longing creates the right atmosphere for a sale. Jelly is able to justify these transactions to herself by emphasising the genuineness of the sentiments being shared. She decides that 'Making things up was okay because it was all about feelings, real feelings and real longing. How they came about, fantasy or not, didn't matter to her. What she hated was that it was all for money' (98). The phone calls become a type of gateway to the much more prolonged relationships she initiates with men working in the film industry, and particularly with Jack Cusano, a Hollywood record producer, whom she calls up under the pretence of having dialled the wrong number, and then seduces through flattering, supposedly spontaneous, observations about his work. That she manages to sustain this acquaintance beyond the first phone call – soon she and Jack are talking every day, and they declare themselves in love – is largely down to Jelly's ability to present herself in a particular way. She knows that her voice can be used for seduction, and from the first word she is careful to sound as alluring as possible: '"Hello", she said. Her voice sliding easily through the "l"s, to the waiting, hopeful "o." She always takes her time. Nothing makes people more impatient than rushing' (36). She also offers 'sultry' (83) little sighs, and smooth conjoining words that carry the conversation forward:

> She rarely used 'uh,' but it was an important wordish sound that introduced a powerful unconscious transaction. Used correctly . . . it invited another to complete the sentence. An intricate conjoining, it was an opening without content, just the pull of syntax and the human need to complete (37).

Jelly has an innate understanding of how to draw men in using just her voice, and in fact her very poor eyesight seems to be compensated for with a heightened response to sensory impressions more generally. She is overwhelmed, for instance, by particular smells, both pleasant and repulsive, and wants things to smell as they actually are: 'An armpit should smell of sweat and hair and skin. A mouth should be clean but not minty. Hair should smell slightly vegetal, plantish. And a room should smell like old wood' (40). Meanwhile the 'rank sting of ammonia under fake pine' could force her out of a shop, 'gasping for air' (40). When her vision permits it, she is perceptive about the specific way red wine colours the lips: it 'found rough surfaces and emphasized them. A crack or dry spot on your lips, patchiness on the surface of your tongue' (55–6). This heightened sensitivity extends also to noises coming from the other end of the telephone: the striking of a match, liquid being poured over ice, a slow sip. In fact, sounds are so important to Jelly that it is only when a word has been said out loud that she can stand apart from it and assess its suitability for the experience being expressed:

> You thought of the word but then you felt it in your mouth, pushed breath into it and said it out loud. The sound of it contained the real meaning – she had to hear the words to know if she had it right (48).

Jelly initiates telephone relationships with men not simply out of idle amusement; she is revolted by her own appearance, and sees an opportunity to create an entirely new identity built not on sight, but on sound – just as her own vision is subordinate to her other senses, the men she attracts are also denied the capacity to see her. In *Eat the Document*, as we saw, Mary's total adoption of alternative identities leads to isolation and the fading of selfhood. In *Innocents and Others*, by contrast, Jelly feels liberated rather than trapped by the false image of herself she presents to Jack. Although she does not directly lie, she allows him to assume certain things about her: that she is younger than her real age of forty-one; that she is a graduate student at Syracuse University; and that she is not middle-aged and overweight, but young, blonde and lithe. At his request, she also sends him photographs, but these are of her friend Lynn, taken one

day at the beach. Lynn looks exactly as Jelly supposes that Jack imagines her to look: she is slim but still curvy, with the 'most appealing
combination of almost too pouty lips, heavy-lidded eyes, and an
innocent spray of freckles across her tiny nose' (149). In the photos
Lynn is tanned, relaxed and dressed in a white bikini. But this is not
simply a fake identity, pieced together for the purpose of fooling
Jack. For Jelly these photographs are the visual embodiment of
how she really feels: there is, she believes, a fundamental mismatch
between her mind and her body, so the image she presents to Jack
does not feel like deception, but instead accords exactly with her
own self-perception. The photograph represents the truer version,
much more so than the 'old and damaged' (83) body she sees in the
mirror. It therefore makes no sense to think of the photographs (and
the assumptions about herself she allows Jack to make) as lies:

> she felt blond and supple and young when she talked to Jack. She felt
> elegance in her hands and wrists. Here is what she did not feel: she
> did not feel dowdy and heavy ... That was the truth, and the rest
> was not of import to either of them (83).

Here, as with her conversations with potential timeshare customers,
it is feelings and emotions that count above all else: an impression one
gives, regardless of what lies behind it. Jelly sets less store by vision,
regarding her actual appearance as an aberration, inconsistent with
the imagined (but much more real-seeming) version of herself. In
Eat the Document, Mary's appearance becomes the most important
thing about her – her clothes and hair are integral to the creation of a
new identity, and her real, inner self is repressed in order to maintain
this image. For Jelly, on the other hand, appearance comes second to
selfhood: she complains of feeling 'invisible' (83) in her own body,
and chooses an image that will tally with (rather than stifle) her vivid
sense of self-perception.

The Jelly and Jack relationship is part of the story Meadow tells
in her film *Inward Operator*, made in 1998, but she constructs the
narrative in such a way as to render Jelly both a 'con artist' (193)
(because she manipulates several men using the same technique), and
as pitiable: in filmed interviews with them both, Jelly now seems a
'tumid, faded person' who is 'so much less appealing than worn, old
Jack' (194). The film, as a visual medium, is unable to fully capture
the emotions that governed Jelly's behaviour. As we have seen,
Jelly's actual appearance has never been consistent with the image
of herself she holds in her mind, and as a life-long film fan, cinemas
have always been spaces of liberation for her, allowing her to sit in

the dark and 'forget she had a body, forget she was in a place' (200). But Meadow's film turns the camera on her for the first time; now 'blown up and public' (200), she is forced to confront how she looks to others, and hurries out of the cinema.

This reconsideration of the recent past is Meadow's filmmaking signature (just as it is Spiotta's approach to fiction). Meadow's career includes documentaries on Argentina's 'Dirty War', focusing in particular on the people who kidnapped children and brought them up as their own; on the bombing of Nagasaki, with Meadow herself dressing up as Truman and reading from his journal; and on the Kent State shootings in 1970, when National Guardsmen fired at unarmed students protesting the invasion of Cambodia as part of Nixon's Vietnam War campaign. It is striking that this last subject should take up so much space in *Innocents and Others* given Spiotta's earlier novel's exploration of New Left resistance to Vietnam and its long-term impact. Even to a country inured to seeing violent clashes between police and protestors, these shootings at Kent State were undeniably shocking: unarmed students being shot and killed by young Guardsmen. It produced one of the most famous images of the era: a fourteen-year-old girl, Mary Ann Vecchio, kneeling over the body of Jeffrey Miller, who had just been shot dead. Nixon's response to the events was deeply callous: his press secretary Ron Ziegler stated that 'when dissent turns to violence, it invites tragedy' (qtd. in Karnow 611). While protests had been widespread across the country following the decision to attack Vietnamese bases in Cambodia, these erupted following Kent State, with nearly four million students involved in a general campus strike. Stanley Karnow notes that 'More than four hundred universities and colleges shut down as students and professors staged strikes, and nearly a hundred thousand demonstrators marched on Washington, encircling the White House and other government buildings' (611–12).

Meadow's 1992 film, titled *Kent State: Recovered,* takes as its central point of focus a (fictional) individual named Marvin Joseph. In the version of the shootings taking place within Spiotta's novel, Marvin was believed by many to have started the tragedy by firing a shot at the Guards, inciting them to turn, kneel and fire at the students. He admits to Meadow that he had previously sold photographs of protesting students to the FBI, which already marked him out as an informer. Unlike the other witnesses to the event Meadow gets hold of, each of whom are interviewed by her in a plain room, this suspected agent provocateur is filmed in his own house in order to render him as ordinary as possible – no different from anyone watching the film. Meadow's purpose, here and throughout her film career, is to revisit sites of national protest or mourning in order to find an alternative angle. She knows that filmgoers would expect Marvin to be a 'bad guy', and this would have created a 'fully satisfying narrative' (169) where the tragic events made sense: there would be a single person to blame, and the audience could leave the cinema feeling that the events had been understood once and for all. Meadow's approach, however, is to fashion the material in a way that suits the version of events she decides to tell; she thinks of the Kent State film as a

> stylized, constructed thing, a version of reality. Not a pure, untainted object. You cut, you put this next to that, you edit this out, you ask, you enact, you show an image. It was a fictiony thing: a fictional thing comprised of pieces of real life (168).

There are, however, some clear problems with this approach when dealing with real-life events. Meadow repeatedly fails to consider the hurt that she causes by carefully editing the facts in order to tell a particular version of the story, and thereby reinterpreting events in a subjective manner. Many of her subjects (such as Jelly) do not wish their story to be told at all, and after *Inward Operator* Meadow admits to feeling 'uncomfortable with the outcome' – but not because it had 'gone badly for her subjects' (which it had) but because 'she [Meadow] had orchestrated so much of it' (183). For her 2001 Argentina film, meanwhile, titled *Children of the Disappeared*, Meadow chooses to emphasise the 'human everydayness', the 'non-monstrousness' of the perpetrators (186), eliciting a predictably negative response among critics: one article describes it as 'a defense of genocide', under the headline 'Handmaiden to Monsters' (221). Throughout each of these projects Meadow remains aware of the influence these films are likely to have on cinema-goers, who are liable to radically alter their perception of the real-life events upon watching them:

> people can know something and visual images will override anything they know. Cinema truth is deceptive that way. It can tell you something but show you something very different. And you can bet you will walk away believing in what you saw (172).

This makes her disregard for a 'neutral rendering' (172) potentially troubling: not only is objectivity wilfully abandoned, but her new, constructed account of real-life past events also seeps into the public consciousness.

Meadow perceives herself to be pulling away the rubble of received opinion, reconfiguring historical moments in order to achieve a supposedly more considered version of events. Her films are worthy, serious pieces of work: they set out to enact change. But there is a narcissism involved in all of this, too: she needs to 'feel the pain of her devotion' (71), as though the commitment and suffering that goes into the filmmaking process will automatically enrich the final cut. She will willingly get up at 5am in order to lie in the mud to record the sound of a train approaching, or travel to Argentina alone and with just a camera to film footage, or watch the same film twenty times in a row without stopping. In an earlier edit of the Kent State movie, she had built herself into the story by inserting audio of the questions she asked interviewees, and footage of her behind the camera filming some of the material. Meadow's concern here is with emphasising her own centrality to the particular version of the story being told: by showing her workings she can remind the audience that 'Of course it was cut a certain way, constructed by her' (173). Her friend Carrie, on the other hand, also a filmmaker, is less dogmatic in her approach to narrative: she has no desire to subvert or challenge the limits of filmmaking or to put herself into the story, and is content to work within a given format; this brings her a string of successes with films including *Girl School*, *Lindy's Last Chance* and *A Baby!* – the titles giving a sense of their mainstream appeal. 'I wanted seduction, not challenge', Carrie notes at one point, before observing that her audience is a 'Tarzana housewife who cracks a lot of silly jokes after a few glasses of white wine on girls' night out' (217).

This conflict in *Innocents and Others* between the two approaches to filmmaking – one single-minded and provocative, the other entertaining and conciliatory – mirrors a tension that is also at the centre of *Eat the Document*. In the latter novel, Miranda slowly realises that for all Nash's facilitation of youth protest groups, he has no intention of executing any of the actions; the plans they discuss in their meetings at Prairie Fire Books are for the sake of the adolescent participants ('keeping their own resistance vital' (131)), rather than a means to trigger wider societal changes. In Nash's previous life as filmmaker Bobby Desoto in the 1970s, his approach appeared at first to resemble Meadow's: complicating the accepted political narrative and making audiences feel empathetic towards unexpected or demonised figures. But on closer inspection, Bobby/Nash resembles Carrie much more than he does Meadow: for both of them it is sufficient if the films (or indeed the protest discussions at the shop twenty-five years later) function simply as diversions, pieces of entertainment – compelling, but not necessarily inflammatory. When Josh discovers Bobby's old films, he notices they have 'very funny absurd political voice-overs', and concludes that he was a 'prankster' (215). Both novels consider whether an apparently more committed, earnest approach to politics and art is necessarily useful. In the 1970s sections of *Eat the Document*, Mary, Bobby's then-girlfriend, urges him to take a straightforward approach, creating films that highlight corporate malfeasance in order to generate an active response. She gradually persuades him to leave his whimsical, ambiguous films to one side and instead take more direct, violent action; it is then that he comes to her with plans to plant bombs in carefully-targeted houses, and this leads to the death of a housekeeper, an innocent bystander. This devastation finds a type of parallel in *Innocents and Others*, as Meadow slowly realises that her uncompromising approach to film-making has caused other people tremendous pain: she made *Inward Operator* knowing that it would humiliate Jelly, and (in another project) by filming her boyfriend Deke for seven hours while he gets progressively more drunk, she records him confessing to a serious crime, the consequences of which only occur to her at the first audience screening: 'Her goading and her relentlessness and the insistence on an all-night shoot. It was a kind of ambush, no matter how consensual, no matter how willing' (141). Meadow's car accident towards the end of the novel is caused by her not paying enough attention to other cars on the road – a physical manifestation of the reckless destruction she has wreaked throughout her career by not stopping to consider the feelings of others.

Spiotta's novels do not allow for easy interpretations. In *Eat the Document* Mary's commitment to a model of Sartrean authenticity might seem a commendable response to the Vietnam War. She devotes herself to violent acts as the means to alter a political and social landscape fundamentally at odds with her own values. But the price that she and others must pay for this commitment ultimately seems too high: her own life is wrecked, and even this sacrifice appears meagre compared to the actual loss of life from the explosion. The softened stance towards corporate greed adopted by 1990s teenagers includes anti-consumerist protests that are diverting but entirely harmless – a more palatable response, perhaps, in a decade when disasters such as the Oklahoma City bombing in 1995 reminded Americans of the devastation caused by domestic terrorism. In fact, reading about the Weather Underground's activities through a contemporary lens (one coloured by repeated, and lethal, acts of terrorism on American soil) is unlikely to work in the group's favour. It seems doubtful, for instance, that Spiotta's contemporary readership will look favourably on Mary's exploits having seen images of the Oklahoma City bombing and other more recent high-profile explosions such as Times Square in 2008 and the Boston Marathon in 2013, as well as the series of bombs set off in New York and New Jersey during September 2016. The Weather Underground's declaration that only corporate and government buildings would be targeted also seems neither commendable nor restrained given that it was the Twin Towers and the Pentagon that were attacked in September 2001, resulting in massive loss of life. *Eat the Document* was written against a post-9/11 political narrative shaped by President George W. Bush's famous rallying cry that 'Either you are with us, or you are with the terrorists', and it might therefore have been easier, if far less probing, to cast members of the Weather Underground as simple villains.[23] But by interrogating their particular motivations, and encouraging us to partially sympathise with them, Spiotta instead chooses to complicate Bush's supposedly self-evident opposition. Meadow Mori, in Spiotta's later novel, cuts a similarly complex figure. Her commitment to a single-minded artistic approach produces stunning results that force the audience to reassess their own response to government decision-making. Meadow's Kent State documentary was released in 1991, just after President George H. W. Bush launched the combat phase of the First Gulf War, and the film 'struck a nerve with some critics' who quickly identified the parallels between US involvement in Vietnam and its current invasion of Iraq: 'after everyone watched the clinical footage of the Desert Storm air strikes', we are told, Meadow's film was nominated for an Academy Award (173). But as was the case with Mary, the novel also forces us to confront the hurt her films cause, and to consider whether a declaration of commitment is ever justification enough.

Notes

1. In this chapter I refer to the group as the 'Weatherman' when I describe events taking place before they went underground, in 1969; otherwise, I call them the 'Weather Underground'.
2. George Cotkin has noted that Sartre's existential ideas became fashionable in America from around 1945 onwards through frequent discussion of Sartre and Simone de Beauvoir in publications such as *Life*, *Newsweek*, the *New York Times Magazine* and *Time*, as well as

Vogue and *Harper's Bazaar* (92). Interest in the pair ranged widely, from discussions of their 'bohemian café' lifestyle in the fashionable Paris streets (92), to intense deliberation over the philosophical ideas; this accounted for their dominance in both the 'serious journals' and the 'popular press' (Cotkin 98). The *Partisan Review*, in particular, translated many essays from Sartre, Albert Camus and de Beauvoir during the 1940s. Camus and Sartre were profoundly influential on the 1960s generation: Cotkin quotes from activists including Jerry Rubin, Tom Hayden and Todd Gitlin to highlight the impact of existential thinking on the formation of their ideals (and those of many thousands of others) at this time. Robert F. Kennedy, who for a short period during the 1968 Democratic primaries (before his assassination in June) seemed to be this generation's saviour, 'turned in his late thirties to Camus for moral guidance', Cotkin tells us, and his reading shaped his policies towards the poor and capital punishment, and his renewed faith in political commitment: 'Added to his already considerable energy, existentialism suggested to Kennedy that he must define himself through his actions, by his courage to act within an absurd world' (Cotkin 228).

3. Cotkin also notes that 'alienation stalked the American landscape' in the 1960s, 'part and parcel of modern life when the power of consumerism and advertising promoted a false sense of identity' and 'An anchored, inner-directed self seemed out of reach' (238). Universities were implicated in this: it was widely felt among America's youth that 'power operated to impose consensus' and 'Students depicted the modern mega-university as a factory designed to produce complacent components for the new industrial state and the war machine' (238).

4. Rossinow traces the roots of this search for authenticity among 1960s students back to Christian existentialism, with youth Christian groups regarding the 'path out of alienation' in terms of 'salvation' (6). Rossinow writes that 'In the world of Christian existentialism, salvation was returned to its original, therapeutic meaning: the healing of a wound, the bridging of the awful separation of the human from the divine. Sin was translated as alienation, and salvation now meant authenticity' (6).

5. Participatory democracy was the political model of the New Left, but the *Port Huron Statement* is frustratingly vague about how this would work in practice. Instead, the manifesto is content to offer affirmatory remarks about participatory politics 'bringing people out of isolation and into community', and that 'channels should be commonly available to relate men to knowledge and to power' (8). Robert J. Lacey has described participatory democracy as 'largely a theoretical concept with little hope for real-world application' (228–9). But we might include an emphasis on political discussion at a local level, and the encouragement of ordinary people to engage themselves in the issues

that affect their lives through, for instance, becoming better informed about policy issues, and challenging their government representatives to listen to their views and act accordingly.

6. Stanley Karnow describes how in 1965 the head of *Life* magazine Hedley Donovan had written that '"the war is worth winning" and that victory was within sight'; within two years, this view had changed: in October 1967, Karnow writes, the magazine adopted a 'new corporate policy toward the war', declaring that 'the commitment was "not absolutely imperative" to the defense of strategic U.S. interests – and thus a difficult challenge "to ask young Americans to die for"' (489). Meanwhile the *New York Times* had already begun its negative coverage on the conflict after assistant managing editor Harrison Salisbury visited North Vietnam and reported on the civilian deaths. Karnow writes that 'For a while in early 1967 it seemed that Salisbury had replaced Ho Chi Minh as the administration's prime adversary' (490).

7. This was a surprise assault by Communist soldiers which began on the night of 30 January, when around 80,000 moved into more than a hundred cities and towns in South Vietnam.

8. Chapter two of Ron Jacobs's 1997 *The Way the Wind Blew* offers a succinct account of the Weatherman's takeover of the SDS during the 1969 National Convention; chapter four of Dan Berger's *Outlaws of America* gives a fuller description; Mark Rudd's book *Underground: My Life with SDS and the Weathermen* is more subjective but also detailed.

9. The group was unexpectedly in the headlines again in 2008 over Barack Obama's apparent association with its former leader and fellow Chicago resident, Bill Ayers, an accusation that was later disproved.

10. This is an example of Sartrean 'bad faith' – the individual deceives themselves by not acknowledging that they always possess the freedom to choose certain aspects of their existence.

11. Rossinow uses the term 'wholeness' to describe 'the opposite of alienation in an internal sense . . . inner wholeness was the state of authenticity' (4).

12. George Cotkin points to the example of Benjamin Braddock in Mike Nichols's 1967 film *The Graduate* as an example of someone who rebels against 'conformist expectations' and the 'emptiness of suburban life' (250) and a comfortable but ultimately stultifying future in 'Plastics' – a word which 'captures the manufactured, mass-produced, inauthentic, unreal quality of the world that is the source of Ben's alienation and discontent' (251). In the 1990s version depicted by Spiotta, on the other hand, Jason chooses conformity.

13. These acronyms seem designed to resemble those of the many groups broadly connected with the New Left during the 1950s and '60s such as the SDS (Students for a Democratic Society), SNCC (Student Nonviolent Coordinating Committee), BPP (Black Panther Party),

NAACP (National Association for the Advancement of Colored People), and the RYM II (Revolutionary Youth Movement II).

14. For a detailed discussion of coalition building (both successful and otherwise) of more than 200 protest groups in the run-up to Seattle, see Margaret Levi and Gillian H. Murphy's 2006 article 'Coalitions of Contention: The Case of the WTO Protests in Seattle'.

15. Chapter three of Wood's 2012 book *Direct Action, Deliberation, and Diffusion: Collective Action after the WTO Protests in Seattle* gives full details of the tactics used and their adoption in subsequent protests.

16. Deliberative discussion, when used effectively, encourages open dialogue around strategy from a broad spectrum of organisations and viewpoints. For further description, analysis, and examples of deliberation in modern and contemporary contexts, see John S. Dryzek 115–161; James S. Fishkin 29–64; Francesca Polletta (2002) 176–201; Polletta (2006) 82–108; and Wood 75–91.

17. Wood's chapter 'The Seattle Cycle: 1998–2002' charts this increase in the use of 'black bloc, blockades' and 'puppetry tactics' in 'global day of action protests', although these approaches were dramatically curtailed after 9/11 (32).

18. For details of the main networks which adopted (or considered adopting) tactics used in Seattle, see Wood 40–48.

19. David Graeber's 2013 book *The Democracy Project* focuses heavily on the various protest tactics developed during Occupy (such as the use of social media, breakout groups to brainstorm ideas, tools such as hand signals and straw polls, the People's Mic for communicating across large groups, and a horizontal structure based on consensus, with the emphasis on compromise rather than voting for or against a particular policy).

20. Graeber argues that although it seemed as though Occupy disappeared practically overnight, the movement spent the next several months working out a new direction and identifying more reliable allies. The liberal establishment had supported the occupation, and this was one of the main reasons why the movement gained so much media attention. But Graeber also notes that when it became clear that the 'principled rejection of electoral politics and top-down forms of organization' was not 'simply a passing phase', they lost interest: 'The real business of the movement would begin', liberals felt, 'once Occupy became a conduit for guiding young activists into legislative campaigns, and eventually, get-out-the-vote drives for progressive candidates' (140). Graeber also cites other reasons for the slow-down in support after the camps were cleared. These include much more intimidating, even violent, police tactics (including police smashing protesters' heads against concrete, sexual attacks on female protesters, and broken bones sustained from police beatings), and an almost total media blackout which meant these assaults stayed largely under the radar of most Americans. By taking

part in marches, one was automatically risking police violence; this led to dwindling numbers, particularly among older people and children, and media sources reported this decline without acknowledging the reasons why.

21. The New Left did not, on the whole, regard feminism and women's rights as important issues, and this was certainly the case with the Weather Underground. Dan Berger writes of it that 'Hostility to feminism characterized the organization from the beginning, even though many of the members – including many of those most committed to the politics – were women and feminists' (292). Jeremy Varon offers a similar take on this: 'in Weatherman, the women were confined mostly to the "second-tier leadership", had to mute or disavow certain of their feminist beliefs, and, no matter their activist credentials, had to prove their commitment once again by showing their ability to engage in "independent" actions as part of "women's cadres"' (59–60). Varon also suggests that 'while the group's sexual politics provided a space for women to assert desire and explore relationships with one another, they also invited the sexual exploitation of female workers' (60).

22. Ron Jacobs explains that in a bid to 'crush any vestiges of bourgeois ideology' (45) within the movement, national leaders travelled around the country to locate local members who seemed the 'most willing to cooperate with the leadership and place them in positions of power' (45–6).

23. Bush made this comment on several occasions – for instance in his address to a joint session of Congress and the American people on 21 September 2001, and during his Middle East policy statement on 24 June 2002. For a more complete discussion of Bush's anti-terrorism rhetoric, particularly his focus on the 'us' versus 'them' dichotomy, see Valentina Bartolucci's 'Terrorism Rhetoric under the Bush Administration: Discourses and Effects'.

Chapter 4

AIDS Activism and Looking Back in Tim Murphy and Garth Greenwell

Tim Murphy's 2016 novel *Christodora*, set mainly in New York and spanning the period from 1981 to 2021, takes as its subject the HIV/AIDS crisis and its long-term impact on the city and its residents. In one of the novel's early scenes Ava Heyman, from the city's Department of Health, is puzzling over a recent spate of Kaposi's sarcoma in young gay men while her new intern, Hector Villaneuva, looks on. The novel shows how this rapidly develops into a full-blown epidemic while the Reagan administration and New York's mayor Ed Koch continue to ignore the issue – refusing to allocate funding for research and treatment, or even acknowledge that the crisis exists. When we next encounter Hector (after several years have passed) he has left the Health Department and is now a dynamic and popular figure in the AIDS Coalition to Unleash Power (ACT UP), campaigning for a co-ordinated national policy, and lobbying the government to provide funding for education about the disease, affordable treatment and more clinical drug trials. In one of *Christodora*'s pivotal scenes, which takes place at a packed ACT UP meeting, Hector is presenting the latest reports on clinical trials when he spots Ava in the crowd. By this stage she is vilified by Hector's fellow activists for her department's inaction, but Hector steps in to her defence, explaining to the crowd that her eagerness to attend the meeting suggests they might be able to work together. This ACT UP scene is the site of convergence with the novel's other main narrative strand: also at the meeting is Ysabel Mendes, or Issy, a distraught young Latina woman with HIV who stumbles into the event desperate for advice about treatment. Hector takes her under his wing, and she later becomes a prominent activist herself, lobbying Congress for research funding, and successfully changing the definition of AIDS to include women's symptoms, thereby qualifying them for welfare, treatment and new drug trials. Murphy's narrative is presented out of sequence, the chapters jumping back and forth through time; Garth Greenwell's 2016 novel *What Belongs to You* (the second novel this chapter examines) also contains a number of temporal shifts: events are told from the position of reconstituted memory, as the narrator, who remains unnamed throughout, recalls his experiences in the Bulgarian capital of Sofia, where he lived for a number of years, teaching English at an American school. On the novel's first page he recalls walking down the steps to the bathrooms of the National Museum of Culture and encountering Mitko, a hustler. The conflation of 'desire and unease' (5) the narrator felt at this point – attracted to Mitko, yet nervous in case he turned violent – becomes the novel's central thematic concern. As with *Christodora*, sex and disease are tightly bound up in this novel: Greenwell's narrator grew up in Kentucky during the height of the AIDS crisis, and his first, entirely innocuous experience with another boy, known to us only as K., led to K. feeling sick the next day and demanding to be driven home. The narrator's father rejected him soon after, having read his diary and discovered he was gay. These early experiences (which are recalled in an extended flashback in the middle of the novel) are part of the reason the narrator left America and moved abroad. But his obsession, in Sofia, with the homeless Mitko, who turns up at the narrator's apartment unexpectedly, and whose behaviour veers from affectionate to violent and cruel, reawakens latent feelings of shame about his sexual orientation, and its association in his mind with dread and disgust.

The first half of this chapter considers the long-term impact of the years 1981 to 1996 on the characters in Murphy's novel, each of whose lives are shaped by the terror and rage of the period. It considers how the novel's non-sequential structure foregrounds the recurrence of addiction and delayed grief across different decades, and focuses attention on the extreme changes in each character's life from their having lived through the crisis. The chapter then explores the novel's concern with being 'out of time', either in the sense of dying prematurely, or (conversely) surviving longer than anyone expected, and feeling discombobulated in a world when so many friends and acquaintances have already died. The vast number of deaths Hector has witnessed are presented as textual absences in this novel, as this chapter will go on to consider. This replicates the official silence about the crisis – years of inaction by government and health authorities which delayed the search for effective treatment, while the grief and fear of those affected went largely unacknowledged. The second half of this chapter turns to Greenwell's novel, which contains an extended flashback at its core, when the narrator's experiences in Bulgaria trigger unwelcome memories from his childhood and adolescence. This section of the chapter considers the lasting effect of the narrator's rejection by his homophobic father. Despite being openly gay, at moments of crisis the narrator's adult reactions replicate the humiliation and defencelessness he felt growing up in the American South. When he tests positive for syphilis while in Sofia, having been infected by Mitko, his feelings of shame, coupled with the disapproving attitude of various doctors, recalls prevailing social attitudes during the 1980s and '90s, when AIDS was blamed on gay men; this aspect of the novel also calls to mind Susan Sontag's 1989 essay *AIDS and its Metaphors*, as the chapter will explore. The AIDS crisis operates as a site of traumatic return for the protagonists in these two novels, although their engagement with that period differs greatly. *Christodora* takes a direct approach: Murphy's characters are prominent activists, leading figures in the fight for treatment. Greenwell's novel takes a more oblique angle: same-sex desire is linked with a more generalised form of illness, the narrator's experience of those years continuing to affect him, but in less obvious ways that pertain to subtleties in his own impulses and responses.

While this chapter's focus is primarily historical and literary rather than theoretical, Heather Love's 2007 book *Feeling Backward* must be acknowledged here, as it argues for the importance of establishing a 'politics of the past' (21) in queer criticism – a recognition that past injury, both 'personal and collective', and the feelings of shame, loneliness and self-loathing this generated, persist in the present time (19). She suggests that the damage wrought by homophobia throughout history has been repurposed, '"turned" to good use in an antihomophobic political project' (18) which focuses on positive affirmation, the reversal of shame into pride in the post-Stonewall era. Her book argues instead that an acknowledgement of 'Backward feelings' (27) is also now needed, because the alternative, the 'politics of optimism', both 'diminishes the suffering of queer historical subjects', while 'at the same time, it blinds us to the continuities between past and present' (29). These ideas are present in Sarah Schulman's 2012 book *The Gentrification of the Mind*, too, where she suggests that the AIDS period urgently needs to be historicised, because neither the suffering of that period, nor the 'consequences of AIDS on the living' (11) have been fully conveyed or measured. When the focus is solely on what has been achieved in terms of equal rights, Schulman argues, and a whole generation of 'younger gay people, especially artists' is 'told that things are better than they are' (7), they are content to simply assimilate into mainstream society. For Schulman this equates to 'an acceptance of banality, a concept of self based falsely in passivity' (13–14), leading to a 'diminished consciousness' both about the wicked failures of the government during the AIDS period and (connectedly) 'about how political and artistic change get made' (14). Drawing on aspects of Schulman's thesis, as well as the work of David France, Deborah B. Gould, Michael Warner and Susan Sontag (among others), this chapter considers the continuing relevance of that period and the manifold ways this past shapes and delimits characters' lives even decades later.

I.

Hector, in Murphy's novel, is a leading member of ACT UP, which was established in New York in 1987 with the purpose of launching a 'militant response' to the AIDS crisis (France 252). Because his work for this and subsequent organisations takes up much of the novel, having a profound impact on the direction of his life and of others such as Issy and Mateo, it will be useful to outline some details of ACT UP's aims and strategy.[1] This political activist group adopted civil disobedience tactics to demand 'drugs into bodies' – its slogan and its *raison d'être*. ACT UP was by no means the first group to address the growing crisis; Gay Men's Health Crisis (GMHC), established in writer Larry Kramer's apartment in 1982, enlisted volunteers to provide care and support for the sick, as well as legal advice: in David France's *How to Survive a Plague* (2016) he explains that 'Employers were firing people diagnosed with the disease, insurance claims were being rejected, and landlords were locking patients out of their homes' (52). GHMC also set up an information and counselling hotline to provide up-to-date advice about safe sex and developments in treatment. Meanwhile the Lavender Hill Mob, founded in 1986 by Marty Robinson, used 'zaps' to target organisations with homophobic policies, such as the Centers for Disease Control (CDC) and the Catholic Church. But as the crisis deepened a more radical response, which focused on drugs, was needed. Close to 20,000 Americans had died by 1987, yet the government still refused to provide sufficient funding for research into treatment. France notes that in 1986 'the Reagan administration called for a 22 percent *reduction* in the fiscal year's AIDS budget, including \$29 million cut in treatment and related spending' (217).[2] Reagan refused to even say the word 'AIDS' in public until 1985, the year his friend Rock Hudson died from the disease. And New York mayor Ed Koch was also reluctant to spend money on fighting the epidemic, despite the fact that New York was at the epicentre of the crisis.[3] Meanwhile Burroughs Wellcome, which manufactured the only drug with FDA approval, AZT, was exploiting their monopoly on treatment by charging up to $10,000 per year for the drug.

ACT UP was the furious rejoinder to the political and medical establishment's inaction: around 300 people gathered at the first meeting in Greenwich Village in March 1987, galvanised by this apathetic response to a disease which had already killed thousands. Among the group's main aims were to establish a 'comprehensive and coordinated national policy on AIDS' to bring together all the research being carried out by various national institutions; to create an 'open and accessible register' for those wishing to enrol on new clinical drug trials; and to bring an 'end to discrimination' against people with AIDS (France 253). Many of its members were also part of GMHC, but it represented a significant departure from that organisation in approach and purpose: the acronym ACT UP points to an important part of its strategy, which involved stunts and theatrics to get its message across. To advance its agenda it organised several marches on Wall Street and Washington, die-ins, kiss-ins and countless demonstrations – targets included the FDA headquarters in 1988, City Hall in 1989, the National Institutes of Health (NIH) in 1990 and numerous protests at St Patrick's Cathedral in New York, where Cardinal John O'Connor promulgated a fiercely anti-gay message and opposed the use of condoms.[4] ACT UP's regular Monday night meetings, which could go on late into the night, became more crowded and impassioned as the death toll continued to rise. Those meetings were a central point of contact, where information was communicated about new possible treatments; upcoming protest activities were announced; and fundraising plans were discussed. The emphasis was on empowering individuals to take an active role in the fight for treatment, forcing the FDA and NIH to take notice and start running drug trials. Protests and demonstrations were the most visible means of drawing attention to the cause, but members of ACT UP also investigated the way these medical bureaucracies were organised, in order to prove that there was little or no research being conducted into possible treatments; that the drug approval process was unnecessarily long; and that testing was limited to very small numbers of patients who met the strict criteria, with women in particular excluded. In the chapter from *Christodora* which takes place at an ACT UP meeting, Hector is 'slightly in awe' at the packed-out meeting, and thinks to himself that 'the past few years, there was no cooler place to be' (135, 136). France recalls feeling that 'if anyone anywhere in the globe was doing something promising about the epidemic, the members of ACT UP would know it first and I might learn it from them' (268). Time was of the essence – many of those leading the ACT UP campaigns were living with AIDS, keeping count of their CD4 levels and watching out for signs of *Pneumocystis carinii* pneumonia (PCP), the distinctive lesions of Kaposi's sarcoma or swollen lymph glands.

In a chapter of *Christodora* set in 1992, Hector is asked by his friend Chris to join him in starting a new treatment group dedicated to doing 'really close work with the feds', free from 'the crazies and the rules of order and the side issues' (263). He is describing the Treatment Action Group (TAG), formed by members of ACT UP's Treatment and Data Committee (T&D). For several years T&D had been the clinical wing of ACT UP, lobbying for more drug trials, a swifter drug approval process, and 'parallel track' to provide access to the drugs for those who needed them most during the trial stage, as France explains: 'If scientists found it necessary to limit enrollment to a homogenous patient profile, why not add another arm to that trial – a *parallel track* – allowing any willing party to partake' (305). TAG was a new group, separate from ACT UP, which modelled itself on a 'professional think tank' (France 449), working closely with federal agencies, particularly the NIH. This proved an effective arrangement: in a later chapter of Murphy's novel set at the 1996 International AIDS Conference in Vancouver, the mood is celebratory: that year marked a turning point in the search for effective AIDS treatment, when the protease inhibitor Crixivan, developed by the pharmaceutical company Merck, was found to have a dramatic effect on patients' virus levels when used in combination with other protease inhibitors.[5] But the novel also considers the terrible years before this breakthrough, particularly for characters like Hector. As a member of the Drug Movement Coalition (Murphy's fictional version of TAG), Hector found the frantic schedule of meetings in Washington to be an effective stay on his grief and despair: his leading role in ACT UP, followed by several years of consultancy, provided him with a 'steady ambient wash of self-importance', but also 'anesthetized his grief' (290). Now that a treatment has been found, his own overriding feeling is of redundancy, which finally forces him to confront the 'tidal wave of death' (Watney 150) he has been suppressing and fully register that his beloved boyfriend Ricky, and most of his friends, are all dead.[6] France has described how, while the deaths were piling up during the heat of the 'plague', there was 'little time or inclination for mourning', as 'Opening a vein to the staggering loss could be paralyzing' (433). Therefore 'In the group's activist ethos, one only looked angrily ahead' (433).[7] Once Hector can no longer use work as a distraction, he can feel the 'maw of emptiness and rage . . . opening beneath him' (Murphy 290), and turns to drugs as another means of evading the fact of Ricky's death: the high he gets from crystal meth allows him to imagine his boyfriend is still alive: '*This is it,* Hector's deep-down voice said. *This is how it felt. This* was his memory of holding Ricky . . . How strange to feel it again after four years!' (293).

The novel shows how similar responses to grief are bound to repeat across time, in different contexts, when those deaths are not properly mourned or even acknowledged. Growing up, Mateo was not told much about his mother, who also died from AIDS; in a scene which parallels Hector's use of crystal meth, Mateo's first experience of heroin nearly fifteen years later generates the illusion of being transported back in time to before his mother's death: 'he's exactly where he's wanted to be his whole life but never knew it, back with her, before he was born, inside her; nothing's begun yet, just this warmth and protection, this liquid blanket' (41). For both Hector and Mateo, the effect of taking drugs is to experience a porous relationship between past and present: they can each drift back to an earlier, less painful moment before 'separation or detachment or ache' (41) – before they were struck by the miasma of delayed grief. This melting away of time is experienced by Hector in a different context, too: in Los Angeles in 2012 he is at his lowest ebb, driving around the city while high on a cocktail of drugs, paranoid and anxious, and in terror of being arrested. Finally, he stops the car in front of a massive modern church and stumbles in during mass. As he looks around, astonished, at the homeless people scattered around the pews, his mind turns to the only other time he has been in a church this size: 'St. Pat's in New York, which he and the other activists had stormed on a Sunday years before to protest the archdiocese's AIDS policies, its opposition to condoms, and its hatred of gays' (238). At the demonstration at St Patrick's Cathedral Hector recalls, which took place on 10 December 1989, ACT UP protestors were joined by the Women's Health Action and Mobilization, and thousands gathered outside on the street with banners, while others dressed as church-goers disrupted the service from inside.[8] The momentary temporal collapse between Hector's days as an activist twenty years earlier, and now, a drug addict about to be taken to a homeless shelter, is a stark reminder of how his circumstances have changed over the past two decades.

As that scene in the Los Angeles church shows, *Christodora* moves freely across different periods in order to draw some devastating comparisons – in this case, Hector's dramatic deterioration. And this impression of a roving narrative eye is introduced at the level of structure, too, with the non-chronological arrangement of chapters meaning that glimpses of each character's life are scattered throughout the novel, presented to the reader out of sequence. This redirects focus from where an individual will end up (as this has usually been revealed quite early on), to instead consider the extent of their transformation and the reasons behind it. In one chapter taking place in 2010, Hector is a meth addict living in a basement squat, scaring passers-by as he screams at his vicious dog in the street; Mateo is 'mesmerized' (123) when he stumbles across the scene. The chapter that follows is set more than twenty years earlier, in 1989, when Hector is a full-time member of ACT UP, and being funded to help design clinical trials. In this 1989 chapter he and Ricky are on their way to an ACT UP meeting when they bump into Ava's daughter Milly. They are a strikingly attractive couple, Milly thinks to herself: Hector is 'ridiculously good-looking', with 'considerable muscles in all the right places', and Ricky 'was good-looking too in that classic blond, blue-eyed, forever-a-boy way' (130). After their brief conversation, Milly glances back at them and she too is 'mesmerized' (133), but in a positive sense, as she wonders at them kissing passionately in the street, both of them entirely unselfconscious. This later chapter recasts the previous scene: Hector is both redeemed and rendered more tragic when we understand that this 'mumbling mess' (123), now twenty years older, had previously been a handsome, confident young man who could take control of a meeting, calmly outlining treatment breakthroughs to a large crowd of frightened people. Since we have already witnessed the nadir of addiction and anger Hector will reach by 2010, the focus is on what triggered this alteration in him. And one particular moment in the 1989 chapter seems to anticipate his later isolation: after the encounter with Milly, Hector asks Ricky if he has been tested for HIV yet. But Ricky rebuffs him, determined not to take the test: '"I've told you a hundred times, Hector. I don't want to know. *I don't want to know.*" He was saying it in a nasty singsong. "I don't see the point. *La-la-la, la-la!*"' (134–5). Hector feels the 'wires of lust and fear crossing in his head' (134), finding no answer to his terrified thought: 'What if he lost this?' (133).

Even when the chapters unfold in a chronological order, the effect is still jarring. Murphy reduces the distance between sets of circumstances which are temporally far apart, so that cause and effect are plainly rendered. For instance, a 1984 chapter depicts a sexual encounter between Issy and Chris – an activist friend of Hector's she meets in a nightclub. The two of them have sex in his car before he drives off home, leaving her on the kerb. That chapter is immediately followed by one set in 1995, in Judith House, the care residence on Avenue B set up by Ava for women with AIDS. By this stage Issy has already died from AIDS, having spent her final few months at Judith House. Issy's trajectory has been starkly condensed: by moving directly from the moment of her infection to the place where she died from the disease, her significant achievements as an activist are omitted.

Hector's sense of being 'out of time', cast adrift from normal temporal rhythms, dates from 1996, at the AmFAR conference in Vancouver, when he first tried crystal meth. By 2012 he barely notices time passing: the drugs he has been taking almost continuously since arriving in Los Angeles a week ago (and habitually for over fifteen years) have left him unmoored from even the most basic of temporal rhythms, unable to distinguish day from night:

> as soon as he'd made a meth connection and the glass pipe and torch had come out, he'd lost track of time. After that, it was just the laptop, the porn, the random visitors with their intermittent glances through the blinds at the sun-baked pool in the courtyard, from which they thought they heard laughter but which appeared deserted. Were people playing tricks on them? Hector and his visitors wondered, as the light and dark rotated rapidly outside like in a time-lapse video (236).

While Hector's haziness and imprecision is partly the result of his drug addiction, it can also be ascribed to the fact that the period since he left activism has felt to him devoid of definition or purpose, and this renders it wholly unmemorable. In Deborah B. Gould's 2009 history of ACT UP, *Moving Politics*, she describes the movement in its early years as characterised by 'tremendous solidarity' and 'constructed commonality' (332, 333), which compelled participants to attend meetings, join marches and perceive themselves as part of a larger queer collective under extreme attack. The meetings were a space where anxiety and terror could be harnessed towards an urgent and defiant group energy which might in turn enact real change in the world. ACT UP was also a vital support network – a place to socialise, share experiences, receive comfort for grief and meet new friends and sexual partners. In those earlier sections of the novel Hector looks forward to the meetings as an opportunity to 'have fun and flirt and plan major disruptions and then go dancing along the way', while at the same time 'using [his education] to help save the lives of his own people' (135). The decline of ACT UP came in the early 1990s – caused in part by the formation of TAG, but also 'despair' and 'exhaustion' at the 'endless amassing of dead bodies', as it dawned on ACT UP members that direct action was not saving lives and there was still no effective treatment (Gould 421). The much-needed sense of solidarity and friendship fostered by the move-ment also fell away, leaving former members newly isolated. Hector has already left ACT UP by this stage, and continues to be sustained for several more years by his activist work as part of the Drug Movement Coalition, which also brings with it a readymade group of like-minded friends. But once it is clear that a treatment break-through has been made, Hector looks on disdainfully as his fellow activists are hired for 'cushy jobs as community liaisons or marketing consultants in the bright-eyed new landscape of the chronic manage-able illness' (290). The rapid dispersal of his fellow activists leaves him suddenly alone and bereft of a clear purpose: he seems to have outlasted his own usefulness.[9] In the novel Mateo tracks him down in a housing group for AIDS survivors, and the man who answers the door is bemused: 'You here to see Hector? . . . He never gets visi-tors!' (372). Following the decline of the activist movement, Hector and the other residents have been abandoned, tucked away in a dan-gerous corner of Brooklyn. Hector even asks Mateo what day it is, because while he is able to recall exact dates in the fight for effective treatment during the 1980s and early '90s, and reassures Mateo that he can 'remember a lot' (392) about his mother Issy, the years since then feel inconsequential, and exist in his mind as a blur.

Hector's description of himself and the other residents as a 'bunch of old broke-down ghosts' (388) suggests theirs is a haunting pres-ence, lingering in a world they should have already left. The feeling of living beyond one's own time, when so many others have already died, is akin to the experiences of those who contracted the virus in the 1980s and early '90s but survived just long enough to gain access to effective treatment.[10] Hector looks around at the people who have 'won the AIDS lottery, made it to the finish line, run out the clock' (289). But this sudden, unexpected recovery – known colloquially as the Lazarus effect – left some survivors with a strange feeling of living beyond their anticipated death; their still being alive was uncanny, almost too strange for them (and others) to countenance.[11] The mundane realities of 'bills, mortgages, disability payments, employment prospects' offered tangible proof that they were 'cursed with the divine gift of having a messy life to go on living' (Murphy 289). And meanwhile there were huge swathes of others who were just out of time – dying just before the protease inhibitors were fully developed. Hector recalls that the darkest period was during the early '90s, when 'overwhelming loss mingled confusingly with tidings of the coming respite' (290). This was when Ricky, the 'blond sliver of sunshine on the timeline that Hector envisioned as his life, had missed the drawbridge' (290). Hector considers these AIDS deaths as a 'network of people' who were 'running faster but falling behind' (259), but Issy, who dies around the same time as Ricky, senses her own death lingering directly in front of her. Death for her is 'the specter – *el espectro* . . . the dark pit before her when she was alone' (276). This suggests some of the ways the disease affects the characters closest to it: those who survive, like Hector (who avoided infection) or Chris (a fellow member of the Drug Movement Coalition who has been HIV-positive for more than a decade), feel their lives taking on an eerie quality, as they carry on, disorientated, beyond their allotted time; others (like Issy) experience something akin to premature mourning, disconsolate about their own looming deaths.[12]

II.

Ricky largely withdraws from the text after he becomes ill, aside from a few paragraphs which describe his time in hospital. For Hector the 'very, very worst years of sickness and death' were during 'Clinton's first term' (290), yet his suffering during those years is barely represented in the novel – only recalled very briefly, in retrospect: 'Twenty years ago! How 1992 bled into 1993. Awful fucking 1993' (246). Tavi, Issy's best friend with whom Hector worked at GMHC, died in 1989, and this too is mentioned only in passing. At first glance, then, *Christodora* would seem to be an example of '"counterimmersive" AIDS writing', defined by Joseph Cady as writing which 'typically focuses on characters or speakers who are in various degrees of denial about AIDS' and who 'cushion themselves against the epidemic's fearfulness, and remain distanced from it' (244, 244, 257).

The effect of this writing, which Cady sets up in negative contrast to the more direct category of immersive AIDS writing, is to protect the 'denying reader', exempting them from 'too close a contact with the horrors of AIDS' and making 'no compelling demands on [them] to change' (257). But on closer inspection, that series of textual voids in *Christodora* does not contribute to a broader societal denial about the disease, but rather highlights the effects of that 'cultural disavowal' (Cady 245) on the groups most affected: Hector pushes aside his grief because there is no viable outlet for its expression, and his subsequent descent into addiction exposes the full ramifications of attempting to stifle this pain. The artist David Wojnarowicz, who died from AIDS in 1992, furiously condemned 'society's almost total inability to deal with this disease with anything other than a conservative agenda' (*Rebellious Mourning* 145), and suggested that 'To turn our private grief for the loss of friends, family, lovers and strangers into something public would serve as [a] powerful dismantling tool' which would 'dispel the notion that the virus has a sexual orientation or a moral code' and 'nullify the belief that the government and medical community has done very much to ease the spread of advancement of this disease' (146). At political funerals organised by ACT UP, the bodies of those who had died from AIDS were carried through the streets to generate a visceral public reaction. And the SILENCE = DEATH posters which went up around the city in 1986 (and subsequently became ACT UP's logo) were an attempt to force New Yorkers to recognise the stark consequences of ignoring the crisis; in small letters at the bottom of the poster was a list of the individuals and institutions who remained silent about AIDS: Reagan, the CDC, the FDA and the Vatican. Murphy's novel repeatedly shows public figures refusing to tackle the AIDS crisis and showing little concern for the dead and dying. When Issy leads a delegation at the NIH to petition for women to be included in clinical trials, she feels as though she is 'lining up for confession, waiting for the priest to tell you something mind-blowing that would make your whole life right, except he never did' (269). The NIH delegate is like a Catholic priest who simply 'told you to go off and say some old prayers' (269) rather than offer practical support. And Ava, from the city's Department of Health, admits to Hector that 'I didn't do enough when this emerged. None of us did. Because of who it affected, and we didn't want to get our hands dirty with it' (143).

These moments in the novel capture the neurotic denial about the scale of the crisis, which proved so powerful that for months and even years the general population was unaware that an epidemic was killing thousands of Americans while the government and health authorities stood by.[13] For Sarah Schulman, that policy of indifference and distortion has its contemporary equivalent in the position that that history occupies in the mainstream American consciousness. At the start of her 2012 book *The Gentrification of the Mind* she recalls her dismay at hearing a radio announcer in 2001 suggest that America simply 'came around' to 'People with AIDS' (2), a statement that belies the traumatic years of terror and anger as activists, many of whom already had AIDS and were fast running out of time, had to force the NIH to start clinical trials and the FDA to fast-track their drug approval process and (in the meantime) allow them access to experimental drugs. Having spoken to younger gay people (artists in particular), Schulman realised that this history had been marginalised to such an extent that this generation (who did not live through the period) remained oblivious to its full horror – with the result that the government's inaction has been forgotten, the hundreds of thousands who died are denied an official memorial, and the ongoing effects on those who survived the period are overlooked. Schulman describes this as a 'gaping hole of silence' (46) – an historical void where the AIDS crisis should be. Deborah B. Gould, too, explains that she was motivated to write her history of ACT UP because of her concern that 'the early years of the AIDS crisis, along with AIDS activism from the 1980s and 1990s ... are being forgotten' (45). This 'erasure from national consciousness of AIDS as a crisis', she argues, means that what is lost is 'the memory of a government of a wealthy, ostensibly democratic country unmoved by the deaths of hundreds, thousands, and finally hundreds of thousands of its own inhabitants' because they were seen as 'expendable': namely, 'gay and bisexual men', 'drug users' and 'poor men and women, a disproportionate number of whom were black and Latino/a' (45). This cultural amnesia is incorporated into Murphy's novel through the character of Mateo, who is completely unaware of his mother's activism during the 1980s. Issy was a young, HIV-positive Latina woman who successfully led the campaign for the CDC to change the definition of AIDS to include women's symptoms. But stories like hers are not widely known: in 2021, when at the age of twenty-eight Mateo tracks Hector down to find out more about Issy, he admits that 'I never knew anything about her, where I came from. We didn't really talk about it in my family growing up' (387). This silence led inevitably to misunderstanding: for years Mateo wrongly suspected that his mother became infected because she was promiscuous. And when he finally sees a video of her giving a speech to crowds demonstrating outside the CDC in Atlanta in 1990, he tries to 'see and hear echoes of himself', but finds that 'She's from another world' (385). Hector's repeated directive that 'You need to read your history' (379) verges on unrealistic, Mateo's experience shows, when the official record (and even his own adopted family) de-emphasises the efforts of community-based activists like his mother. Issy's friend Esther Hurwitz has created a website so that the 'thousands of hours of tapes, of interviews and demos' (382) from the period will be publicly accessible, telling Mateo that 'There's not a lot of documentation and I know everyone's forgotten about it, but your mother really was a hero' (387).[14]

Until Mateo grasps the full significance of Issy's life, he is disturbed by a past he struggles to fully comprehend – the image of his mother from an old Polaroid appears in his mind's eye whenever he takes heroin, but she occupies a shadowy space in his consciousness, and is beyond his reach when sober. But Issy's spectral presence in Mateo's life means he instinctively understands that repressed memories can unexpectedly resurface, and this becomes important when he returns to New York after a decade in Los Angeles. He is immediately struck by how particular streets and buildings in the Lower East Side can throw him off his 'present-day linear course' (356), triggering a descent into the 'wormhole of the past' (369) he has tried to paper over: his heroin addiction, stealing from his parents' friends to buy drugs, countless arguments with his adoptive father Jared, failed attempts at rehab and eventually being thrown out of the apartment. Certain storefronts still function for Mateo as 'memory-stabs' (352): he becomes a reluctant historical archaeologist as he encounters 'the old stoops, fire escapes, cornices, and witch-hatted water towers' which still exist 'between the glass spires and wedges' (358), and which pertain to shameful actions a decade earlier. For instance, he feels a 'hot flash' when he crosses Ninth Street in a taxi, even though he does not directly pass the Christodora, his old home: 'It just means I could feel its latitude. Or longitude or whatever' (355). While the new glass buildings Mateo notices all over Greenwich Village and the Lower East Side remind us that downtown New York is now a highly salubrious area, Mateo's return to the city also serves as confirmation that there is a porous relationship between past and present, and as a self-described 'AIDS orphan' (421) who has been haunted by his mother's death since he was first adopted, he seems uniquely well-placed to understand the scale of loss and trauma hidden just beneath the shiny surface of the city.

As a child Mateo lived in the 'Christodora' of the novel's title – a sixteen-storey brick apartment building on Tompkins Square Park built in 1928. Jared's father bought a large two-bedroom apartment in the Christodora in 1986 for just $90,000. This development, the narrator explains, was 'heralded as the inevitable triumph of gentrification' (4). For years the Lower East Side had been almost entirely Puerto Rican (and before that, Jewish), but white, middle-class people started to move into the area during the 1970s, attracted back into the city by the promise of newly-converted housing. And it was coincidental but calamitous, as Schulman explains, that the AIDS epidemic hit 'in the middle of this process', meaning that more and more apartments were becoming available at an 'unnatural speed' (25, 26) as tenants were dying in considerable numbers, particularly in gay enclaves of the city such as the East Village, the West Village and Chelsea. Schulman recalls that 'The process of replacement was so mechanical I could literally sit on my stoop and watch it unfurl' (26) and 'It was normal to hear that someone we knew had died and that their belongings were thrown out on the street' (37).[15] Nowadays, as Mateo discovers, downtown Manhattan is comprised of luxury apartments and expensive shops and restaurants, making it unrecognisable from its previous incarnation as a diverse cultural space – a hub for gay men and women, artists and immigrants. The tony, whitewashed cityscape Mateo returns to, which obscures its dynamic, heterogeneous past identity, stands in metonymic relation to the official AIDS narrative which covers up the transformative role of the gay community in fighting back against 'governmental indifference' to the disease and its victims – each of those pasts have been papered over, subjected to 'gentrified thinking' (Schulman 48, 51). Mateo, who understands better than most that the unresolved past has a habit of resurfacing, finds that when 'the noise of the present clears', he is left 'staring into the abyss of the past' (369), and intuits that beneath the 'tinted glass slivers and shards that have shot up everywhere' (353) there is another story he needs to hear. When he meets Hector at the end of the novel he finds him living in Brownsville, a dangerous area of Brooklyn – presumably the only place he can still afford. And it is there, in 'maybe the last ungentrified neighborhood in New York City' (372) that Mateo finally learns about his mother's fight for the CDC to recognise her symptoms, her illness and her death – information which his internet searches have failed to yield.

III.

On the way to an ACT UP meeting in 1989, Hector recalls the 'years of self-denial and self-containment' he went through in the 1970s before he came out as gay, and at times he feels himself 'falling back, back, back, crashing backward' through those years (133). In the decade after Stonewall the gay rights movement achieved a number of limited but still significant gains, with hundreds of local organisations across the country creating community centres, establishing newspapers, campaigning for equal civil rights and endorsing pro-gay candidates for public office. Gay subcultures were also thriving in all major cities across the US: the establishment of bath-houses, and bars and clubs catering to every sexual kink, meant casual and experimental sex was freely available. This period was immortalised in Andrew Holleran's 1978 novel *Dancer from the Dance*, a conscious rewriting of *The Great Gatsby*, in which drag queen Sutherland and his protégé Malone embark on a hedonistic circuit of drug-fuelled partying and sex in Manhattan and on Fire Island.

But at the same time as gay culture was flourishing across much of America and the western world, the New Right was campaigning vociferously for a return to so-called 'traditional values', stoking fears about a newly permissive society and its 'immoral' sexual practices. In 1977 Christian right conservatives led by Anita Bryant launched a successful campaign to overturn antidiscrimination legislation. This conservative backlash against the gay rights movement was likely to have been a factor in Hector's decision to delay coming out, but for him (and many others) coming out became a moral imperative after the AIDS crisis began in 1981, when gay men were subject to fresh assault: condemnation of the so-called 'gay lifestyle' was frequently articulated in newspaper articles and pamphlets produced during the AIDS crisis, even by those who had once been part of that scene.[16] Men like Hector, terrified after seeing friends and lovers fall ill and die, and furious at governmental inaction, channelled this anger into collection action. Dennis Altman described in 1986 (the year before ACT UP was established) how

> AIDS has begun to alter the shape of gay male life in America ... in terms of creating genuine community. The combination of a desire to help one's 'brothers and sisters' and the anger generated by a sense that no one else cares has given renewed life to gay organizations and brought thousands of new activists into gay communal activities (98).

And Gould explains how feelings of 'gay shame' and the fear of societal rejection was then 'inverted' by ACT UP: the message was that

> the (in)actions of the government and other institutions responsible for the AIDS crisis were shameful . . . lesbians and gay men angrily fighting back were righteous and responsible, and rather than feeling ashamed, they should feel proud of both their sexual practices and their confrontational activism (250).

This usefully describes Hector, in the novel, who is now 'making up for lost time like a starving dog' and wonders to himself, 'How had he gone so long without this? All those nights in the office, boxed away . . . Was this really happening? Could he possibly be so happy?' (133). Hector experienced the late '80s as a thrilling period, and those ACT UP meetings an intoxicating mixture of 'righteous anger and complicated lust, social energy, bitterness, and hurt' (136). But this was not the case for the majority of gay men, for whom coming out was simply not an option: this could mean being fired from their job or disowned by their family. Gay men were regularly beaten up in the street. And those who became sick with AIDS provoked terror and vilification, even among the medical community: some were refused care altogether and even those admitted to hospital might receive minimal attention, with some hospital staff refusing to touch or even go near sick patients. Public figures such as Jerry Falwell, Jesse Helms, William F. Buckley and Patrick Buchanan suggested gay men be quarantined and those with HIV should have their buttocks tattooed to warn others.

It is this homophobic environment which still haunts the narrator in Garth Greenwell's novel *What Belongs to You* (which this chapter will now turn to) even decades later: when growing up during the 1980s and early '90s he recalls, 'Disease was the only story anyone ever told about men like me' (122). As a teenager (and in a different context) the narrator's father had accused him of having 'no pride' (75), but as a grown man Greenwell's narrator does not hide the fact that he is gay; in Bulgaria, when a weak attempt is made to blackmail him, he regards this as 'a threat in a different world, in his world perhaps but not in mine', telling his former lover: 'Mitko, I said, speaking gently, not in fear but in pity, I am an open person, I don't have these secrets, everyone knows what I am . . . from the first day I've told them, everyone knows . . .' (186). This assured response comes from someone who is not afraid of being exposed, and yet homophobic dictums designed to shame him as a child continue to shape his self-perception, remaining a potent characteristic of his gay identity – humiliation has been an enduring corollary to desire since the age of nine or ten, when he first intuited that he was different from others: his friends, able to 'sense the added heat', and noticing how he would seek out their company 'with a new urgency' (71), were 'scared off by the need I felt for them, and soon the best I could hope for was their indifference' (73).

In *What Belongs to You* the narrator recalls the period of his life teaching at a prestigious American school in Sofia, where he embarked on an erratic affair with Mitko, a hustler whom he first encountered in the subterranean bathrooms of the National Palace of Culture, a popular cruising spot. Their relationship has a transactional, unequal quality from the start: he pays to perform oral sex on Mitko (although Mitko takes much more money than was agreed), but the narrator also finds himself powerless over him, whom he finds himself unexpectedly drawn to. His early description of Mitko's body as 'almost infinitely dear' (8) is a phrase that can be understood in two different ways: this hints at the blurring of contractual arrangement and genuine feeling that characterises their relationship. Several days after their first encounter, the narrator invites Mitko over to his apartment and feels 'helpless' and 'ashamed' (24, 25) at Mitko's apparent lack of interest: he already pictures scrubbing his own face of the 'eagerness and servility and need it wore' (29) before he can stand in front of a class again the following day. The narrator's inhibited, passive demeanour in this early scene becomes increasingly familiar as the narrative develops, and a long flashback midway through the novel reveals that these are traits he has learned in his childhood in Kentucky during the early '90s. In Bernadette Barton's article examining the experiences of gay men and women in the Bible Belt, she suggests that growing up gay in the American South is guaranteed to generate feelings of shame, fear and isolation: she describes how 'abusive language about and threatening actions toward homosexuals is reflected from the pulpit and echoed in the pews, on the playground, in the bar, at work, and during family dinner' (466). In this way the fiercely anti-gay doctrine espoused by Christian fundamentalism becomes generalised, and we see in the novel how homophobic discourse permeates the narrator's childhood, rendering his desires a moral outrage which warrant condemnation and even ostracism: he recalls that his life during that period was 'flattened . . . to a morality tale, in which I could either be chaste or condemned' (122). That this was also during the height of the 'AIDS panic' compounded the societal prejudice, so that 'warnings about precaution and prevention', commonplace at the time, 'had long been part of my most private sense of myself' (122). Like Murphy's novel, *What Belongs to You* moves back and forth through time: the events of the novel happened several years earlier and are therefore relayed from a position of reconstituted memory; the flashback within this retrospective narrative goes further back still, describing incidents from the narrator's childhood and adolescence. That flashback is triggered by the narrator receiving a message (while in Sofia) telling him that his father is gravely ill and wishes him to return home; a series of harrowing moments from his early life then intrude on his consciousness, including his first realisation that he was gay; humiliation at the hands of his first love; and his father disowning him and wishing he had never been born.

The extended flashback reveals that the narrator's decades-long retreat into 'uneasy solitude' (73) began when he was still a child. He recalls the closeness he used to feel with his father as having been 'free of suspicion or doubt' (71) until the age of nine or ten, when after a shower together, and while still dripping wet, he hugged his father from behind, and his father, feeling the boy's erection pressing against him, pushed him away, his face 'twisted in disgust' (72). 'That was the end of care' (72), the narrator explains, and the safety he had enjoyed with his father having been withdrawn, the conclusion he reaches is that the affection of others is conditional rather than permanent, and that specific, inescapable aspects of his self-identity mean that that care is likely to be revoked. The withdrawal of his father's affection leads him to feel 'less substantial or less certain of my substance' (73), his core essence having been judged undesirable, and his membership of the family newly precarious. Crucially, his father's response has shaped his own self-perception in the longer-term: he describes how 'his look entered me and settled there and has never left, it rooted beneath memory and became my understanding of myself, my understanding and expectation' (72).

The lasting effects of this early rejection manifest themselves in various ways, but particularly in his refusal to fight back or defend himself: as an adult he tends towards passivity and ambivalence, allowing Mitko to take advantage of him not only financially, but also physically. During a row in a hotel room in Varna, for instance, he does not react when Mitko strikes him across the face and then pins him down on the bed, instead resolving that 'whatever happens next I will let it happen . . . he could have taken whatever he wanted' (54). The narrator recognises that this type of response can be traced back to his childhood, when his father's rejection left him feeling 'somehow less real' (73) and in a state of 'habitual unease' (145)

– less sure of himself and his own defences. After Mitko leaves the room, we get the following passage, explicitly tying his adult reactions to his past experiences:

> So the crisis isn't past, I thought, using that word, crisis; I was right to still be afraid. I was frozen in place, pinned where I stood, a feeling I remembered from childhood, when stillness was the only response to the terror I often felt at night (54).

When Mitko leaves, and the narrator asks the hotel attendant to find another room for him with a better lock on the door, he finds himself 'paralyzed with humiliation' and 'burning with shame' (56, 55), despite the attendant's repeated attempts to redirect the shame back onto Mitko: 'It's a shame there are such people in the world, he said, you have to be so careful, you pay them, you have your fun, and then they should leave' (56). It is entirely appropriate then, that at the end of the novel's long flashback, an extended period of temporal collapse which has delved into the narrator's troubled childhood, he should look down to discover he is 'mired in roots and mud' – 'ankle-deep' in a 'morass' (90). The literal and figurative roots he has stumbled upon while walking through countryside outside Sofia do not ground him or offer any form of stability, but instead trap and confine him, as they have done all along: this unwanted excavation of childhood experiences demonstrate their continued relevance in his adult life, where he is stuck repeating the same patterns of behaviour – ashamed, prone to indecision and, at the crucial moment, reluctant to defend himself.

While the narrator's relocation to Bulgaria repeatedly reminds him of the condemnatory backdrop to his childhood and adolescence, it also prompts him to engage in acts of resistance which replicate earlier rebellions against restrictive cultural norms. He recalls, for instance, that as a younger man back in America, the constant terror of contracting HIV through sex had eventually 'given way to something like carelessness, which I knew was irresponsible, though I mostly took the usual precautions' (110). And many years later in Sofia, he regularly cruises in the public bathrooms at the National Palace of Culture; later in the novel he also masturbates in a McDonald's toilet with Mitko standing behind him, and is thrilled by the 'risk': the unlocked door 'heightened my pleasure as Mitko pressed his whole length against me' (133). That he chose to masturbate in a branch of McDonald's, a global symbol of western capitalism and synonymous with all-American values, reframes this incident as an act of rebellion against the social norms he grew up with in early '90s Kentucky, some of which are still maintained in Bulgaria. Post-communist Bulgaria remains culturally conservative: while it is not illegal to be gay, and discrimination on the grounds of sexual orientation has been prohibited since 2004, there is still widespread societal prejudice and an emphasis on 'traditional family values', endorsed by the Orthodox Church and bolstered by far-right political groups. During the first Sofia Pride march in 2008, a petrol bomb was thrown at participants, and in 2013 the event was postponed because of security concerns. In practical terms, therefore, Bulgaria remains a hostile and unsafe environment for gay people, with homophobic violence rarely followed up by the police.[17] In Greenwell's story 'Decent People', set in 2013, and published in his 2020 collection *Cleanness*, the narrator is attending an anti-government demonstration in the centre of Sofia when he notices a small group of LGBT activists among the crowd. When he reaches the group (most of whom he has met before), one of them, S., begins to fulminate about the cancelling of Sofia Pride, describing it as 'total bullshit . . . it says we have to choose between being gay and being Bulgarian, fuck that, it's so fucking homophobic' (62). Yet his defiance ('we're doing Pride anyway . . . they should know we're here, they shouldn't be able to ignore us') is punished: the narrator encounters his activist friends again at the end of the story, but this time sitting on the ground, S. having been attacked by men in masks who labelled the group 'dirty queers' (62, 81); meanwhile the police are nowhere to be seen. Even discreet intimations of gay desire are off-limits: in another story, the narrator's lover extends his hand towards him as they sit in a restaurant having lunch, but they both know that it would be 'imprudent' (90) to actually touch.

These risks are also described in *What Belongs to You*: towards the end of the novel Mitko relays the explicit language people already use to describe him: 'they've said . . . why are you hanging out with that faggot, and he used the term *pederast*, here as elsewhere it's the preferred term of abuse' (185). Mitko's dark warnings about the 'bad people' who 'might make trouble' (186) for the narrator hint at the dangers of being openly gay in Bulgaria. But it also triggers another flashback, calling to mind the language used by his father many years earlier, when he read his diary:

> So you like the little boys, that voice said, the voice almost of instinct, the voice of the look he had given me once and of what had once fouled the air . . . A faggot, he said, if I had known you would never have been born (99).

It is a long-standing trope in gay novels that foreign settings are more amenable to self-realisation and expressions of same-sex desire; we see this in the work of E. M. Forster, Christopher Isherwood, Thomas Mann and James Baldwin, and more recently in Edmund White's novel *The Married Man* (2000), André Aciman's *Call Me By Your Name* (2007) and *Enigma Variations* (2017), Caleb Crain's *Necessary Errors* (2013) and Darryl Pinckney's *Black Deutschland* (2016). In Greenwell's novel, by contrast, the narrator's experiences in Bulgaria reawaken memories of his father's virulent homophobia, and the lessons he was taught about his sexuality – aspects of a past he has 'worked hard to forget' (63) but which cannot be unlearnt entirely.

IV.

Murphy's novel is unambiguously about AIDS: about the experience of living through the crisis and the appalling after-effects for those who survived the period. *What Belongs to You* takes a more oblique approach to the subject: AIDS is not mentioned until fairly late in the novel, and then only briefly. The narrator in Greenwell's novel is much younger than *Christodora*'s Hector, reaching adulthood in the mid-'90s, and therefore did not experience the crisis up close in the same way that Hector did. And while Hector is openly gay and part of a larger group of like-minded activists, Greenwell's narrator remained isolated when younger, making desperate efforts to conceal his gay identity in a Red state. But like *Christodora*, sex is explicitly linked with illness throughout Greenwell's novel – in the first instance, when the narrator (by this stage a teenager, still in Kentucky) forges an intense friendship with another boy, known to us as K. The ramifications of this bond (which is described in the novel's extended flashback) are far-reaching. Before they had even met, the narrator intuited that things were likely to go wrong, feeling 'an anxiety that gnawed at me and for which I could find no cause, that gnawed at me more deeply precisely because I could find no cause' (75–6). When K. comes to stay, they sneak out at night and gleefully rip Republican yard signs from people's gardens – this is an election year, almost certainly 1992 – but again the narrator's happiness contains a kernel of fear: when K. hangs his arm around his neck, he feels 'almost frightened by the happiness that overtook me, that filled me up and charged me and at the same time carried a threat' (78). Gestures of affection, even at their most innocuous, cannot be dissociated from perceived risk. The narrator was in his early teens at this point, and well versed in the stark warnings about gay sex that were circulating at the time. From the start, Kaposi's sarcoma was dubbed the 'gay cancer' and AIDS the 'gay plague'; the acronym GRID, which was replaced by AIDS in 1982, stood for 'gay-related immune deficiency', which suggested that queerness and AIDS was a straightforward example of cause and effect. This metonymic link between queerness and disease took on an additional meaning in the narrator's particular Southern context, where to be gay was to be sinful, morally sick. On the waterbed the boys share that night, K. asks the narrator to rub his back; this leads to them hugging, and in a gesture partly reminiscent of the incident after the shower with his father, the narrator falls asleep embracing K. from behind. But by the next morning, K. has fallen ill: the narrator wakes up to find him heaving 'nauseous breaths' (82) by the side of the bed, and he shrugs the narrator off, asking to go home. Despite there being no obvious cause, the narrator instinctively feels 'shamed' (82) about the situation and about the mess K. has made, and tries to clean it up before his father sees it; finally, he throws a towel over it, 'thinking that if I could do nothing about the smell I could at least hide the sight of it away' (83).

Susan Sontag's 1989 essay *AIDS and its Metaphors* functions as a useful intertext for Greenwell's novel, and this scene with K. in particular. Sontag examines how particular diseases have been culturally interpreted in ways which induce shame, moral judgement and the fear of contagion: during the nineteenth century, for instance, 'Sinister characterizations of the organic proliferated . . . to describe both the disease and its cause' (41). Certain diseases were 'thought to be caused by an "infected" (or "foul") atmosphere, effusions spontaneously generated from something unclean' (41). This 'miasma theory' (42), which posited that illness was caused by a 'disease-carrying atmosphere' that was 'Usually identified . . . by its bad smell' (41), was a way of 'moraliz[ing] a disease' (42), suggesting that the illness was linked to filth, therefore that the infected person must have been dwelling in dark and squalid parts of the city. The ill person was also then marked out as unclean, liable to contaminate the atmosphere for others. This goes some way to explaining the scene in the car when K. is being dropped home. The narrator quickly notices that the air in the car is 'foul', as K'.s 'vomit' and 'sweat' have combined to create a 'bitter and strong' smell (83), yet it is the narrator whom his father steadily observes in the rear-view mirror, rather than K., and he grimaces when their eyes meet; this betrays his suspicion that the unpleasant smell has emanated from the narrator, rather than from his friend. The narrator is subsequently accorded pariah-like status – the uncleanness in the air apparently signals his engagement in 'unclean' or transgressive behaviour, and its potency is such that it pollutes the atmosphere for others. K., who has already fallen ill after sharing the narrator's bed, takes no further chances, ignoring the narrator's questions and turning away, as though simply acknowledging his friend's presence might further compromise his own wellbeing: 'I felt him [K.] identify me as foulness. It was as though he felt my father was health and I contagion' (84). The 'foulness in the air', the narrator also realises, is 'not just a bodily foulness but something stranger and heavier' (83) – it is both literal and metaphorical, as Sontag suggested, emblematic of something unpleasant about the narrator's character which should be avoided. And, crucially, that foulness seems to be ineradicable, as though intrinsic to the narrator: when he winds down the window he notices that 'The air was cool as it flooded in but the foulness still remained' (83). In the pages that follow this incident, K. makes the immediate and conscious decision to be 'free of the foulness' (89) he encountered through the narrator, embarking on a heterosexual relationship he specifically asks the narrator to witness, proving to him that he is no longer part of his 'unclean' world.

K.'s mysterious but short-lived illness occurred immediately after an affectionate but ultimately chaste night with the narrator; this incident, which we learn about in the novel's longest sustained flashback, is a forerunner for the narrator's relationship with Mitko, in Sofia, which brings further (and more serious) illness into the narrator's life. When Mitko arrives unexpectedly at the narrator's apartment one evening, two years after they last spoke, to explain that he has syphilis, the narrator finds himself 'drawing back without thinking, a reflex against contagion and against the word, too, feeling horror at a nineteenth-century disease I only knew about from books' (108–9). It is significant that Greenwell chose syphilis as the particular disease his narrator contracts from Mitko: in her essay, Sontag frequently compared syphilis with AIDS, describing them both as 'meaning-laden' diseases (92), generally construed as judgements on 'moral laxity' (54) and associated with uncleanness, sexual transgression and promiscuity. Dennis Altman made the similar point in 1986 that in terms of the 'metaphorical weight' attached to AIDS, the 'parallels' with syphilis 'are actually quite remarkable' (140). He explained that 'It did not take long for syphilis to be linked to sexual contagion, and hence to punishment by God' (140–1), and even in the present day, 'venereal diseases are still seen by some as divine retribution' (141). Syphilis was often linked to prostitution, while AIDS was linked to sex between men, the 'gay plague' functioning as some type of vengeance for 'immoral' sexual behaviour, with ramifications too for the society which had licensed it.[18] Although the narrator has syphilis, the novel is therefore clearly also about AIDS: his illness reminds him of warnings about sexual activity during the AIDS crisis of the 1980s and early '90s, when 'desire and disease seemed essentially bound together, the relationship between them not something that could be managed but absolute and unchangeable, a consequence and its cause' (122). To have sex, the narrator had been taught, was to invite disease into one's life, hence he found the 'thrill of release so intense it was almost suicidal' (123) when he had sex for the first time. This synonymy appears to be confirmed when Mitko pulls down his underwear to show him the discharge caused by syphilis, and the narrator notices that it looks exactly the same as the discharge generated by sexual arousal:

> Mitko took it in one hand and pinched the base with two fingers, pulling them slowly up the length of it. It was the gesture I remembered as the final act of sex, milking the last of a desired substance, and I watched as a single drop emerged at the tip, cloudy and white, indistinguishable from semen, really, and maybe it was the very similarity that so repulsed me (109).

Mitko's eroticised display seems to offer visible proof of the link between sex and disease – their 'symptoms' look exactly alike.

Many years earlier, the narrator's father had treated him as an agent of contagion, 'grimacing' as he watched him steadily in the rear-view mirror. Now the narrator in turn looks at Mitko and imagines how 'It must be terrible . . . to find oneself a source of such pollution, to have it flow out unchecked' (109). And days later, having tested positive for syphilis himself, he regards himself as a pollutant, washing his hands 'compulsively' and making 'obsessive use of the little bottles of antiseptic gel that most teachers keep close by' (127). When he masturbates in the bathroom of a McDonald's, he immediately regrets it, and compulsively wipes the entire area clean:

> I was sick, I was infectious, and children came here . . . I stepped into the stall and unwound a mass of toilet paper, which I wet at the sink and used to wipe down the lever I had just touched, as well as the wall where I had braced myself, though there could be no danger there; and then I began wiping down the porcelain itself, inside and

out. I knew the whole performance was excessive, I was wiping surfaces unlikely ever to be touched, but I kept at it as the paper dissolved in my hand (134).

His fixation on hygiene, which is at odds with any logical understanding of how the disease spreads, recalls Sontag's observation about AIDS that 'When the focus is transmission of the disease, an older metaphor, reminiscent of syphilis, is invoked: pollution' (17). The narrator is capable of talking rationally about the way syphilis spreads, telling Mitko that 'I have it from you . . . probably my friend has it from me, and you got it from someone, too; it's an infection, I said, there's no guilt, you don't need to be sorry' (132). Yet this does not reflect the way he really feels about the disease: he is horrified about having syphilis, regarding himself as infectious and dirty: 'I felt unclean, I wanted to hide myself away' (127). He is also guilt-ridden about having infected his boyfriend, R., thereby corrupting the 'cleaner life he and I had made together' (145–6), and imagines that R. is experiencing similar feelings of 'apprehension' or 'remorse' (143). Sontag also noted that 'Infectious diseases to which sexual fault is attached always inspire fears of easy contagion and bizarre fantasies of transmission by nonvenereal means in public places' (27). Clearly the narrator is haunted by the scare warnings and misinformation which circulated in the early years of the AIDS crisis, when the cause was still unknown: among the theories posited was that the epidemic was spread by germs in the pipes of the bathhouses, that contaminated nitrate inhalants (poppers) were to blame, and that it could be caught by kissing or even hugging – it was common for medical staff to refuse to touch or go near AIDS patients in their care. After his syphilis diagnosis, the narrator instinctively feels, 'for all I had learned of the disease, that even touching someone might contaminate them' (127).

As well as making him feel unclean and posing an imagined risk to innocent bystanders, the narrator's diagnosis also exposes him as having engaged in 'deviant' (Sontag 25) sexual behaviour. Sontag made the point that

> to get AIDS is precisely to be revealed, in the majority of cases so far, as a member of a certain 'risk group,' a community of pariahs. The illness flushes out an identity that might have remained hidden from neighbors, jobmates, family, friends (25).

The narrator's diagnosis of syphilis likewise seems to reveal to others his past sexual encounters and in this way serves as a 'physical confirmation of shame' about his sexual identity: when he approaches the reception desk at the sexual health clinic, his embarrassment is 'strong and deep-seated, part of that larger shame of which my whole story with Mitko, from our first encounter to this deferred consequence, was merely the latest iteration' (127, 118). That word 'shame', which the narrator uses repeatedly throughout this novel, recalls Eve Kosofsky Sedgwick's argument in *Epistemology of the Closet* (1990) that 'homo/heterosexual definition has been a presiding master term of the past century' which operates in a climate of 'urgent homophobic pressure to devalue one of the two nominally symmetrical forms of choice' (11, 9). And Michael Warner has written extensively about the 'politics of shame' (7), sexual shame in particular, which positions gay people lowest on the 'hierarchy of respectability' (49). Warner, writing in 1999, mapped this onto the 'desexualized identity politics' (24) he suggested had taken over America's gay rights movement: because certain sexual acts generate moralistic disapproval, and bring shame and indignity on those perceived to engage in them, the approach of 'gay political groups' was to 'repudiate sex': rather than challenging the stigma, their goal was to integrate, and they figured that social acceptance would come through downplaying, or even rejecting, this aspect of their identity (48). At first glance, this shame or embarrassment regarding sex does not appear to describe the narrator – after all, in the first scene of the novel he recalls cruising in Sofia's public bathrooms, where he meets Mitko. But though he regularly engages in public sex, he quite reasonably considers those bathrooms to be circumscribed spaces, noting that they 'are well enough hidden and have such a reputation that they're hardly used for anything else' (4). And that familiar sense of humiliation, 'that aura or miasma of shame' (127) still attaches itself to him whenever his sexual conduct spills over into heterosexual spaces. We saw this for instance at the hotel in Varna, where he was mortified at having to call on the attendant's help to keep Mitko away from him. And the scene at the sexual health clinic provokes a similar type of response: when the nurse loudly runs through his list of tests in front of a crowded waiting-room, he finds himself embarrassed by her 'inflated tone' (119), because he imagines that by announcing to the room his possible infection, she is also publicly disclosing his sexual conduct.

The narrator re-encounters these responses the following day when he visits a second clinic for confirmatory tests. At first, he rejects the doctor's attempts to embarrass him, stating 'Yes, I had contact with him. I wouldn't accept the shame she seemed to want me to feel, and she acknowledged this, I thought, dropping her gaze as she walked past me to open the door' (141). Yet after he tests positive for a disease he has caught from having sex with another man, her attitude towards him hardens and she abruptly orders him to lower his trousers:

> Go on, I need to see your dick, using a word that while not quite vulgar wasn't clinical either. It shocked me a little, though it wasn't just the word that was a breach in decorum, it was also the pronoun she used, the informal *ti* . . . I felt the difference it made now, it was like a change of temperature, and it eroded further the dignity I wanted to preserve. I lost that dignity entirely as I exposed myself, and then lifted my penis for her to inspect, pulling it to the right and the left as she directed, exposing all surfaces to her view (147).

The narrator's indignity is not just caused by the intimate inspection, but also by the sexual acts that have led up to it: he is being deliberately shamed for his behaviour. The doctor's conduct also calls to mind scenes in Murphy's novel which described the hostility on the part of certain authority figures who were slow to acknowledge the AIDS crisis, to allocate proper funding for research into possible treatments or to provide care for the sick. Some twenty years later in Greenwell's novel, the doctor is demonstrably unsympathetic – even censorious – towards the narrator, adopting a 'tone of officious formality' after his results come through; before handing over the prescription, she also offers the following disclaimer, apparently learnt by rote: 'In making these recommendations . . . I'm following the guidelines of the Ministry of Health and Prevention, *zdraveopazvaneto*, I'm not sure of the best translation; should you wish to follow another treatment, I cannot accept responsibility for the consequences' (149). In a final moment of humiliation, the narrator is instructed by the doctor to write his name in a ledger: all cases of syphilis must be reported to the government. The Bulgarian authorities seem to be using surveillance (albeit in an unsophisticated form) to track all instances of sexual nonconformity in the country. In some of the most notorious homophobic responses to the AIDS crisis, media outlets and social commentators suggested that anyone carrying the disease should be publicly identified and kept away from those who were infected. Proposals included mandatory HIV testing, and quarantine for those who tested positive.[19] In the novel the narrator is required to sign an official ledger, the implication is that he poses a danger to the health of the country – a potential contaminant of the body politic which might necessitate his expulsion; his instinctive response is to wonder 'if this would complicate my stay in the country' (150).

The doctor's exasperation seems to be partly down to the fact that she disapproves of the sexual behaviour which led to the narrator's infection. And this evokes the broad cultural resolve, in a slightly earlier period, to lay the blame for AIDS on those who had it, but particularly gay men: prominent figures even within the gay community advocated limits to sexual activity in order to curb the spread of the disease.[20] Although Greenwell's narrator now recognises that this vilification was based on prejudice and fear, his early conditioning is difficult to expunge, and at times his narrative reads like a declaration of guilt – in the first few pages of the novel he admits that 'the whole bent of my nature is toward confession' (11) and this is palpable when his father finds his journal and forces him to admit that he is gay:

> Is it true, he asked when he had finished speaking, giving me a choice, or a semblance of a choice. He presented it to me as if it were something that might be spoken away and made right . . . Yes, I said, laying claim to myself, it is true, yes (99).

But rather than priestly absolution, his admission brings with it rejection, his father adopting a 'snarling voice' (99) to wish he had never been born. When he was tested for HIV the first time as a teenager, he had felt 'sure of the news she [the nurse] would bring'; when the results turned out negative, he felt 'not relief, exactly, but disappointment, or something so bewilderingly mixed I still have no good name for it' (123). That temporary impulse to test positive suggests he had absorbed moralising lessons about the consequences of being gay (and particularly having sex) and was seeking the punishment he believed he deserved: 'I wanted the world to have a meaning, and . . . the meaning I wanted it to have was chastisement' (5, 123).

In a 2017 interview about the novel Greenwell said of his narrator that

> He knows that the lessons he was taught about himself as a child were false lessons, that they're bankrupt lessons. But they are still lessons that shape him. He will never get to be someone who was not taught those lessons.

Like his narrator, Greenwell also taught in Sofia, and in the same interview he described the uncanny experience of re-encountering, in Bulgaria, the homophobic culture of his youth:

maybe the spark of this novel was this weird kind of vertiginous experience I kept having living in this very foreign place, Bulgaria, of being reminded of the place where I grew up, which was Kentucky in the early '90s.

The authority of the Bulgarian Orthodox Church (which remains intolerant towards gay people, regarding same-sex desire as 'anathema to Christian principles') has declined in recent years and 'homonegativity' among the population is also decreasing (Spina 39, 40). Nevertheless, when the narrator stumbles upon a half-built cathedral in Sofia, his instinct is towards self-reproach, as though he is responding, unconsciously, to the Orthodox Church's teaching, and by extension his encounters with religious doctrine back home: Christian fundamentalism in Kentucky, and the conservative moral position taken by the Catholic Church during the AIDS crisis. As he breaks into the construction site to admire the arch of the cathedral, his mind returns, apparently unprompted, to his having caught syphilis and – even worse – having passed it on to his boyfriend:

> I looked up at the arch, and something in me responded to the familiar shape of it, though I haven't been to a church in years, or not as anything but a tourist. I thought of R., wondering if he had gotten tested yet, if he was waiting for the result . . . I worried it would make him regret having met me at all; I wondered if I thought it should (144–5).

The apparently unconscious flow of thought from religion to disease to remorse suggests that cautionary and moralistic threats about the consequences of being gay, familiar to him from growing up in the American South, are once again part of his surroundings. The narrator is a good deal older than he was back in Kentucky, when his sexual orientation was enough for his family and friends to expel him from their lives. When recalling his night with K., he remarks that 'we were younger it occurs to me even than my students' (81), a comment which contains the muted hope that any of those students who share his own experience of being closeted might also enjoy freer, more open lives in the future – although this will likely necessitate them leaving the country, just as he had left America. But that scene in the cathedral also establishes the potency of homophobic lessons forced on him during those formative years, and their unexpected recurrence in another place and time.

The two novels considered in this chapter were both published in 2016, and therefore after some important milestones had been reached: in 2013, the Defense of Marriage Act, which had been signed into law by Bill Clinton in 1996, was ruled unconstitutional by the Supreme Court. And two years later, in 2015, the Supreme Court legalised gay marriage in all fifty states. But focusing attention solely on the victory for gay marriage risks ignoring the substantial past hurt that was inflicted on the gay community and the discrimination that still exists across parts of America today. This is the point made by Sarah Schulman, who fears that younger gay men and women are blithely assimilating into a 'cultural structure' in which 'there is no nationwide antidiscrimination law' and which, within living memory, had 'allowed us [gay people] to be destroyed' (6, 114, 156). For Schulman, that period of history is now largely 'invisible', never 'integrated into the American self-perception' (158, 70): it has been left off the school history syllabus, denied a permanent memorial equivalent to those built to commemorate deaths in Vietnam and 9/11, and the government's response never investigated, let alone apologised for. But this 'mammoth act of self-deception' (Schulman 51) is not feasible for the individuals who lived through those years, as both Murphy and Greenwell can testify: for their protagonists (whose experiences of the period were themselves very different), the unresolved past tends to re-emerge, unexpectedly and uninvited, resisting even the most vehement efforts to leave it behind.

Notes

1. In researching the ACT UP sections of this chapter, I found the following texts particularly useful: David France's *How to Survive a Plague*, Lillian Faderman's *The Gay Revolution*, David Eisenbach's *Gay Power: An American Revolution* and Deborah B. Gould's *Moving Politics*.
2. Lillian Faderman records that in 1983, when more than a thousand people had died from AIDS, 'the National Institutes of Health (NIH) hadn't yet funded a single grant to study the epidemic' (422). Federal money was scarcely more forthcoming as the AIDS epidemic spread, as Dennis Altman recorded at the time: although funding for research increased from $5.5 million in 1982 to $96 million in 1985, this was paltry when seen in the context of the overall budget: 'in 1985 the National Institutes of Health alone spent over $3 billion and AIDS expenditure has been less than 1 per cent of the total expenditure of the Public Health Service' (112).
3. France writes of the situation in 1983 that 'In the thirty months of the plague, a time in which 1,340 New Yorkers were diagnosed and 773

were already gone, Koch had spent just $24,500 on AIDS' (122). His one initiative was a Salvation Army-run programme 'to provide home attendant care to AIDS patients', but this was cancelled as no one had installed phone lines, meaning no one could sign up for the service (122). Comparing this response with that of San Francisco underlines Koch's unwillingness to deal with the problem in what was the worst affected city in the US: San Francisco spent over $4 million in the same period, despite the fact that 'the city by the Bay had just 12 per cent of the nation's caseload compared to New York City's 42 per cent' (France 122). Dennis Altman wrote (in 1986) that before 1985, when a 'slew of programs involving housing, outpatient and hospital care and education' was announced, costing an estimated $6 million a year, 'Mayor Koch's strategy had seemed to consist largely of claiming that someone else – usually Washington – should take responsibility for the epidemic' (131).

4. Members of ACT UP were not afraid to use crude publicity stunts to convey their message: in 1991 they covered the house of Senator Jesse Helms, who blocked all bills relating to AIDS funding, with a giant condom on which was written: 'Helms Is Deadlier Than a Virus'.

5. Early results from taking Crixivan were breathtaking: patients who had been too weak to get out of bed found their CD4 levels quickly rise and their viral load crash. When taken with other protease inhibitors (developed by pharmaceutical companies such as Hoffman-La Roche and Abbott), the virus had less opportunity to mutate to develop resistance, meaning that the combination drugs were capable of suppressing the disease for long periods. For more on this, see France 487–9 and 493–509.

6. In an article originally published in 1996, Simon Watney addressed the 'growing experience of multiple loss among gay men' which he described as '*secondary* social symptoms caused by proximity to illness and death among one's friends and acquaintances on a constant, recurrent basis, over time' (216). He explained that 'morbidity and frankly self-destructive behaviour are likely to be frequent symptoms of cumulative loss', as 'Some may . . . become wholly stupefied by the scale of death around them' (224). Written in 1986, Dennis Altman's book *AIDS and the New Puritanism* reminds us that because the epidemic was largely concentrated among certain groups (such as gay men and drug users), this meant that the people affected 'have felt a disproportionate amount of personal loss' (1). We might compare this with Vietnam, where a family may have lost a son or a father, but not an entire community of friends. Sarah Schulman has also described the impact of this 'mass death experience of young people' from 1981 to 1996, when 'the people who witnessed our lives as we witnessed theirs . . . sickened and died constantly for fifteen years' (45). She notes that 'the losses are so numerous and cumulative' that we must assume

'Every gay person walking around who lived in New York or San Francisco in the 1980s and early 1990s is a survivor of devastation and carries with them the faces, fading names, and corpses of the otherwise forgotten dead' (54, 45).

7. Douglas Crimp, who was a member of ACT UP, suggested in his 1989 essay 'Mourning and Militancy', that activism, while absolutely vital, 'may be a means of dangerous denial' (18), disrupting and displacing the process of mourning. He argued that 'for many gay men dealing with AIDS deaths, militancy might arise from conscious conflicts *within* mourning itself' (10), caused by their being subject to contempt and even violence 'during their hour of loss' (8), and by the fact that their grief is complicated by the fear that they might 'share the fate of the mourned' (10).

8. For accounts of the 'Stop the Church' protest, see Bradford Martin 177–9; Faderman 433–5; France 391–3; Gould 285–6; and Hirshman 205–6. Many thought this action crossed the boundaries of acceptability, particularly when a protestor spat out a communion wafer and dropped it on the ground.

9. In the final pages of France's book he explains that after 1996 'many of the survivors . . . found themselves staggering into an unfamiliar land, exhausted, disoriented, lost' (512), and 'Drug addiction became a secondary epidemic' within the HIV community: he describes how Peter Staley, one of the most recognisable figures in ACT UP and later one of the founders of TAG, 'fell unexpectedly into the thrall of methamphetamine' in the early 2000s, 'at a time when he felt most alienated from the community of activists that had nourished him' (514).

10. In an interview with the writer Edmund White, who was diagnosed with HIV in 1985, Schulman uses the striking phrase, 'Now that you are hopefully outliving your own death . . .' (Schulman 118).

11. France describes how in 'the plague's original epicenter' of St Vincent's Hospital in Greenwich Village, 'a remarkable proportion of patients lying on the AIDS ward rose unexpectedly and went home' (511) once a selection of the protease inhibitors became widely available.

12. A very similar image appears in Andrew Holleran's *Grief* when the narrator is shown a photograph of a friend who died from AIDS. In the photo, taken near the end of his life, he appears 'gaunt and haunted, looking down at something outside the frame – contemplating his own death' (116).

13. David Eisenbach discusses this issue at length in the chapter 'The Conspiracy of Silence Redux' in his book *Gay Power: An American Revolution*.

14. This is not dissimilar to the ACT UP Oral History Project, codirected by Schulman and Jim Hubbard. They have interviewed nearly 200 surviving members of ACT UP, and made those interviews freely available for download.

15. In *Close to the Knives* (1991) Wojnarowicz described walking in the city after Peter Hujar's death, and entering the 'dying section of town where bodies litter the curbsides and dogs tear apart the stinking garbage by the doorways' (76).

16. Larry Kramer's attacks on gay promiscuity were the most notorious. His novel 1978 *Faggots*, a satire on New York's sexually voracious gay subcultures, came out several years before the AIDS crisis even began, and he later argued in favour of celibacy: in articles for the *GHMC Newsletter* (which he also edited) and the *New York Native*, he argued that 'sex is not the fabric holding our community together' and a 'temporarily suspended sexual liberty' (qtd. in France 80, 81) was needed to stop the spread of infection. Dennis Altman in 1986 made the point that using terms like 'sexual compulsion' when criticising 'gay men's behavior' was 'a particularly insidious form of argument, since it reinforces the popular belief that AIDS is the direct result of unrestrained promiscuity, and effectively pathologizes behavior that in another time or place would be perfectly harmless' (159).

17. For further discussion of this, the following articles are particularly useful: Nicholas Spina, 'The Religious Authority of the Orthodox Church and Tolerance Toward Homosexuality'; Shaban Darakchi, 'Emergence and Development of LGBTQ Studies in Post-Socialist Bulgaria'; and Sasha Roseneil et al., 'Changing Landscapes of Heteronormativity: The Regulation and Normalization of Same-Sex Sexualities in Europe'. The authors of that last article explain that 'there is very little discussion of anti-gay violence and no policy initiatives to combat it' in Bulgaria, and that there are instances of 'police violence against homosexuals, the collection of personal information from homosexual victims of violence that does not relate to the case, and refusal to register acts of homophobic violence' (181).

18. Sontag argues that 'AIDS is understood in a premodern way, as a disease incurred by people both as individuals and as members of a "risk group" – that neutral-sounding, bureaucratic category which also revives the archaic idea of a tainted community that illness has judged' (46).

19. Reporting of HIV cases is now commonplace across the US: positive results are reported to the state health department, and this information is then de-anonymised and submitted to the CDC.

20. In 1985 Jeffrey Weeks noted that 'What is so very striking about the moral panic around AIDS is that its victims are often being blamed for the illness' (45); he quoted from activist Konstantin Berlandt that 'no one blamed war veterans for Legionnaire's Disease, no one attacked women over Toxic Shock Syndrome' (qtd. in Weeks 49). Sarah Schulman wrote a 1991 article titled 'Laying the blame' (later reproduced in her book *My American History: Lesbian and Gay Life During the Reagan/Bush Years*), in response to Magic Johnson's announcement

that he was HIV-positive; she described the 'split' which had been 'set in stone by the US media' between '"guilty" (homosexuals, bisexuals, IV users and anyone who has sex with them) and "innocent" (babies and haemophiliacs or other people who have had blood transfusions)' (35).

Chapter 5

Anxious Futures in Colson Whitehead and Omar El Akkad

Towards the end of *10:04* one of Ben's graduate students recalls a remark he once made that 'we shouldn't worry about our literary careers, should worry about being underwater' (217). When Ben tries to remember making that comment he imagines 'I must have been joking around in class – half joking' (217). This flippancy is typical of Ben, who tries to downplay his own anxieties about the future throughout the novel, with varying levels of success. It so happens that one reason for him to be fearful – those storms brewing over New York – turn out to have little impact on his life, but as both Colson Whitehead and Omar El Akkad suggest in their respective novels *Zone One* (2011) and *American War* (2017), the near future remains a deeply frightening prospect, particularly if America continues down its current path of neoliberalism and environmental destruction. Previous chapters in this book have considered the effects generated by a past which retains its grip over the present, continuing to disturb characters many years later. In this chapter the 'past' being considered is now: the early decades of the twenty-first century. These two novels highlight the mid- to long-term ramifications of poor decision-making in the contemporary period: they both take place in a near-future America which is struggling because of governmental failures over the past twenty or so years. And yet at the same time the novels also draw on particular episodes in America's history: they share with the fictions explored in previous chapters that urge to turn backwards, blurring temporalities so that earlier periods seem at times to be pushing their way into this one.

Mitchum Huehls has described how 'the historical novel of futurity renders the present as the prehistory of the future' (146), and he draws attention to the vastness of current crises (most obviously 'global capital and climate change') to explain this turn towards the future in recent historical fiction: 'The subject's relation to the past will no longer suffice. Only the future provides a perspective capacious enough to account for historical dynamics that exponentially exceed the scope and scale of the human' (147). In this, Huehls has taken his cue from Fredric Jameson, who suggests, in *The Antinomies of Realism* (2013), that 'the philosophical question about future history and indeed about the future history of the planet itself is one which all true historical novels must raise today' (qtd. in Huehls 147). For Jameson, 'the historical novel of the future (which is to say of our own present) will necessarily be Science-Fictional': it 'must be seen as an immense elevator that moves us up and down in time, its sickening lifts and dips corresponding to the euphoric or dystopian mood in which we wait for the doors to open' (Jameson, *Antinomies* 298, 301). To achieve this effect, it 'demands a temporal span far exceeding the biological limits of the individual human organism: so that the life of a single character – world-historical or not – can scarcely accommodate it' (301). While the novels examined in this chapter are each concerned, to varying degrees, with the planet's future, they offer neither the multi-narrative structure nor the broad temporal sweep Jameson describes, and they also fail to present us with what we might regard as 'futuristic' visions of America – cleaner, more efficient, or more technologically advanced. In *American War*, which begins in the year 2074, El Akkad considers how the US will fare if it continues to ignore calls to reduce its carbon emissions. Among the dire projected consequences are civil war, mass poverty and homelessness and America's total disappearance from the world stage. In this paradoxically regressive future America, the technological advances we now take for granted seem uncanny – a haunting reminder of the modern world from which the country has now retreated. The novel's backwards turn is further underscored by its depiction of the country's descent into a second civil war which resembles, in its ideological rhetoric and in the split between North and South, the 'first' Civil War, which was fought more than two centuries earlier, in 1861–65. Time periods are therefore mixed: as well as casting ahead to the effects of extreme climate change and looking to the past for historical parallels to its fictional civil war, the novel also describes tactics used more recently during the 'War on Terror' launched by President George W. Bush in 2001 – in the novel, drone killings leave millions of Americans dead and a version of Guantánamo Bay (rather euphemistically called Sugarloaf Detention Facility) continues to operate. *Zone One* is ostensibly set at some future time just after a zombie plague has wiped out much of the global population; the central protagonist, a young Black man nicknamed Mark Spitz, has so far managed to survive, and is hired as a 'sweeper', with responsibility for clearing Manhattan of zombies, or 'skels'. But the narrative also appears to be set in the early years of the twenty-first century – specifically, immediately after the 2008 financial crisis: just as banks were kept running after the crash, money continued to influence politics, and no real changes were made to finance laws or labour regulations, the novel's interim government similarly adopts a strategy premised on continuity, using the same language and structures as before the plague in a bid to smooth over the devastating changes that have been wrought.

While the two novels explored in this chapter focus on some of the more visible and far-reaching governmental policies in recent times, their aim is not to historicise the contemporary period; instead they employ analogy as the means to interrogate decisions relating to (for instance) climate change, foreign policy and neoliberalism, and to stress their ongoing impact. This approach sets them apart from Alexander Manshel's category of the 'recent historical novel', which refers to books set in the 'very recent past' and feature specific real-life crises that 'fix it [the narrative] precisely on this or that day, in this or that year'; for Manshel, this 'commitment to the nonfictional event' lends such novels 'a certain authenticity' but also 'threatens their very fictionality' (n.p.). *Zone One* and *American War* are similarly focused on events and issues shaping America in the twenty-first century, but they tend instead to disguise – however lightly – the crises they describe. This affords them more latitude, allowing them to recontextualise particular events – so for instance in *American War*, the US military response to 9/11 is reconfigured as an internal conflict, with the North facing off against a group of four Southern states. In *Zone One*, which this chapter will turn to first, Whitehead's post-plague America appears at first to run along similar lines as it does now: familiar workplace structures have clicked back into place, with the proliferation of marketing buzzwords and the emphasis on measuring productivity. Huehls notes that in some 'historical novels of futurity . . . the future world looks almost exactly the same as our present one, usually with one dramatic difference that effectively throws into relief the historical truth of our present' (148). In *Zone One*, this is zombies, the presence of which highlights 'capitalism's enduring perpetuity', because even in the wake of a zombie plague, and despite the death of millions, things still return to normal through 'the seamless continuation of capitalism' (Huehls 148).

Policy wonks based in Buffalo are employed to 'rewind catastrophe' (Whitehead 35) and come up with clever ways to 'hone the future' – 'rebranding survival' by 'tossing ideograms up on whiteboards' in a bid to 'stir the masses . . . to pledge their lives to reconstruction' (79). The reconstruction project also has an uplifting anthem, official mascot and a clothing range which has been 'well crafted' using 'cheap child labor' (38). This enterprise deliberately ignores the fact that even the most basic necessities of everyday life have been destroyed: most people are dead, and the survivors live in makeshift camps – flimsy protection from zombie invaders. But as this chapter will also argue, Mark Spitz becomes a point of resistance to the government's publicity machine: his efforts to hold onto memories of his past, and his compulsive return to places which trigger recollections of life before the disaster, renders him a powerful witness to the scale of the deterioration, and governmental attempts to cover this up. Whitehead's novel does not really claim that there is any longer an 'alternative' to what Mark Fisher terms 'capitalist realism' (*Capitalist* 2), yet his protagonist's repeated encounters with sites of 'broken time' fleetingly expose the 'lost futures' (Fisher, 'Hauntology' 19, 16) which have been supplanted by inertia and inevitability. These moments of temporal disjunction haunt Mark Spitz, reminding him, however uneasily, that a different, more optimistic world was once conceivable.

I.

Part of *Zone One*'s central thesis is that even a zombie apocalypse is not powerful enough to destroy the structures of neoliberalism which hold sway over all aspects of American politics and society.[1] In this novel, great swathes of the global population have been wiped out, with much of the world now uninhabitable, and yet the capitalist structures we recognise as our own continue to operate, zombie-like and essentially uninterrupted, with no public acknowledgement that these are now functioning in an entirely different, post-apocalyptic context.[2] Mark Spitz's remit changes each week as he moves from grid to grid, and his small team of sweepers are constantly assessed on their productivity, with targets relating to the number of 'skels' they find in each section: they are required to fill out 'Incident Reports' after every 'engagement', recording 'the ages of the targets, the density at the specific location, structure type, number of floors' (30), and this data is used to forecast how quickly the city might be cleared. After a zombie encounter on the fifteenth floor of an office block, Mark Spitz's colleague Kaitlyn quickly pulls out a notebook, while the third member of their team, Gary, reminds them to 'make sure the paperwork is right' (28). Their line managers (now given martial titles such as 'General' and 'Lieutenant') sit through 'daily planning sessions' where they cover 'briefings and strategy' (28) relating to 'reconfiguration' (28–9) – that is, how to get the city ready for people to move back in. Meanwhile marketing executives are tasked with coming up with new terminology which will nor- malise global extinction, while workplace jargon – the language of twenty-first-century neoliberalism – is applied to a post-apocalyptic context, with new 'Buzzwords' emerging (53) and management- speak continuing to flood the popular discourse: 'I'm sure you've been briefed'; 'Get in on the ground floor'; 'They're really cracking down on nonessential air travel' (186, 82, 166). Office 'banter' has survived the zombie plague, too, with casual harassment of young female employees still the norm: 'Bozeman appraised her ass as she went inside. "Wouldn't mind some of those Buffalo wings", he said' (193).

As was the case before the plague, those who thrive in this familiar yet simultaneously post-apocalyptic environment are the 'adaptables'– people like Mark Spitz, whose defining characteristic is his mediocrity: as a young boy 'He nailed milestone after develop- mental milestone' and 'child behaviorists would have cherished him . . . He was their *typical*, he was their *most*, he was their *average*' (9). At school, 'He staked out the B or the B chose him . . . He was not made team captain, nor was he the last one picked' (9) and since then he has remained in the 'well-executed muddle, never shining, never flunking, but gathering himself for what it took to progress past life's next random obstacle' (10). This ability to adapt himself to each new situation makes him ideal for this 'reconstructed' envi- ronment where flexibility is key: able to shape-shift at a moment's notice, he finds work as a sweeper and carries it out with reasonable efficiency. In *Capitalist Realism* (2009) Mark Fisher describes how in the 'post-Fordist reorganization of work', the 'slogan which sums up the new conditions is "no long term"': workers no longer learn 'a single set of skills' which they use throughout their career, but have to 'periodically re-skill as they move from institution to institution, from role to role', and a 'premium' is therefore placed on 'flexibility' (32). After the plague Mark Spitz is 'casualized' and 'outsourced' (Fisher 33), along with other members of the precariat: he describes his fellow sweepers as 'Soldiers of the new circumstance', whose former occupations had been similarly insecure: 'food bloggers', 'erstwhile cheerleaders' and 'dispatchers from international delivery companies' (Whitehead 31).

Mark Spitz is fully accustomed to this precarious employment. Before the plague he had been hired for a role in which he had no obvious expertise, quickly learning on the job. The position had been invented by his 'supervisor's supervisor' during the company's 'annual retreat' (151), that facile workplace ritual designed to improve productivity and strengthen teamwork; as such, Mark Spitz's remit had been vague and devoid of obvious purpose ('to monitor the web in search of opportunities to sow product mindshare and nurture feeling of brand intimacy'), as well as unstable: he was a 'probationary hire', therefore his pay rise would take twice as long to be approved (149, 151). This role comes under the category of what David Graeber has termed 'bullshit jobs', which 'Contemporary capitalism' is 'riddled with' (6), proliferating in recent decades and continuing to grow in number. These jobs (a large percentage of which tend to be in consultancy, finance, policy, IT, marketing and PR) have no obvious function or value, Graeber claims – they are 'primarily or entirely made up of tasks that the person doing that job considers to be pointless, unnecessary, or even pernicious' (5). They are 'Jobs that, were they to disappear, would make no difference whatsoever', and where the 'jobholder must feel obliged to pretend that there is, in fact, a good reason why her job exists, even if, privately, she finds such claims ridiculous' (5–6, 8).[3] These jobs still exist in vast numbers after the plague. Mark Spitz and his small team are never very clear why they have been given a particular instruction by their line manager, who himself is in the dark, guided by 'trickled-down objectives'; this willingness to carry out tasks they do not fully understand – 'Speculation was above his pay grade' (111), Mark Spitz acknowledges – renders them particularly well-suited to the work.

The interim government's creation of jobs based around 'obsolete directives' (32) is one means by which they attempt to normalise the lethal new environment. Officials in Buffalo focus on constructing a post-plague future which looks remarkably similar to life before, papering over the zombie apocalypse in a bid to keep the system running, and the jobs they allocate to survivors feel all too familiar. Mark Spitz even thinks it conceivable that his 'social-media persona', cultivated while working in 'Customer Relationship Management' (151, 149) for a major Pacific Northwest coffee chain, still exists somewhere, punch[ing] the clock, gossiping with the empty air and spell-checking faux-friendly compositions, hitting Send. 'Nothing cures the Just Got Exsanguinated Blues like a foam mustache, IMHO'. 'Sucks that the funeral pyre is so early in the morning – why don't you grab a large Sumatra so you can stay awake when you toss your grandma in? Wouldn't want to sleep through that, LOL!' (151).

In this dark parody of the peppy, pseudo-personal social media messaging used by large conglomerates, Whitehead suggests that post-plague America is merely 'an extrapolation or exacerbation' of our world, rather than 'an alternative to it' (Fisher, *Capitalist* 2). Fisher might have been discussing *Zone One* when he noted that in Alfonso Cuarón's film *Children of Men*, 'ultra-authoritarianism and Capital are by no means incompatible: internment camps and franchise coffee bars co-exist' (2). The film 'connects with the suspicion that the end has already come' and 'the thought that it could well be the case that the future harbors only reiteration and re-permutation' (3). In Whitehead's novel a similar feeling arises: survivors are housed in makeshift refugee camps with euphemistic names such as New Vista, Happy Acres and even Bubbling Brooks; this rebrands the crisis, as does the new merchandise – 'hoodies and sun visors and such' – printed with a logo almost identical to a 'very popular design trend' from before the plague (79).

The novel therefore obliquely gestures towards recent crises such as the 2008 financial crash, which did not lead to an overhaul of the banking system, but instead a bailing out of the 'too big to fail' organisations in what amounted to a 'massive re-assertion of the capitalist realist insistence that there is no alternative' (Fisher, *Capitalist* 78). The figure of the zombie operates in two ways in this novel: firstly, as an existential threat the government is trying to downplay; and secondly, as a way of conceptualising the survival of neoliberalism, particularly after the crash.[4] In Graeber's book on the Occupy movement, *The Democracy Project*, he writes that 'Considering the state of crisis the U.S. economy was in when Obama took over in 2008, it required perversely heroic efforts to respond to a historic catastrophe by keeping everything more or less exactly as it was' (95). And yet 'Obama did expend those heroic efforts, and the result was that, in every dimension, the status quo did indeed remain intact' (95). As Graeber points out, Obama's slogan 'Be the change!' was not followed up by substantive policy shifts; this led to the Occupy Wall Street protests in 2011, which registered public fury and disappointment about the fact that progressive rhetoric had translated into fiscal conservatism. The novel's reconstruction motto 'We Make Tomorrow!' (48) and the phrase 'The future was the clay in their hands' (65) likewise fail to signal any type of structural change post-plague; instead 'they in Manhattan' were hoping to 'transport the old ways across the violent passage of the calamity to the safety of the other side' (48).

Because the official policy is to carry on as though no disaster has occurred, with authorities using the same language and structures as the means to smooth over the crisis period, Whitehead's survivors often find themselves unable to distinguish between the pre- and post-plague eras. The novel deliberately blurs temporality in order to mimic the effects of this confusion, leaving the reader continually uncertain as to which period is being described. The narrator describes for instance how

> The dead had paid their mortgages on time, and placed the well-promoted breakfast cereals on the table when the offspring leaped out of bed in their fire-resistant jammies. The dead had graduated with admirable GPAs, configured monthly contributions to worthy causes, judiciously apportioned their 401(k)s across diverse sectors according to the wisdom of their dead licensed financial advisers (25).

In that passage the narrator is ambiguous as to when everyone became 'dead', or 'zombie'-like, the implication being that they were only ever half-alive, their days descending into mindlessness as year after year they followed the same trajectory as their peers. That same temporal ambiguity is a feature of Mark Spitz's 'mundane' dream about taking the subway home: 'Some of the dead entered the train politely and others were quite rude as they shouldered into the car when he tried to gain the platform. Everybody trying to eke it home' (108, 109). The description applies both to exhausted New York commuters on any given weekday (with a knowing nod also to T. S. Eliot's 'dead' walking over London Bridge) and to the skels Mark Spitz encounters post-plague.[5] The past and the present have collapsed into each other, barely differentiable.

Despite Mark Spitz's proficiency in adapting to the terms of his post-apocalyptic employment, he rejects the interim government's position that his life was always simply 'an interminable loop of repeated gestures' (50), that things now are exactly as they were before the catastrophe, and that there has never been an alternative to this current state of capitalist exhaustion. This post-plague world, he slowly realises, is actually far worse than anyone will acknowledge. The narrative takes a close third person perspective as Mark Spitz considers that when the government describes survivors as the 'American Phoenix', who together represent a 'new day', this is nothing more than a euphemism which ignores the full horror: these are 'half-mad refugees', he thinks, 'a pathetic, shit-flecked, trauma-tized herd' (79). When Mark Spitz traverses New York, the past has a tendency to bubble up unexpectedly, reminding him of pleasing moments when his life had seemed full of excitement and promise. For instance, he feels that 'his subconscious steered' as he takes a detour to 'Forlorn Tribeca' on his way uptown, passing by the 'corner lounge where he'd met Jennifer for drinks once after work' (148). And when he reaches Canal Street subway station during a sweep, 'the yellow tile of the station entrance generate[s] a familiar calm in him', as he recalls a time when he was still a teenager trying to finding his way around, and 'the steps leading to a subway plat-form offered refuge from the madness of the streets above, sparing him the skyscrapers' indictment of his shabby suburban self' (206). While he had hoped one day to assimilate into office work, to 'be one of their tribe', at that stage he was still 'eager', a 'rube' (206). 'Back then', the narrator explains ominously, 'if the worst happened, his phone would transmit the coordinates of his murdered body to the satellite and back down to the authorities and eventually to his parents on Long Island' (206). But even this now seems somehow 'quaint' – 'to die while looking for cool T-shirts' (206). These vestiges of Mark Spitz's past life reappear throughout the novel, with the city generating what Tim Murphy called 'memory-stabs' (*Christodora*, 352), specific streets and buildings reminding Mark Spitz of a time before the plague, particularly his younger, optimistic years trying (and failing) to make it in New York. The memories are often casual, seemingly minor flashes of recall: during a routine sweep of an office building on Duane Street he is struck by the underwear one of the skels is wearing,

> the same brand of panties his last two girlfriends had favored, with the distinctive frilled red edges. They were grimed and torn. He couldn't help but notice the thong, current demands on his attention aside. He'd made a host of necessary recalibrations but the old self made noises from time to time. Then that new self stepped in. He had to put them down (14).

But Mark Spitz protects memories of his 'old self' when he can – he is careful not to give away his story of the 'Last Night' (when the plague hit and his family died), even refining it into three different versions depending on who he is with. The 'Silhouette' he shares with 'survivors he wasn't going to travel with for long'; the 'Anecdote', which is 'robust and carrying more on its ribs' (112), is told to 'those he might hole up with for a night'; but the 'Obituary' is 'sacred in its current guise': it is

> heartfelt, glancing off his true self more than once, replete with digressions about his lifelong friendship with Kyle, nostalgia for the old A.C. trips, the unsettling and 'off' atmosphere of that last casino weekend, and a thorough description of the tableau at his house and its aftermath (113).

By safeguarding the 'Obit' for a meaningful encounter with someone by whom he 'wanted to be remembered' (113), Mark Spitz is preserving and honouring his most traumatic memory.

These kernels of the past contain a totemic power Mark Spitz is careful to hold onto. They also delimit his ability to subscribe to the national myth of reconstruction, which insists that there is not, and never has been, a viable alternative to this capitalist malaise, and that Mark Spitz's post-plague apathy is an inevitable continuation of life before. Mark Spitz is periodically reminded that he and his friends had once had 'hopes' – that there was a time when the 'complete eradication of aspiration' (204) had not yet materialised. These 'stories of the past', the narrator explains at one point, 'were another stencil to lay over the disaster, to remind them of the former shape of the world' (48). In one key moment Mark Spitz locates a branch of the restaurant, specialising in 'fine American fare' (154), where his family would go for the 'impulse visits and birthdays and random celebrations, season upon season' (153):

> He pressed his forehead against the glass and gazed down upon himself: a five-year-old lump of boy-matter; the slovenly tangle of him at sixteen; some vague creature attending his parents' thirtieth who pinched balloons when he thought no one was looking. He grew dizzy in his mesh. He felt like a little kid who'd split for the restroom and then forgot where his parents were sitting. Another family had replaced his own when he reached the table, no kin of his at all, they hailed from the badlands, sizing him up, suspicious and foreign (155).

Revealed in this moment of 'broken time' (Fisher, 'Hauntology' 19) is the lost possibility of another type of future – the restaurant had been the 'stage for cherished theater', where reassuring family dynamics had been ritualised: his father's jokes about the calorific cheeseburgers, his mother's mild disapproval of this 'so-called humor', his own crayoning on the place mat (Whitehead 154, 155). In Fisher's *Ghosts of My Life* (2014), he argues that in the twenty-first century, 'cultural time has folded back on itself' (9), with the music industry (the example he turns to most readily) seemingly incapable of producing anything that sounds new.[6] Twenty-first-century culture, Fisher concludes, 'doesn't feel like the future'; instead it is 'oppressed by a crushing sense of finitude and exhaustion' (8). But what is lost here is not simply musical innovation, but something much more serious, because contained within the 'experimental culture' (8) of the twentieth century was the possibility of a whole new mode of thinking: as Fisher explained in his 2012 article 'What is Hauntology?', the 'digital cul-de-sacs of the twenty-first century' stand in metonymical relation to 'all the lost futures that the twentieth century taught us to anticipate . . . the capacity to conceive of a world radically different from the one in which we currently live' (16). Fisher returns repeatedly to the phrase 'the time is out of joint', which Derrida borrowed from *Hamlet* for use in his book *Specters of Marx: The State of the Debt, the Work of Mourning and the New International*, translated in 1994. This phrase can usefully be applied to the episode in Whitehead's novel when Mark Spitz looks down on the spectral scene of his lost family life. As he gazes at the restaurant table he acknowledges that 'He had been here in other lives that were now pushing into this one'; this prompts him to consider 'What did he love, what place had been important to him?' and the narrator concludes, melancholically, that 'Yes, he loved his home', before fantasising that 'Perhaps he'd end up there, installing himself in his worn perch on the right-hand side of the sofa' (155). This lamentation for a different, more hopeful future – a future that he knows has already been 'cancelled', to borrow Fisher's term – is a brief moment of resistance to the capitalism which has 'colonized the dreaming life of the population', and 'seamlessly occupies the horizons of the thinkable' (Fisher, *Capitalist* 8).

Mark Spitz's hauntological experiences are a reminder that life was not always characterised by mundanity and indifference.[7] He is struck, elsewhere in the novel, by the old storefronts across the city which successfully evaded modernisation, and wonders if 'the city itself was as bewitched by the past as the little creatures who skittered on its back' (223). One such store belongs to a fortune teller (now zombie) whom he and his unit have been ordered to kill. Like the building, the fortune teller is an anachronism – not just because her occupation seems quaintly old-fashioned, New York's version of Madame Sosostris, but also because the notion of predicting the future seems utterly redundant when that same future has now been cancelled. The fortune teller represents an earlier time when life had seemed open-ended, ripe for speculation, which may be why Mark Spitz hesitates rather than killing her immediately and why, within minutes, he starts to sense the presence of his uncle's old apartment on Lafayette, a few blocks away.[8] As a boy he had 'daydreamed' (3) about living in that apartment and became 'giddy' (4) when visiting with his parents, so he is stunned to find himself sweeping at a building nearby which stands 'unruined' (64) amidst the destruction; his uncle's apartment is a 'pulsing presence' (226) throughout the novel, and the surrounding streets offer him 'a vision of what might be' which makes him slip into a brief 'reverie' (26), distracting him from his sweeping.

II.

Whitehead's novel is a commentary not just on the dominance of neoliberal structures, but also the swiftness with which governments and banks double down on them following a crisis. And the novel extends its satirical vision to consider the issue of climate change – another (connected) major catastrophe facing the US (as well as the rest of the globe) which successive administrations have failed to address. Nathaniel Rich's 2019 book *Losing Earth* documents the period 1979 to 1989, when the Reagan administration doggedly blocked all significant legislation to reduce carbon emissions and downplayed the clear scientific evidence pointing to a warming planet caused by fossil fuels, while his successor Bush refused to back plans for a 1989 global agreement to stabilise emissions – a treaty that would have kept planetary warming to 1.5 degrees. In the years following, the country's biggest fossil fuel corporations (among them Exxon and API) formed a series of 'front groups' with names such as Global Climate Coalition (GCC), Citizens for the Environment and the Global Climate Information Project – 'their cynicism laid bare by their parodic names', as Rich puts it – to lobby successive governments against signing any agreements on emissions reduction (184). Rich argues that 'Everyone knew' about the impact of fossil fuels on climate change, 'and we all still know', yet find it difficult to accept (191). In the novel Mark Spitz is a witness to the tangible consequences of decades of fatal inaction, as he notices the air has turned grey from the ashes of incinerated skel bodies which float into the atmosphere. The toxic rain that falls is literally manmade: it consists of human particles, having 'captured ash on the way down' (120), and Mark Spitz feels that 'the dust of the dead ... was in his lungs, becoming assimilated into his body' (187). Several critics have interpreted this swirling dust as a reference to the air pollution of Lower Manhattan in the days and weeks after 9/11.[9] But Mark Spitz's growing awareness of the 'slurry', the 'dead weather' (63, 189) falling down around him can also be seen in the context of climate change: the 'residue from the rain when it dried' reminds him, significantly, of the 'brown globs of oil' on his body after swimming in the ocean around Florida after a 'big spill' (63). During a 'heavy-flow' day, when there were a 'lotta skels coming in' (190, 189), Ms. Macy asks Lily, a member of the Disposal Unit, about the body bags they use to transport the dead: '"We should really recycle those", Ms. Macy said, pointing to the biohazard bin. It took Mark Spitz a second to realize she referred to the body bags intermingled with the wall corpses' (190). Lily's bland and distracted reply that 'I know, it's terrible' (190), as she carries on using them, replicates the tendency among most people to not think too deeply about the clear existential threat facing the planet.

During the plague's first winter Mark Spitz had hidden for months in a toy store while the snow fell steadily outside. In one of the novel's many flashbacks we are told that his fellow survivor Mim described the drifts as 'Kinda retro', and the narrator reminds us that this was how winters had been 'in the good old days' before they became progressively milder (194, 193–4). 'People [had] got used to' those warmer winters, the narrator explains: 'the unopened bags of sodium chloride gathering cobwebs next to the kids' boogie boards in the garage' and the 'nightly news footage of the venerable ice shelf splashing into the frigid seas', which only made the final cut 'if there were no more pressing outrages, or a celebrity death' (193). This well-documented indifference towards dramatic shifts in weather patterns might be explained as some type of pre-traumatic tension, where the easiest option is simply to do nothing; but of course billions of corporate dollars have gone into discrediting (or denying) the scientific evidence and conducting large-scale disinformation campaigns. Mark Spitz's colleagues seem able to ignore the ashy rain, 'its constancy and pervasiveness': they pay no heed to the 'long, gray, plummeting streaks' falling down on them and downplay the ash though it lands like 'dandruff on their shoulders' (187, 120, 187). But Mark Spitz, alert to any sign of deterioration, becomes fixated on the toxic weather. The climate change situation before the plague was already reaching tipping point, yet there had still existed a viable alternative: if humans opted to change course, planetary warming might have been kept to a manageable level. But effective solutions to the climate crisis cannot take place without a radical overhaul of the current system of free market capitalism, and as Whitehead's novel emphasises, the stubborn persistence of the latter means sacrificing the former.[10] An alternative to environmental disaster is no longer conceivable by the end of *Zone One*. The polluted air has infiltrated Mark Spitz's imagination and clouded his vision as he perceives human ash to be 'everywhere. In every raindrop on his skin and the pavement, sullying every edifice and muting the blue sky: the dust of the dead' (187).

The worsening disaster of climate change, and the sustained refusal on the part of government and corporations to address the crisis, is the most pressing issue of the contemporary period. John Wills suggests that at the beginning of the twenty-first century America is faced with a choice: 'to continue to react with ambivalence to an unfolding climate crisis or aspire to a new position in the world as a green republic' (196). The latter option now seems impossible to imagine, and in El Akkad's *American War* (which this chapter will now turn to), which is set near the end of the current century, the ramifications of continuing down the wrong path are writ large. In the novel America is ideologically split between North and South: when the government based in Columbus, Ohio put forward the Sustainable Future Act, a bill designed to prohibit the use of fossil fuels (the main contributor to climate change), this was defiantly rejected by Mississippi, Alabama, Georgia and South Carolina, which instead seceded to form the Free Southern State. This determination to continue using fossil fuels takes place against the backdrop of wild storms, land erosion and extreme drought. El Akkad's narrator explains that 'The new maps looked like the old ones, but with the edges of the land shaved off – whole islands gone, coastlines retreating into their continents. In the old maps America looked bigger' (19). Lower Louisiana in particular has mostly eroded into the sea, so that it now consists of 'thin strips of asphalt that disappeared at high tide, ghost towns propped on manmade hills, crumbling bridges that nosedived into the water' (55). When the novel opens, Sarat and her family are living in an old corrugated iron shipping container in coastal Louisiana, where the 'sea's mouth opened wide over ruined marshland, and every year grew wider, the water picking away at the silt and sand and clay' (9). They have no electricity or running water, and their pantry contains bags of sorghum cereal they have milled themselves. In the winter, during the regular storms and heavy rain, the shipping container's roof sounds like 'the bowl of a calypso drum'; during the summer the heat is unbearable, 'like a steel kiln' (10).

American War can be read as an example of 'cli-fi', or climate fiction, a burgeoning branch of literature which also includes Margaret Atwood's MaddAddam trilogy (2003–13), Kim Stanley Robinson's *Science in the Capital* trilogy (2004–07), Barbara Kingsolver's *Flight Behavior* (2012), Richard Powers's *The Overstory* (2018) and Jenny Offill's *Weather* (2020). But while drought and rising seas have become the norm in *American War*, the disaster of climate change is not the novel's central focus. Instead El Akkad uses the dispute over fossil fuels as the trigger for a civil war between North and South which has allowed the global order to reorganise itself in surprising ways: dozens of Middle Eastern countries have taken advantage of America's preoccupation with its domestic conflict and have joined together to form the Bouazizi Empire, a vast territory 'stretching from the Gibraltar Pass in the state of Morocco all the way to the edges of the Black and Caspian Seas' (26). The Bouazizi Empire's lasting success is contingent on America continuing to plunge its attention and resources into the civil war, therefore it has been arming rebels in the South (who would otherwise have been overpowered by Northern forces some time ago) in order to keep the war going. America in the novel is thus at the receiving end of its own real-life policy of selling arms to volatile foreign powers, a programme which has increased exponentially since 9/11, with the US arming states which have used these weapons to 'promote oppression, commit human rights abuses, and perpetuate bloody civil wars' (Thrall and Dorminey 6).[11] In the novel the Bouazizi Empire capitalises on (and contributes to) America's volatility, selling arms to the weaker side in order to advance its own geopolitical agenda without recourse to direct involvement.[12]

Where Whitehead satirises the financial crisis and its aftermath, El Akkad takes aim at US foreign policy, specifically the wars in Afghanistan and Iraq, the tactics and effects of which are reproduced in this novel, but this time on American soil.[13] The fictional war is presented as an ideologically-driven dispute about fossil fuels, but it was actually triggered by the assassination of President Daniel Ki in 2074 by a Southern rebel insurrectionist, Julia Templestowe, after which the North embarked on a sustained strategy of military aggression against the South – most notably, firing on a crowd of unarmed protesters at Fort Jackson, killing at least 59 people; massacring thousands of refugees at Camp Patience; and detaining and torturing suspected rebel fighters. The North's military assault on the South, sparked by the assassination of President Ki, but narrativised as a clash between binary ideological positions, is therefore broadly (though not precisely) analogous to the US invasions of Afghanistan and Iraq, exploits which were also precipitated by a major and symbolic act of terror – the events of 9/11, perceived as an 'existential threat' to the country (Bolton 171). In the days and weeks after 9/11, the Bush administration posited the terrorist attacks as clear justification for the 'war on terror' which was pitched to a largely supportive American public as an ideological battle against the 'forces of evil', while Bush declared to the rest of the world that 'Either you are with us, or you are with the terrorists'.[14] In practical terms this meant committing billions of dollars and thousands of troops to complex and prolonged wars in Afghanistan (begun in October 2001) and particularly Iraq (March 2003), as well as the capture and detainment without trial of suspected terrorists in Abu Ghraib, Bagram and Guantánamo Bay, and in CIA-operated 'black sites'. In the novel the conflict takes place in America, with a Middle Eastern superpower pulling the strings, yet the Northern show of might against the South resembles the US invasion of Iraq, with the North applying its superior military resources to attack the South and destroy its infrastructure, beginning with drone strikes and ground assaults, before finally occupying Southern territory. During the Iraq invasion, US and allied forces had captured Baghdad and other major Iraqi cities with relative ease by May 2003, yet their continued occupation of the country created mounting opposition from resistance forces – most infamously when Sunni fighters ambushed a group of American security contractors from Blackwater Security in Fallujah in March 2004, killing them and burning their bodies.[15] In the novel, occupying Blue soldiers stationed in strategically-located watch towers and on patrol in Southern towns and cities are increasingly at risk from insurgencies, with attacks on Northern military bases and regular skirmishes on the border. Sarat, by this stage a rebel insurrectionist, even succeeds in killing General Joseph Weiland, a senior member of the Ohio government, as he visits a Northern operating base on the Tennessee line. The protracted Blue occupation has also converted the Free Southern State into a fertile recruitment ground for terrorists, with anti-Northern recruits, 'the makings of hellfire strapped to their chests' (191), carrying out suicide bombings every few days. These attacks even extend into Northern territory, with 'martyrs' (191) recruited to cross into 'Blue country' with the job of 'turning one of their city squares to rubble' (233). Constant in-fighting between rebels and Free Southerners has further destabilised the region, which is now a complex tangle of shifting loyalties, as both sides vie for political and military control.

III.

American War presents us with a deliberate interrogation of US foreign policy at the start of the twenty-first century (particularly the war in Iraq), but to do so it repeatedly draws on episodes in America's past, most notably the American Civil War (1861–65), which was fought between secessionist Southern states and Northern 'Blues', just like the novel's fictional conflict. This historical parallel hints at the fact that El Akkad's divided America is still wedded to centuries-old ideological rhetoric. Certainly, the same language is used by the novel's Southern secessionists as was employed during the 1860s: Adam I. P. Smith has described the romantic nationalism of Southerners just prior to the American Civil War, who would often become 'Drunk on their own rhetoric' as they claimed in excited terms that 'finally they could take control of their own destiny' (60). He notes that Southerners 'routinely talked of their distinct identity and values, defining themselves explicitly or implicitly in opposition to Yankees' and 'What defined Confederate nationalists was ... their loyalty to the project, the potential or, most potently, the reality of the Confederate state' (159). In the novel, Sarat imagines the Northerners to be 'of a different breed, a different species' (164), and the Free Southerners describe the war as a 'glorious Southern rebellion' (187) and give passionate toasts to the 'Southern spirit and the great and noble cause of freedom' (203). Rebel insurrectionists, who perceive themselves as more committed to the Southern cause than Free Southern State leaders (whom they fear will eventually capitulate to the demands of the North), vow to continue fighting, keeping up the violence near the border. This rebel identity is built on consciously nostalgic ideals which Sarat, for one, finds highly persuasive: after a few lessons about 'the old mythology of her people ... of unmatched generosity and jubilant excess; of whole pigs smoked whole days and of peaches and pecans and key lime pie' (135), she starts talking about 'my people' (168) and calling out those who 'ain't even from the Red' (240).

These rebels, but also the Free Southerners who agree an end to the war, both resemble adherents to the Lost Cause, a mythology about the past which emerged after the Civil War, as 'diehards' worked hard to construct a 'Confederate version of the history of the war' (Blight 259). Reconciliationists used the 'language of vindication and renewal', as well as 'sheer sentimentalism' to turn a 'narrative of loss' into a 'narrative of order, revival, and triumph' (266). In the novel, during peace negotiations with the North, Free Southerners attempt to wrest control of the narrative: 'all they wanted to do was haggle over the wording of the Reunification Day speeches and the preamble of the peace agreement', trying to reinscribe their war effort as an honourable, just cause:

> Every day they'd come up with something new they wanted included in the public record – one time it'd be some nonsense about courage in the face of aggression, the next time it'd be about the necessity of self-defense and the protection of long-cherished ways of living (280).

Loyalty to the Free Southern State continues long after the war is ended, as the narrator Benjamin discovers when he returns South decades later to visit an old friend of his aunt Sarat: 'I drove past dust farms and shack-towns, places riddled with postwar poverty and the occasional three-star flag hanging limp from trailer-side posts – reminders that in so much of the Red, the war stopped but the war never ended' (329). The description deliberately evokes the aftermath of the Civil War, particularly rural regions of the former Confederacy, where even now the flag is sometimes seen. In the novel rebels and Free Southerners alike also attend the 'Yuffsy', a violent monthly cage fight between twelve contenders which the novel describes as the 'South's true outlaw sport', and although 'bound by no written code', is in reality regulated by

> an elaborate system of unsaid conventions . . . an honor code concerning sucker punches and the length of time a man may avoid his opponents. A fighter clearly headed for the exit should be left alone, for example. But there was no actual punishment for violating these rules (208).

This is an updating of the Southern code of honour, an established system of justice which called for a chivalrous response to personal insults and attacks against one's moral standing: Anne E. Marshall has described how the violence and bloodshed which resulted from these disputes (they were often resolved through duels) was bestowed with 'a patina of gentility' through the honour code (75).[16]

Although the war in the novel is very deliberately referred to as the 'second' of its kind, none of the characters seem to be conscious of the historical parallels. In this respect El Akkad's future Americans resemble Whitehead's interim government, which also has a highly selective historical memory: in that novel, the fact that the clean-up operation is given the official title 'reconstruction' suggests that government strategists have forgotten the original programme of Reconstruction after the Civil War, from 1867 until 1877, when the high optimism of the Thirteenth, Fourteenth and Fifteenth Amendments swiftly gave way to white supremacist violence and thereafter the denial of Black civil rights during Jim Crow, with the institutionalisation of segregation, disenfranchisement and convict-leasing. Given that no one in Whitehead's government seems to acknowledge the existence of that first period of Reconstruction (if they did, why would they name their own project after it?), the novel reminds us of the country's tendency to overlook specific episodes in its own history of racial violence and control, including those with ramifications which continue into the present day. While El Akkad's narrator seems to be conscious of his country's history, the other characters are not: they are unaware that the dispute over fossil fuels has resurrected divisions which are centuries old. Sarat's mother Marina sounds like an 1860s Northerner content to let the Confederate states go when she thinks to herself that perhaps 'there had never been a Union at all', but instead 'long ago some disinterested or opportunistic party had drawn lines on a map where previously there were none, and in the process created a single country fashioned from many different countries' (18). And this being the case, 'How bad would it really be . . . if the federal government in Columbus simply stopped wasting money and blood trying to hold the fractured continent together?' (18).

The Free Southern State's stubborn attachment to fossil fuels, which it justifies as allegiance to time-honoured values, renders it an anachronism – a throwback to an earlier period in America's history. But the South is retrogressive in a more tangible sense, too: its limited resources, already depleted because of the inhospitable climate, have been channelled towards the war effort, and in Camp Patience, the major refugee camp in Mississippi, technology is now practically non-existent, forcing them to communicate via handwritten notes – Sarat makes good money delivering messages on foot. Elsewhere El Akkad has described how 'being on the losing end of a war is very much akin to moving backwards in time' and in this fictional environment electronic items from our own era (such as Martina's 'barely functional tablet' (74)) seem anomalous: these remnants of a more advanced world take on a haunting quality, quasi-futuristic when set against the makeshift beds, communal shower blocks and yellowing copies of magazines long out of date.[17] This is particularly the case with the 'Birds' which circle above them: these are drones which had once been operated remotely by Union engineers, but the control unit was destroyed a long time ago by a group of Southern rebels, and the solar-powered machines now 'flew rogue, abandoned to the skies, their targets and trajectories random' (41). The arbitrary but deadly violence unleashed by these machines underlines the pointless destruction of war: the narrator describes how people in the South tried to understand why a particular location had been targeted before they realised it was simply 'dumb luck' (241). More generally the Birds are also an uncanny presence for citizens of the South, pertaining to a different, more developed world from which they have retreated.

The novel thus highlights the reckless folly of prolonging a costly and destructive war over the right to burn fossil fuels – an activity which will only exacerbate the climate crisis already depleting most of the South's resources and leaving millions of its citizens displaced.[18] Camp Patience, where Sarat and her family live for many years, consists of makeshift tents, and the Bouazizi Empire has taken the place of the US as a global superpower, sending aid shipments to the war-torn South with supplies of water, food and blankets. It is also a cultural hub: in Camp Patience Sarat finds Dana reading a magazine feature on her mother's tablet about 'Black Sea chic and the newly resurgent fashion scene of the far northern Bouazizi' (147). The Bouazizi Empire's success is down to its decisive response to the climate crisis. While the Free Southern State stubbornly continues its use of fossil fuels, with gas-guzzling muscle cars driven around as a badge of pride, the Bouazizi Empire adapted its energy strategy when the desert became too hot, abandoning its depleted supplies of oil in favour of solar power: Sarat learns from her textbooks about the 'parched sandscapes [which] were now lined with wave after wave of solar panels – blinding amber nets that caught the energy needed to feed and finance the empire' (140). America has been left behind: the Southerners are now the victims of what Rob Nixon terms 'slow violence', and its refugee camps and crumbling infrastructure make it particularly vulnerable to foreign meddling.[19] After Sarat is released from Sugarloaf, an agent from the Bouazizi Empire persuades her to release a virus in Columbus during the Reunification Ceremony. Rather than pretend that his government genuinely supports the

Southern cause, he admits that it is acting purely in 'self-interest', as a protracted American war will assist them in their power grab: 'My people have created an empire. It is young now, but we intend it to be the most powerful empire in the world. For that to happen, other empires must fail . . . if it were the other way around – if the South was on the verge of winning – perhaps I would be having this conversation in Pittsburgh or Columbus' (306).

This chapter has suggested that while both of these novels take the early years of the twenty-first century as the 'history' they look back on, other, earlier periods continue to make their presence felt. Initially *Zone One* appears to repudiate this historical sense, with the novel deliberately conflating the ruined city where Mark Spitz carries out his sweeping with the era before the plague struck; the survivors' inability to distinguish between two different periods testifies to the dread and mundanity of life even before the plague, and the reassertion of the same deadening structures immediately after the crisis. By eradicating that sense of a 'before' and 'after', the government hopes to destroy its citizens' perception that life might have been different for them – freer, more dynamic and less predictable. In that sense we might regard *Zone One* as another example of neoliberal workplace satire, with only the zombies setting it apart from other novels exploring the stultifying effects of office life, such as Joshua Ferris's *Then We Came to the End* (2007), Dave Eggers's *The Circle* (2013), Jillian Medoff's *This Could Hurt* (2018) and Halle Butler's *The New Me* (2019). Whitehead's novel is also remarkably prescient: as an illustration of how governments and corporations avoid making substantial changes after a crisis, it anticipates the political rhetoric surrounding our own 'plague', the Covid-19 pandemic, where the phrase 'new normal' is routinely used to describe our emergence out of restrictions and lockdowns, with scarce indication that this will differ substantively from life pre-Covid. And yet in the novel Mark Spitz is able to conjure up functional memories of life not just before the apocalypse, but also before he became trapped in a series of unfulfilling jobs; this reminder that his own future had once seemed unfixed and full of promise leaves him simultaneously reassured and melancholic. In many respects El Akkad's near-future America is equally as disturb-ing as *Zone One*: climate change, civil war and foreign interference have left parts of the American South in ruins. The novel presents this looming disaster in broadly realist terms which Fredric Jameson would likely regard as inappropriate or even anachronistic: the start of this chapter quoted from the final chapter of *The Antinomies of*

Realism, where Jameson suggests the historical novel 'of our own present' should adopt a 'Science-Fictional perspective' (298), with planetary shifts and multiple interlocking narratives. El Akkad's novel, by contrast, spans a single lifetime, and he even reproduces (fictional) historiographic documents, such as newspaper articles about the conflict, to lend his narrative a more authentic feel. Yet as with the other novels explored throughout this book, *American War* also foregrounds its historical consciousness: while the narrative takes place several decades into the future, and its sharpest criticisms are directed at contemporary policies, it does so by drawing on the language and landscape of America's divided past, resulting in a haunting picture of national decline.

Notes

1. Erica Sollazzo describes how 'Corporations, like the proverbial cockroach that survives a nuclear explosion, survive Whitehead's apocalypse and continue to wield the same kind of power in relation to "Buffalo" as they did before' (466). Her 2017 article on the novel argues that Whitehead draws on three crises particularly germane to New York – 'the financial meltdown, September 11, and gentrification', and uses these 'as a launch pad from which to critique certain insidious effects not just of capitalism but, more specifically, of unchecked corporate influence' (460). One effect of this is that citizens are turned into 'de-individuated consumers', or 'zombified consumers' (462); another is that government becomes ineffective – a 'toothless entity' – when faced with corporate malfeasance (465).

2. As Theodore Martin puts it, 'This is the running joke and central conceit of *Zone One*. The plague did not transform or unmake the modern world; it "only honed" its elemental features' (181). Martin suggests that the 'eerie sameness of the post-apocalyptic world is, for Whitehead, a direct consequence of the instinct to survive. Survival is first and foremost a rule of repetition, an image of things kept constant', and 'The survivor's impulse to "continue to be" the way she was both predicts and guarantees the larger continuities of the entire socioeconomic system, the inevitable reappearance of "goods and vital services"' (181). Genre fiction is an ideal mode for conveying the 'repetitions of late capitalism', Martin explains, because 'What is genre but an explanation of how it is possible to see the same thing over and over again? And what is genre fiction but the primal scene of those "repeated gestures" that enable capitalism's continued survival, no less than our own?' (182). Mark Spitz's familiarity with the generic conventions of horror films becomes key to his survival, as he has understood

from them the 'rules' of how to behave in a catastrophe (182). And this *'genre-fication'* extends to the modern workday, also characterised by repetition (184).

3. Graeber talks about the feelings of 'purposeless' and 'moral confusion' (*Bullshit* 74) that these jobs tend to generate, and concludes that 'They cause misery because human happiness is always caught up in a sense of having effects on the world; a feeling which most people, when they speak of their work, express through a language of social value' (243).

4. This latter application of the zombie trope has been widely used. In Fisher's 2013 article 'How to kill a zombie: strategizing the end of neo-liberalism', he argues that 'Since 2008, neoliberalism might have been deprived of the feverish forward momentum it once possessed, but it is nowhere near collapsing. Neoliberalism now shambles on as zombie – but as the afficionados [sic] of zombie films are well aware, it is some-times harder to kill a zombie than a living person'. Chris Harman's 2009 book *Zombie Capitalism* is a critique of global capitalism from a Marxist perspective; he argues that '21st century capitalism as a whole is a zombie system, seemingly dead when it comes to achieving human goals and responding to human feelings, but capable of sudden spurts of activity that cause chaos all around' (12). John Quiggin's *Zombie Economics* (2010) uses the term 'zombie ideas' to describe optimistic claims about market liberalism that were disproved by the 2008 finan-cial crisis but 'are already reviving and clawing their way through up the soft earth' (4).

5. Other critics, among them Theodore Martin and Andrew Hoberek, have also noticed this 'constant confusion of workers and zombies' in the novel (Martin 185).

6. He cites as an example the Arctic Monkeys' 2005 song 'I Bet You Look Good on the Dancefloor', which when he first watched the video, he 'genuinely believed . . . was some lost artifact from circa 1980' (9). The singer Adele's music, too, is 'not marketed as retro', and yet 'there is nothing that marks out her records as belonging to the 21st century either'; instead, it is 'saturated with a vague but persistent feeling of the past' (14).

7. Katy Shaw's 2018 book *Hauntology* looks at a range of twenty-first-century texts that 'profile the spectral' in order to consider 'how and why the spectral is being used to represent the changing anxieties and hopes of the new millennium in twenty-first century English literature' (3). While her focus is on hauntological literature by English writers, her description of the spectre might also be applied to Mark Spitz in this particular scene: Shaw writes in her introduction that 'The appearance of the specter, a thing from the past in the present moment, marks a burden of the past on the present, and opens up the present to the many possibilities of that which came before'; she later adds that 'The specter returns from the past to make us act in the present, it

presents us with a possibility, an acknowledgement of the past and a re-imagining of the future' (8, 13).

8. Andrew Strombeck reads *Zone One* as a 'palimpsestic novel rooted in New York's long 1970s' (274), and considers this scene with the fortune teller in the context of the city zoning instigated by the Municipal Assistance Corporation after the 1975 financial crisis: 'Insisting on her right to occupy the eclectic, non-functional space of her shop, even after she is bitten, the fortune teller represents an idiosyncratic remnant that refuses the blank logic of city planners' (264). Whitehead's fascination with how the past exists amongst New York's reconditioned buildings and streets is even more pronounced in his non-fiction work *The Colossus of New York*, which Tamar Katz reads as example of 'urban nostalgia', imagining 'an earlier city now lost to us but potentially retrievable' (815, 821). While parts of Katz's analysis could be applied also to *Zone One*, her focus is on the 'built environment of the past', with how 'The private nature of urban memory turns out to make the continuity of a physical city possible' (825); I would suggest that Mark Spitz's memories are less about recovering the city than about his own memories of a now-vanquished life, irrespective of setting.

9. Sollazzo for example suggests that the 'Flurries of ash [which] swirl around Zone One' are 'a reminder of the debris that once covered lower Manhattan' (468); Tim S. Gauthier argues that 'the novel critiques and comments on the protracted reconstruction efforts that followed the events of that Tuesday morning in September 2001' (111).

10. Naomi Klein's 2014 book *This Changes Everything* argues that the urgent call to take action on climate change coincided with the 'triumph of market fundamentalism' (20) which 'systematically sabotaged our collective response' (19). She offers the stark assessment that 'we have not done the things that are necessary to lower emissions because those things fundamentally conflict with deregulated capitalism, the reigning ideology for the entire period we have been struggling to find a way out of this crisis. We are stuck because the actions that would give us the best chance of averting catastrophe – and would benefit the vast majority – are extremely threatening to an elite minority that has a stranglehold over our economy, our political process, and most of our major media outlets' (18).

11. These are the findings of A. Trevor Thrall and Caroline Dorminey, the authors of a 2018 report on US arms sales for the Cato Institute, who discovered that while a risk assessment must be carried out before any sales can go ahead, 'the risk assessment process is rigged to not find risk' (3), and that Libya, Iraq, Yemen, and the Democratic Republic of the Congo have bought an average of $1.8 billion of weapons since 9/11, despite those countries being 'classified by the various metrics as: "terror everywhere", "not free", "most fragile", "large impact from terrorism", and as being involved in high-level conflicts' (5–6).

12. Thrall and Dorminey describe how 'in instances where the United States has an interest in conflicts already underway, arms sales can be used in attempts to achieve military objectives without putting American soldiers (or at least putting fewer of them) in harm's way. This tactic has been a central element of the American war on terror, with sales (and outright transfers) of weapons to Afghanistan and Iraq to support the fight against the Taliban, al Qaeda and ISIS, as well as to Saudi Arabia for its war in Yemen' (10).

13. According to El Akkad the 'central thesis statement of the book is that there is no such thing as an exotic, foreign form of suffering'. And to make that point, he explains, 'I simply took things that were happening to people far away, and I brought them close to the heart of the current superpower . . . I took the conflicts that have defined the world in my lifetime. And these are conflicts in which US involvement has either been indirect or from a great distance. And I made them as close to home as I could possibly think of, which is a civil war, where you're fighting yourself'.

14. This declaration was made in Bush's address to a joint session of Congress and the nation on 20 September 2001; the full transcript can be found on pp. 65–73 at https://georgewbush-whitehouse.archives.gov/infocus/bushrecord/documents/Selected_Speeches_George_W_Bush.pdf

15. Peter L. Bergen describes how this ambush led US Marines to fight for control of the city in April, and again in November that year during the Second Battle of Fallujah, by which stage 'thousands of jihadist insurgents' controlled the city, and US Marines engaged in 'the heaviest urban combat . . . since the battle of Hue in Vietnam' (165). Bergen explains that 'retaking Fallujah came at a tremendous cost; thousands of the city's buildings were destroyed and hundreds of thousands of its inhabitants fled, including Abu Musab al-Zarqawi and other members of al-Qaeda' (165).

16. Southern honour dated back to the antebellum period, but persisted in Lost Cause mythology, taking on a more political bent. For more on the political significance of code of honour, specifically its use during Reconstruction as a 'political weapon against the Republican Party' (802), see Adam Fairclough's 2011 article '"Scalawags", Southern Honor, and the Lost Cause: Explaining the Fatal Encounter of James H. Cosgrove and Edward L. Pierson'.

17. El Akkad, a war correspondent for many years, expanded on this point in the same interview: 'You look at places like Kabul. You look at pictures from the 70s, from the 60s, and it feels like a place that is futuristic relative to present-day Kabul. This is what war does'.

18. In Roy Scranton's famous article from 2013, 'Learning How to Die in the Anthropocene', he identified similarities between the destruction of war-torn Iraq and the devastation caused by climate change in the US.

He describes watching the footage of Hurricane Katrina on the news: 'This time it was the weather that brought shock and awe, but I saw the same chaos and urban collapse I'd seen in Baghdad, the same failure of planning and the same tide of anarchy . . . The grim future I'd seen in Baghdad was coming home: not terrorism, not even W.M.D.'s, but a civilization in collapse, with a crippled infrastructure, unable to recuperate from shocks to its system'.

19. Nixon's 2011 book *Slow Violence and the Environmentalism of the Poor* looks at the 'slowly unfolding environmental catastrophes' which 'present formidable representational obstacles that can hinder our efforts to mobilize and act decisively' (2). He defines 'slow violence' as 'a violence that occurs gradually and out of sight, a violence of delayed destruction that is dispersed across time and space, an attritional violence that is typically not viewed as violence at all' (2). This creates 'long dyings – the staggered and discounted casualties, both human and ecological that result from war's toxic aftermaths or climate change' (2–3).

Conclusion

This study began by reflecting on the incidence of protests and demonstrations over the past two decades, with several of the chapters examining movements such as Occupy Wall Street, Black Lives Matter and the 1999 Seattle WTO protests alongside historical examples of political activism including the civil rights movement, the New Left and ACT UP. Generally speaking, these protests (past and present) have been in opposition to government policies that have promoted economic and social inequality, failed to protect particular groups of people, or deprived citizens of their rights. But perhaps the most notorious protest in recent times was governed by an altogether different set of objectives. On 6 January 2021 a mob of angry Trump supporters, persuaded by repeated (and unfounded) claims that the 2020 election had been 'stolen', marched to the United States Capitol in a bid to stop Congress from formally certifying Biden's victory. This anti-democratic protest turned violent during clashes with police on the steps of the Capitol and several hundred of the rioters then broke into the building, where they hunted down lawmakers, smashed up offices, occupied the Senate chamber and looted and destroyed artworks, statues and other public property. Their attempt to break into the House of Representatives chamber led to an armed standoff with police while members of Congress were escorted to safety, and in total more than a hundred police officers were injured during the riot, and five people died. Trump was impeached a week later for incitement of insurrection: for months he had refused to accept the election result, alleging widespread electoral fraud and filing dozens of lawsuits to challenge the result, even petitioning the Supreme Court to overturn the results in five states won by Biden. On the day of the riot Trump held a rally outside the White House where he had urged his supporters to 'stop the steal', telling them that 'We fight like hell. And if you don't fight like hell, you're not going to have a country anymore'.

The chaotic scenes at the Capitol were televised live on all the major networks, with journalists and political commentators responding to the footage in real time. Stunned by what they were seeing, many were quick to characterise the event as outlandish and unprecedented, entirely unreflective of America's national character: on CNN David Axelrod, former advisor to Obama, claimed that 'This is not an American scene', the implication being that while a familiar enough spectacle in volatile foreign states, this type of violent unrest was aberrant in domestic politics. Representative Mike Gallagher, a Republican, made this point directly when he told CNN anchor Jake Tapper that 'I've not seen anything like this since I deployed to Iraq', a view shared by fellow Republican Adam Kinzinger: 'This is something that . . . you guys would be covering right now if it was happening maybe in Belarus or anywhere else around the globe'. When Biden took to the stage in Delaware to condemn the riot he employed similar rhetoric, telling the assembled press corps that 'The scenes of chaos at the Capitol do not reflect a true America, do not represent who we are'. He warned that this was an 'assault on the most sacred of American undertakings, the doing of the people's business', and described how 'Like so many other Americans I am genuinely shocked and saddened that our nation, for so long the beacon of light and hope for democracy, has come to such a dark moment'. But while the riot was certainly unique in its scale and context, as an attack on American democracy (and indeed on the Capitol Building) it was by no means without precedent, and as with the other contemporary crises this book has considered, taking a broader view can help to uncover striking historical parallels – in this case, situating the riot as merely the latest attempt by white supremacists to disenfranchise other Americans. Historians, among them Eric Foner and Kevin Kruse, were quick to offer correctives to the media framing of the riot: both were among those quoted in a *National Geographic* article a day or two later, which pointed out that America has witnessed repeated, often violent efforts to overturn election results (for example those won by Black candidates during Reconstruction), as well as consistent attacks on (and even denial of) voting rights.[1] Perhaps the most obvious example was the Compromise of 1877, devised as a way to resolve the disputed election of 1876, which brought about the end of Reconstruction and the disenfranchisement of Black Americans across the South. Widespread race-based voter suppression continued up to and during the civil rights era, and the targeting of particular groups of voters continues to this day – an obvious example being the continuing disenfranchisement of former felons, a policy which disproportionately affects Black men.

The aim here is not to suggest that America is worse than it perceives itself to be, but instead to reaffirm the importance of placing moments of contemporary crisis in correspondence with historical antecedents. The siege at the Capitol was part of a longer history of white supremacist violence that was reignited, but by no means invented, under Trump's presidency; one of the Capitol intruders even advertised the riot's ideological origins by carrying a Confederate flag through the building, explicitly connecting the pro-Trump movement with the history of slavery, sedition and white supremacy. Identifying these types of historical parallels lays bare the stubborn persistence of acts and attitudes supposedly belonging to an earlier period in time, while contributing to a more thorough understanding of the nation's vexed twenty-first-century character.

Notes

1. This article was written by Rachel Hartigan and published under the title 'Was the article on the Capitol really "unprecedented"? Historians weigh in'. See also the *New York Times* article '"Sedition": A Complicated History' by Jennifer Schuessler, which was published the day after the riot, on 7 January.

Bibliography

Aarnes, William. 'Withdrawal and Resumption: Whitman and Society in the Last Two Parts of *Specimen Days*'. *Studies in the American Renaissance* (1982): 401–32.

Alexander, Michelle. *The New Jim Crow: Mass Incarceration in the Age of Colorblindness*. New York: The New Press, 2012.

Altman, Dennis. *AIDS and the New Puritanism*. London and Sydney, Pluto Press, 1986.

Anderson, Perry. 'From Progress to Catastrophe'. *London Review of Books* Vol. 33, No. 15, 28 July 2011, 24–28.

'A Premature Attempt at the 21st Century Canon'. *Vulture*, 17 Sept. 2018.

Bartolucci, Valentina. 'Terrorism Rhetoric under the Bush Administration: Discourses and Effects'. *Journal of Language and Politics* 11.4 (2012): 562–82.

Barton, Bernadette. '"Abomination" – Life as a Bible Belt Gay'. *Journal of Homosexuality* 57.4 (2010): 465–84.

Bergen, Peter L. *The Longest War: The Enduring Conflict between America and al-Qaeda*. London: Simon & Schuster, 2011.

Berger, Dan. *Outlaws of America: The Weather Underground and the Politics of Solidarity*. Oakland: AK Press, 2006.

Blackmon, Douglas A. *Slavery by Another Name*. New York: Doubleday, 2008.

Blight, David W. *Race and Reunion: The Civil War in American Memory*. Cambridge, MA and London: The Belknap Press of Harvard University Press, 2003 (2001).

Bolton, M. Kent. *U.S. National Security and Foreign Policymaking After 9/11*. Lanham, MD and Plymouth, UK: Rowman & Littlefield Publishers, 2008.

Bonilla-Silva, Eduardo. *Racism without Racists: Color-Blind Racism and the Persistence of Racial Inequality in America*. Lanham, MD: Rowman & Littlefield, 2018. 5th ed. (2003).

Bonilla-Silva, Eduardo, and Victor Ray. 'When Whites Love a Black Leader: Race Matters in *Obamerica*'. *Journal of African American Studies*. 13.2 (2009): 176–183.

Boxall, Peter. *Twenty-First-Century Fiction: A Critical Introduction.* Cambridge: Cambridge University Press, 2013.

Brown, Wendy. *Undoing the Demos: Neoliberalism's Stealth Revolution.* New York: Zone Books, 2015.

Buchanan, Larry, Quoctrung Bui, and Jugal K. Patel. 'Black Lives Matter May Be the Largest Movement in U.S. History', *New York Times*, 3 July 2020.

Burn, Stephen J. *Jonathan Franzen at the End of Postmodernism.* London: Continuum, 2008.

Cady, Joseph. 'Immersive and Counterimmersive Writing About AIDS: The Achievement of Paul Monette's *Love Alone*' in *Writing AIDS: Gay Literature, Language, and Analysis*, ed. Timothy F. Murphy and Suzanne Poirier. New York: Columbia University Press, 1993, 244–64.

Clayton, Dewey M. 'Black Lives Matter and the Civil Rights Movement: A Comparative Analysis of Two Social Movements in the United States'. *Journal of Black Studies* 49.5 (2018): 448–80.

Coates, Ta-Nehisi. *We Were Eight Years in Power: An American Tragedy.* London: Hamish Hamilton, 2017.

Cohen, Samuel. *After the End of History: American Fiction in the 1990s.* Iowa City: University of Iowa Press, 2009.

Cotkin, George. *Existential America.* Baltimore and London: Johns Hopkins University Press, 2003.

Crimp, Douglas. 'Mourning and Militancy'. *October* 51 (Winter 1989): 3–18.

Crowell, Steven. 'Existentialism', in *The Stanford Encyclopedia of Philosophy* (Summer 2020 Edition), Edward N. Zalta (ed.), available online at https://plato.stanford.edu/archives/sum2020/entries/existentialism

Darakchi, Shaban. 'Emergence and Development of LGBTQ Studies in Post-Socialist Bulgaria'. *Journal of Homosexuality* 67.3 (2020): 325–34.

De Boever, Arne. *Finance Fictions: Realism and Psychosis in a Time of Economic Crisis.* New York: Fordham University Press, 2018.

DeLillo, Don. *Libra.* London: Penguin, 2018 (1988).

Dos Passos, John. *Manhattan Transfer.* London: Penguin, 2000 (1925).

Dryzek, John S. *Deliberative Democracy and Beyond: Liberals, Critics, Contestations.* Oxford: Oxford University Press, 2000.

Eaglestone, Robert. 'The Past' in *The Routledge Companion to Twenty-First Century Literary Fiction*, ed. Eaglestone and Daniel O'Gorman. London: Routledge, 2019: 311–20.

Eisenbach, David. *Gay Power: An American Revolution.* New York: Carroll & Graf Publishers, 2006.

El Akkad, Omar. *American War.* London: Picador, 2017.

—. Interview for FutureLearn MOOC 'How to Read a Novel', 2018.

Eliot, T. S. *The Waste Land and Other Poems.* London: Faber and Faber, 1999 (1922).

Erkkila, Betsy. *Whitman the Political Poet*. New York and Oxford: Oxford University Press, 1996 (1989).

Faderman, Lillian. *The Gay Revolution: The Story of the Struggle*. New York: Simon & Schuster, 2016 (2015).

Fairclough, Adam. '"Scalawags", Southern Honor, and the Lost Cause: Explaining the Fatal Encounter of James H. Cosgrove and Edward L. Pierson'. *The Journal of Southern History* 77.4 (Nov. 2011): 799–826.

Fisher, Mark. *Capitalist Realism: Is There No Alternative?* Hampshire: Zero Books, 2009.

—. *Ghosts of My Life: Writings on Depression, Hauntology and Lost Futures*. Hampshire: Zero Books, 2014.

—. 'How to kill a zombie: strategizing the end of neoliberalism'. openDemocracy 18 July 2013.

—. 'What is Hauntology?' *Film Quarterly* 66.1 (Fall 2012): 16–24.

Fishkin, James S. *Democracy and Deliberation: New Directions for Democratic Reform*. London and New Haven, CT: Yale University Press, 1991.

Fosl, Catherine. *Subversive Southerner: Anne Braden and the Struggle for Racial Justice in the Cold War South*. Lexington, KY: The University Press of Kentucky, 2006 (2002).

Foucault, Michel. *The Archaeology of Knowledge*. Trans. A. M. Sheridan Smith. London: Routledge, 1997 (1972).

France, David. *How to Survive a Plague: The Story of How Activists and Scientists Tamed AIDS*. London: Picador, 2017 (2016).

Gauthier, Tim S. 'Zombies, the Uncanny, and the City: Colson Whitehead's *Zone One*' in *The City Since 9/11: Literature, Film, Television*, ed. Keith Wilhite. Madison, NJ and Teaneck, NJ: Fairleigh Dickinson University Press, 2016: 109–26.

Gitlin, Todd. *Occupy Nation*. New York: It Books/HarperCollins, 2012.

Gould, Deborah B. *Moving Politics: Emotion and ACT UP's Fight against AIDS*. Chicago and London: The University of Chicago Press, 2009.

Graeber, David. *Bullshit Jobs: A Theory*. London: Penguin, 2019 (2018).

—. *The Democracy Project: A History, A Crisis, A Movement*. London: Penguin, 2014 (2013).

Greenwell, Garth. *Cleanness*. New York: Farrar, Straus and Giroux, 2020.

—. Interview for FutureLearn MOOC 'How to Read a Novel', 2017.

—. *What Belongs to You*. London: Picador, 2016.

Hamacher, Werner. '"NOW": Walter Benjamin on Historical Time'. *The Moment: Time and Rupture in Modern Thought*, ed. Heidrun Friese. Liverpool: Liverpool University Press, 2001: 161–96.

Harman, Chris. *Zombie Capitalism: Global Crisis and the Relevance of Marx*. London: Bookmarks Publications, 2009.

Hartigan, Rachel. 'Was the assault on the Capitol really "unprecedented"? Historians weigh in'. *National Geographic*, 8 Jan. 2021.

Hartman, Saidiya V. *Scenes of Subjection: Terror, Slavery, and Self-Making in Nineteenth-Century America*. New York and Oxford: Oxford University Press, 1997.

Hirshman, Linda. *Victory: The Triumphant Gay Revolution*. New York: Harper Perennial, 2013 (2012).

Hoberek, Andrew. 'Living with PASD'. *Contemporary Literature* 53.2 (2012): 406–13.

Holleran, Andrew. *Grief*. New York: Hyperion, 2006.

Huehls, Mitchum. 'Historical Fiction and the End of History' in *American Literature in Transition, 2000–2010*, ed. Rachel Greenwald Smith. Cambridge: Cambridge University Press, 2017: 138–51.

Jacobs, Ron. *The Way the Wind Blew: A History of the Weather Underground*. London and New York: Verso, 1997.

Jameson, Fredric. *The Antinomies of Realism*. London and New York: Verso, 2013.

—. 'Culture and Finance Capital'. *Critical Inquiry* 24.1 (Autumn 1997): 246–65.

—. *The Political Unconscious: Narrative as a Socially Symbolic Act*. London and New York: Routledge, 2006 (1981).

—. *Postmodernism, or, The Cultural Logic of Late Capitalism*. Durham, NC: Duke University Press, 1995 (1991).

Karnow, Stanley. *Vietnam: A History*. London: Guild Publishing, 1988 (1983).

Katz, Tamar. 'City Memory, City History: Urban Nostalgia, *The Colossus of New York*, and Late-Twentieth-Century Historical Fiction'. *Contemporary Literature* 51.4 (Winter 2010): 810–51.

Kauffman, L.A. *How to Read a Protest: The Art of Organizing and Resistance*. Oakland, CA: University of California Press, 2018.

—. 'We are living through a golden age of protest'. *Guardian* 6 May 2018.

Kelly, Adam. 'Formally Conventional Fiction' in *American Literature in Transition, 2000–2010*, ed. Rachel Greenwald Smith. Cambridge: Cambridge University Press, 2017: 46–60.

Klein, Naomi. *This Changes Everything: Capitalism vs. the Climate*. London: Penguin, 2015 (2014).

K'Meyer, Tracey E. *Civil Rights in the Gateway to the South: Louisville, Kentucky, 1945–1980*. Lexington, KY: The University Press of Kentucky, 2011 (2009).

Kunzru, Hari. Interview for FutureLearn MOOC 'How to Read a Novel', 2018.

—. *White Tears*. London: Hamish Hamilton, 2017.

Lacey, Robert J. *American Pragmatism and Democratic Faith*. Dekalb, IL: Northern Illinois University Press, 2008.

Lawrence, D. H. *Women in Love*. London: Penguin, 2007 (1920).

Lee, Jonathan. 'For Literary Novelists the Past Is Pressing'. *New York Times*, 13 June 2021.

Lerner, Ben. *10:04*. New York: Faber and Faber, 2014.

—. 'The Dark Threw Patches Down Upon Me Also'. *No Art: Poems*. London: Granta, 2016. 257–67.

Levi, Margaret, and Gillian H. Murphy. 'Coalitions of Contention: The Case of the WTO Protests in Seattle'. *Political Studies* 54 (2006): 651–70.

Love, Heather. *Feeling Backward: Loss and the Politics of Queer History*. Cambridge, MA and London: Harvard University Press, 2009 (2007).

Lowery, Wesley. *They Can't Kill Us All: The Story of the Struggle for Black Lives*. New York: Back Bay Books, 2016.

Lukács, Georg. *History and Class Consciousness: Studies in Marxist Dialectics*. Trans. by Rodney Livingstone. London: Merlin Press, 2010 (1971).

—. *The Historical Novel*. Trans. Hannah and Stanley Mitchell. London: Merlin Press, 1989.

Manshel, Alexander. 'The Rise of the Recent Historical Novel'. *Post45* Sept. 2017. https://post45.org/2017/09/the-rise-of-the-recent-historical -novel/

Marable, Manning. *Race, Reform, and Rebellion: The Second Reconstruction and Beyond in Black America, 1945–2006*. 3rd ed. Jackson: The University Press of Mississippi, 2007 (1984).

Marshall, Anne E. *Creating a Confederate Kentucky: The Lost Cause and Civil War Memory in a Border State*. Chapel Hill: The University of North Carolina Press, 2010.

Martin, Bradford. *The Other Eighties: A Secret History of America in the Age of Reagan*. New York: Hill and Wang, 2011.

Martin, Theodore. *Contemporary Drift: Genre, Historicism, and the Problem of the Present*. New York: Columbia University Press, 2017.

Martínez, Elizabeth 'Betita'. 'The WTO: Where Was the Color in Seattle?' *Colorlines* 3.1 (30 Apr. 2000): 11.

Miller, James E. *Walt Whitman, Updated Edition*. New York: Twayne Publishers, 1990.

Morgan, C. E. *The Sport of Kings*. London: 4th Estate, 2016.

Murphy, Tim. *Christodora*. New York: Grove Press, 2016.

Nixon, Rob. *Slow Violence and the Environmentalism of the Poor*. Cambridge, MA and London: Harvard University Press, 2011.

Onwuachi-Willig, Angela. 'Policing the Boundaries of Whiteness: The Tragedy of Being "Out of Place" from Emmett Till to Trayvon Martin'. *Iowa Law Review* 102.3 (2017) 1113–185.

Pannapacker, William. 'The City', in *A Companion to Walt Whitman*, ed. Donald D. Kummings. Oxford: Blackwell, 2006: 42–59.

Polletta, Francesca. *Freedom Is an Endless Meeting: Democracy in American Social Movements*. Chicago: University of Chicago Press, 2002.

—. *It Was Like a Fever: Storytelling in Protest and Politics*. Chicago and London: University of Chicago Press, 2006.

Quiggin, John. *Zombie Economics: How Dead Ideas Still Walk Among Us.* Princeton, NJ and Oxford: Princeton University Press, 2010.

Rich, Nathaniel. *Losing Earth: The Decade We Could Have Stopped Climate Change.* London: Picador, 2020 (2019).

Rolph, Stephanie R. *Resisting Equality: The Citizens' Council, 1954–1989.* Baton Rouge: Louisiana State University Press, 2018.

Roseneil, Sasha, Isabel Crowhurst, Tone Hellesund, Ana Cristina Santos, and Mariya Stoilova. 'Changing Landscapes of Heteronormativity: The Regulation and Normalization of Same-Sex Sexualities in Europe'. *Social Politics: International Studies in Gender, State and Society* 20.2 (Summer 2013): 165–99.

Rossinow, Doug. *The Politics of Authenticity: Liberalism, Christianity, and the New Left in America.* New York: Columbia University Press, 1998.

Rothstein, Richard. 'The Making of Ferguson: Public Polices at the Root of Its Troubles'. *Economic Policy Institute*, 15 October 2014. Available online at https://www.epi.org/publication/making-ferguson/

Rudd, Mark. *Underground: My Life with SDS and the Weathermen.* New York: Harper, 2010 (2009).

Sartre, Jean-Paul. *Being and Nothingness.* Trans. Hazel E. Barnes. London: Methuen & Co. Ltd, 1984 (1943).

Schaeffer, Susan Fromberg. *Buffalo Afternoon.* London: Penguin, 1990 [1989].

Schuessler, Jennifer. '"Sedition": A Complicated History'. *New York Times,* 7 Jan. 2021.

Schulman, Sarah. *The Gentrification of the Mind: Witness to a Lost Imagination.* Berkeley, Los Angeles, and London: University of California Press, 2013 (2012).

—. 'Laying the blame'. *Guardian* 19 Nov. 1991: 35.

Scranton, Roy. 'Learning How to Die in the Anthropocene'. *New York Times,* 10 Nov. 2013.

Sedgwick, Eve Kosofsky. *Epistemology of the Closet.* Berkeley, CA, Los Angeles and London: University of California Press, 2008 (1990).

Sharpe, Christina. *In the Wake: On Blackness and Being.* Durham, NC: Duke University Press, 2016.

Sharpe, William Chapman. *Unreal Cities.* Baltimore and London: The Johns Hopkins University Press, 1990.

Shaw, Katy. *Hauntology: The Presence of the Past in Twenty-First Century English Literature.* Cham: Springer International Publishing/Palgrave Macmillan, 2018.

Smith, Adam I. P. *The American Civil War.* Basingstoke and New York: Palgrave Macmillan, 2007.

Sollazzo, Erica. '"The Dead City": Corporate Anxiety and the Post-Apocalyptic Vision in Colson Whitehead's *Zone One*'. *Law & Literature* 29.3 (2017): 457–83.

Sontag, Susan. *Aids and its Metaphors*. London: Allen Lane, 1989.

Spina, Nicholas. 'The Religious Authority of the Orthodox Church and Tolerance Toward Homosexuality'. *Problems of Post-Communism* 63.1 (2016): 37–49.

Spiotta, Dana. *Eat the Document*. New York: Scribner, 2006.

—. *Innocents and Others*. New York: Scribner, 2016.

Stevenson, Randall. *Modernist Fiction: An Introduction*. London: Prentice Hall, 1998 (1992).

Strombeck, Andrew. 'Zone One's Reanimation of 1970s New York'. *Studies in American Fiction* 44.2 (Fall 2017): 259–80.

Students for a Democratic Society. *The Port Huron Statement*. New York: SDS, 1964.

Tesler, Michael. *Post-Racial or Most-Racial? Race and Politics in the Obama Era*. Chicago and London: The University of Chicago Press, 2016.

Thrall, A. Trevor and Caroline Dorminey. 'Risky Business: The Role of Arms Sales in U.S. Foreign Policy'. Cato Institute: *Policy Analysis* 836 (13 Mar. 2018): 1–28.

Trelease, Allen W. *White Terror: The Ku Klux Klan Conspiracy and Southern Reconstruction*. Baton Rouge and London: Louisiana State University Press, 1995 (1971).

Varon, Jeremy. *Bringing the War Home: The Weather Underground, the Red Army Faction, and Revolutionary Violence in the Sixties and Seventies*. Berkeley: University of California Press, 2004.

Varvogli, Aliki. 'Radical Motherhood: Narcissism and Empathy in Russell Banks's *The Darling* and Dana Spiotta's *Eat the Document*'. *Journal of American Studies* 44.4 (2010) 657–73.

Vermeulen, Pieter. 'How Should a Person Be (Transpersonal)? Ben Lerner, Roberto Esposito, and the Biopolitics of the Future'. *Political Theory* 45.5 (2017): 659–81.

Warner, Michael. *The Trouble with Normal: Sex, Politics, and the Ethics of Queer Life*. New York: The Free Press, 1999.

Watney, Simon. *Imagine Hope: AIDS and Gay Identity*. London and New York: Routledge, 2000.

Weeks, Jeffrey. *Sexuality and Its Discontents: Meanings, Myths & Modern Sexualities*. London and New York: Routledge, 1999 (1985).

Whitehead, Colson. *Zone One*. London: Harvill Secker, 2011.

Whitman, Walt. 'Crossing Brooklyn Ferry' in *Leaves of Grass*, ed. Jerome Loving. Oxford: Oxford University Press, 2009. 129–34 (1856).

—. *Specimen Days in America*. London: The Folio Society, 1979 (1882–83).

Wills, John. 'America and the Environment' in *American Thought and Culture in the 21st Century*, ed. Martin Halliwell and Catherine Morley. Edinburgh: Edinburgh University Press, 2008: 195–207.

Wilson, Rob. *American Sublime: The Genealogy of a Poetic Genre*. Madison: The University of Wisconsin Press, 1991.

Wojnarowicz, David. *Close to the Knives: A Memoir of Disintegration*. Edinburgh: Canongate, 2017 (1991).

—. 'Postcards from America', in *Rebellious Mourning: The Collective Work of Grief*, ed. Cindy Milstein. Chico, CA: AK Press, 2017: 140–6.

Wood, Lesley J. *Direct Action, Deliberation, and Diffusion: Collective Action after the WTO Protests in Seattle*. Cambridge: Cambridge University Press, 2012.

Woolf, Virginia. *Mrs Dalloway*. Oxford: Oxford University Press, 2009 (1925).

—. *Orlando*. London: Penguin, 2000 (1928).

Wright, George C. *Racial Violence in Kentucky, 1865–1940: Lynchings, Mob Rule, and 'Legal Lynchings'*. Baton Rouge and London: Louisiana University Press, 1990.

Index